JEWISH ORTHODOXY IN SCOTLAND

Scottish Religious Cultures *Historical Perspectives*

Series Editors: Scott R. Spurlock and Crawford Gribben

Religion has played a key formational role in the development of Scottish society shaping cultural norms, defining individual and corporate identities, and underpinning legal and political institutions. This series presents the very best scholarship on the role of religion as a formative and yet divisive force in Scottish society and highlights its positive and negative functions in the development of the nation's culture. The impact of the Scots diaspora on the wider world means that the subject has major significance far outwith Scotland.

Available titles

George Mackay Brown and the Scottish Catholic Imagination
Linden Bicket

Poor Relief and the Church in Scotland, 1560–1650
John McCallum

Jewish Orthodoxy in Scotland: Rabbi Dr Salis Daiches and Religious Leadership
Hannah Holtschneider

Forthcoming titles

The Catholic Church in Scotland: Financial Development, 1772–1930
Darren Tierney

Miracles of Healing: Psychotherapy and Religion in Twentieth-century Scotland
Gavin Miller

Presbyterianism Re-established: The Presbyteries of Dunblane and Stirling after the Williamite Revolution
Andrew Muirhead

edinburghuniversitypress.com/series/src

JEWISH ORTHODOXY IN SCOTLAND

Rabbi Dr Salis Daiches and Religious Leadership

HANNAH HOLTSCHNEIDER

EDINBURGH
University Press

To my father and the memory of my mother and my parents-in-law:

A. Holtschneider 1935– who gifted me a love of stories and dry humour.

H. Holtschneider 1942–2015 who brought me into the world and raised me with integrity.

D. Wilkes 1930–2016 whose curiosity and zest for life continue to live in his granddaughters.

B. Wilkes 1931–2018 whose commitment to life ethical and creative remains a lasting inspiration.

Edinburgh University Press is one of the leading university presses in the UK. We publish academic books and journals in our selected subject areas across the humanities and social sciences, combining cutting-edge scholarship with high editorial and production values to produce academic works of lasting importance. For more information visit our website: edinburghuniversitypress.com

© Hannah Holtschneider, 2019, 2021

Edinburgh University Press Ltd
The Tun – Holyrood Road
12 (2f) Jackson's Entry
Edinburgh EH8 8PJ

First published in hardback by Edinburgh University Press 2019

Typeset in 10/12 ITC New Baskerville by
Servis Filmsetting Ltd, Stockport, Cheshire

A CIP record for this book is available from the British Library

ISBN 978 1 4744 5259 5 (hardback)
ISBN 978 1 4744 5260 1 (paperback)
ISBN 978 1 4744 5261 8 (webready PDF)
ISBN 978 1 4744 5262 5 (epub)

The right of Hannah Holtschneider to be identified as author of this work has been asserted in accordance with the Copyright, Designs and Patents Act 1988 and the Copyright and Related Rights Regulations 2003 (SI No. 2498).

Contents

Abbreviations	vii
Preface and Acknowledgements	ix
Introduction	1
Terminology	3
Setting	4
Recent debates in British Jewish historiography	6
The sources	12
The chapters	15
1 Portrait and Ideology	**19**
Biography and migration	25
Education and ideology	29
Conclusion	37
2 The Chief Rabbi, the London Beth Din and the Battle for Leadership in the 'Provinces'	**40**
Immigration and religious leadership: British Jewry at the turn of the twentieth century	43
Regional *batei din* and the authority of the London Beth Din: a diplomatic journey	49
Conclusion	58
3 Scotland: Local Leaders, Local Communities	**61**
Rabbi Salis Daiches and Edinburgh's Jews	62
A triangle of concerns: Salis Daiches – Chief Rabbi Hertz – Glasgow's Jewish leaders	70
Conclusion	78
4 Traces and Spaces: Jews and/in the City of Edinburgh	**81**
Two Worlds and *Jewish Edinburgh on Foot* as *lieux de mémoire*	87
Movements, locations, language(s)	90
Conclusion	101
Epilogue	**103**

Glossary 108
References and Notes 112
Bibliography 131
Index 141

Abbreviations

HLS Hartley Library Southampton
JC The Jewish Chronicle, weekly newspaper
JTS Jewish Theological Seminary, New York
LMA London Metropolitan Archives
MOEHC Minute Books of the Edinburgh Hebrew Congregation
MOGHC Minute Books of the Garnethill Hebrew Congregation
NLS National Library of Scotland
SJAC Scottish Jewish Archives Centre

Preface and Acknowledgements

Anglophone Jewish religious history, that is the history of religious institutions and the contributions of groups and individuals to their development and outlook, is currently undergoing a spurt of activity, judging by the number of titles in print and in preparation for publishers in the United States with strong Jewish history lists, such as Wayne State University Press and State University of New York Press. Furthermore, there is a sustained stream of articles in Jewish studies journals on smaller communities across North America and Britain and, increasingly, such articles connect community history and biography with the field of Jewish transnational migration history.[1] Thus, cumulatively, we see a small cottage industry making a strong case for the scholarly community to pay attention to religion *in situ*: religion as performed, taught and thought about at a local level by 'religious professionals' and the communities which employed them. Indeed, the study of the lives of individuals, in particular, is now becoming a vehicle for the exploration of the migration and development of Jewish practice, tradition and ideology. The present monograph taps into these same interests: through the exploration of the life of one migrant *rabbi*,[2] born near Vilna,[3] who entered Britain via various staging posts on the European continent, we have the opportunity to investigate the impact of different continental Jewish religious ideologies and ideas about authority in community governance and *halakhah* in early twentieth-century Britain. We know that, within the United Synagogue and the broader sphere of influence of the Chief Rabbi of Great Britain and the Empire, ideas about leadership, authority, *halakhic* competence, education and community structure clashed in the first two decades of the twentieth century. As immigrants outnumbered residents by far, maintaining authority and power was of primary importance for Chief Rabbis Hermann Adler and Joseph Hertz. Not only did their education and religious training differ from the educational opportunities open to Jewish religious functionaries in the United Kingdom, continental rabbis had fundamentally different ideas about the role of a rabbi and his position in a Jewish community. The example of Rabbi Salis Daiches (1880–1945) and the Jewish community of Edinburgh allows us to unravel some of the conflicts over *halakhic* authority and leadership, demonstrating that the Chief Rabbi not only struggled to maintain power but that there were underlying ideological differences that have, thus far, hardly been examined in any detail. I argue that such an analysis is worthwhile because it allows us to trace not only religious ideologies as part of Jewish intellectual history but situates such ideologies within the lived reality of Jewish religious communities.

My family has accompanied the research and writing process with characteristically good humour and, in their different ways, all have taken delight in 'Mama's little rabbi', as my daughters, rather irreverently, are want to call Rabbi Dr Salis Daiches. Indeed, the birth of my youngest child seven years ago coincided with the beginnings of my academic interest in Scottish Jewish history. Having two children in as many years, and consequently being less able to be completely absorbed by research and writing outwith the university's teaching semester, made me look for an exciting and sustainable research topic close to home. I discovered quickly that the research paths of Jewish history in Scotland were not very well trodden: indeed, that there had been little critical or sustained academic interest in the communities on the Celtic Fringe of the British Isles. This is unsurprising, seeing that the Jewish communities in this northern land were and are small and, even recently, an eminent historian of British Jewry[4] has suggested rather forcefully that not much of significance can be learned by engagement with the 'provinces'.[5] Yet, everyone with an interest in British Jewish history I spoke with appeared instantly familiar and interested when the name Salis Daiches was mentioned and immediately began to sing the praises of this immigrant rabbi and his son, literary critic David Daiches. At the same time, I became aware of a 2012 PhD thesis at the University of Ulster which had the history of the Edinburgh Jewish community as its subject. Mark Gilfillan's work, published in 2019 as the monograph *Jewish Edinburgh*, had brought together for the first time a rich tapestry of archival sources relating to the social and economic history of Jews in Edinburgh from 1880 to 1950. Rabbi Salis Daiches, of course, played a major part in this thesis, noting his fame for uniting the rather fractious Jewish communities of Scotland's capital and becoming the first Jewish public intellectual in Scotland with a reach far beyond his own community.

Thrilling as it may be to a historian cum detective to unearth any number of dusty documents, my question was whether there was a new and compelling story to be told that could make a contribution to the field of British Jewish religious history. And so, I began my own investigations in the National Library of Scotland (NLS), the Scottish Jewish Archives Centre (SJAC), the Hartley Library at the University of Southampton (HLS), and the London Metropolitan Archives (LMA), and talked to anyone who would listen to my reflections on my growing research project. Fortunately, my colleague at the University of Glasgow, Mia Spiro, is not only a good listener but was as eager as I to establish a greater presence for Jewish studies research in Scotland and generate interest in the various archival collections hitherto unresearched or definitely underresearched. Together we hatched a plan which succeeded in 2015 with the award of a large joint grant from the Arts and Humanities Research Council (AHRC). We received this funding to explore over the course of three years the collections of the Scottish Jewish

Archives Centre in Glasgow, in particular, under several headings relevant to the study of migration and culture which are significant in contemporary research on Jewish migration and the intersection with local Jewish history and culture. This monograph is one of the fruits of this AHRC project and I am very grateful for the time and resources this funding provided. Without such generous support, the monograph could not have been completed in a timely fashion. In addition, a small grant from the Carnegie Foundation for the Universities of Scotland in 2014 enabled vital preliminary archival research in London and Southampton.

In the pages that follow, I argue that, by focusing our view on British Jewish history in the first half of the twentieth century and, furthermore, on one significant actor in a so-called provincial Jewish community, we can learn a lot about migration history and also about local religious networks; we can learn more about the development of central features of British Jewish religious history: about power relations within Jewish religious institutions and particularly about relations between the assumed centre (London) and the 'provinces' (in this case Scotland) at a time of massive demographic and cultural change in the Jewish communities. This monograph, then, asks the reader to follow the path of one such migrant who entered the United Kingdom in the first decade of the twentieth century, along with many thousands of his co-religionists. What distinguished Salis Daiches was his religious commitment and educational achievements which placed him in key positions in relation to the issues debated in Britain's Jewish communities just before and just after World War I. With immigration stagnating, and immigrants now poised to stay rather than seeing Britain as a staging post in their journey west, Jewish communities had to come to terms with the majority of their congregants now being first-generation immigrants, and to deal with the resulting cultural conflicts with those resident Jews whose families had anglicised one or more generations earlier. Salis Daiches's life journey – from Vilna via Berlin to Britain – and his work highlight central aspects of the processes of adjustment dealt with in the communities across the United Kingdom, and does so from the perspective of the 'provincial periphery'. Thus, I hope that this work provides a complementary perspective to the excellent and detailed explorations of the Chief Rabbinates of Hermann Adler and Joseph Hertz undertaken by Benjamin Elton and Miri Freud-Kandel. This monograph's concern with religion also tallies well with the social histories of modern British Jewry written by Lloyd Gartner and Todd Endelman, chiefly by homing in on a setting outwith larger provincial centres, such as Manchester, which has been skilfully explored by Bill Williams. Religion, in the shape of competing or conflicting religious ideologies, authority structures, expectations and ambitions for the future of local communities, by and large has not been the focus of research on Jewish communities in Britain. By contrast, this monograph identifies competing religious ideologies in the early twentieth century as a crucial element in the history of

British Jewry, countering the tendency to view the religious life of migrants as a function of immigrant communities seeking cultural stability while settling in a new context, and thus as more of a transient social phenomenon.[6] While this was the case for many migrants, the establishment and maintenance of religious institutions generations after settlement, and the care taken in the appointment of religious professionals, speak to the continuing significance of religious observance and education.[7] Salis Daiches, and other contemporary religious officials, were driven by specific religious and ideological commitments that informed their view of religious institutions and the place of Jews in British society.

Over the years, my children have grown and, alarmingly, so much time has passed that my eldest is now more than half way through primary school! Many debts have been accrued in pursuit of this research, intellectual as well as personal, and it is my absolute pleasure to mention by name at least a few of the people concerned. As always, my biggest thanks goes to my first and most critical (in every good sense of the word) reader, my husband George Wilkes. His knowledge, wisdom and insight always help me to see my research more clearly, and this allows me to articulate my findings better. A big thank-you to the AHRC Project Team, Mia Spiro and Phil Alexander: the past three years have been an exciting journey, and I hope we shall continue to work together in the future. Huge thanks go to my colleagues at the School of Divinity, particularly to the members of the Religious Studies Subject Area. Not only have they, over the years, listened to my papers, offered insight and encouragement and provided a space for discussion, they have gracefully and supportively accommodated my absence from the Subject Area to complete this monograph: Naomi Appleton, Arko Longkumer, Steve Sutcliffe, thank you so much for your unwavering commitment to see all four of us thrive in our research. Our project partner, the Scottish Jewish Archives Centre in Glasgow, has supplied enthusiastic and generous expertise in locating documents and placing obscurities in an enlightened context: thank you Harvey Kaplan, Deborah Haase, and Fiona Brodie. Arnold Rifkind of the Edinburgh Hebrew Congregation generously trusted me with a box of handwritten papers by Salis Daiches and the rabbi's letterbook, all now safely deposited in the National Library of Scotland and thus united with the archives of the Daiches family; he also allowed me to borrow the Minute Books of the Edinburgh Hebrew Congregation (MOEHC) so I could trace discussions about the building of the synagogue in Salisbury Road. I gratefully acknowledge the National Library of Scotland, the University of Southampton, and the Chief Rabbi's Office for permission to quote from their archives. I am extremely grateful to Jenni Calder, academic and novelist, and Salis Daiches's granddaughter, who generously gave her time to discuss her grandfather's legacy and her family's relationship with Scotland. Her enthusiasm for my research cheered me on immensely. A huge thank you to Piotr Leśniak who created the beautiful map accompanying Chapter 4.[8]

Research for this monograph has been presented in various stages of the research process at conferences and invited seminars. The audiences at the conferences of the British Association for Jewish Studies in 2014, 2016 and 2017, the Parkes Institute Research Seminar at the University of Southampton in 2015 and the Scottish Religious Cultures Conference in 2016 have offered helpful comments and gently guided me away from a few obvious mistakes! Particular thanks in this context goes to Joachim Schloer, who encouraged me to submit a first article on Salis Daiches to *Jewish Culture and History*, and to Tony Kushner for inviting me to present in Southampton. Friends and acquaintances in the Edinburgh Jewish Literary Society (the Lit.) have contributed their insights on the history of the religious Jewish community in Edinburgh and have been patient (and perhaps also delighted) to listen to more than one talk on Rabbi Salis Daiches. Particular thanks go to David Bleiman and Anthony Gilbert for help with the archives of the Edinburgh Jewish Literary Society, to Charles Raab for his thoughts on the correspondence between the Chief Rabbi and colonial congregations, and to Wendy and Norman Crane and John Danzig for reflections on the finances of the Edinburgh Hebrew Congregation. I am grateful to Michael Adler, Gillian Raab and Elaine Samuel for embracing the idea of a Jewish walking tour in Edinburgh with enthusiasm and drive and for dedicating countless hours of plotting, researching, writing and walking throughout 2017. As we walked, the tour's reservoir of stories grew with each instalment because of our wonderfully participatory audience who contributed their own memories of growing up in Edinburgh. Particular thanks also to Ellen Galford for sharing her experience of constructing Edinburgh's LGBT+ walking tour and for her anecdote about the 'Yiddish Parliament'. Stewart Brown further enlightened the tricky question of what constituted a decent salary for a minister of religion in interwar Edinburgh by offering helpful comparisons with what ministers of the Kirk expected to be paid and receive in benefits when serving in the Scottish capital. Michael Tobias's and Gillian Raab's research on Scottish-Jewish demography and on the census records was helpful specifically when writing Chapter 3, and I am indebted to Gillian, in particular, for insightful discussions about the meaning of statistical data for social history. I thank Benjamin Elton for correspondence about rabbinical beards, and Adam Mendelsohn for sharing prepublication proofs of his article on Jews in Great Britain and the anglophone world. My thanks go to the two anonymous reviewers who read the manuscript for Edinburgh University Press and offered helpful and generous feedback which made the final writing stages so much more rewarding, and to Scott Spurlock who welcomed my book into the series Scottish Religious Cultures, to Jen Daly and the editorial team at EUP for shepherding this book through to publication.

I greatly appreciated the research assistance of Deborah Butcher and Jonathan Tuckett who compiled meticulous lists of relevant documents when the archival records threatened to overwhelm me. A huge thank you goes to Jeremy Kidwell who, with characteristic patience, wit and clarity, explained the benefits of database software to me so that I was able to order my collections of documents, literature and notes, and thereby to build up a searchable network of connections across various forms of evidence. This, in turn, makes me peculiarly indebted to data-management software in the same way as previous generations of scholars might have thanked their card indexes and other physical data-management tools and the skills of real-life research assistants! My online writing group provided me with encouragement and accountability for progressing this book while being committed to administrative and teaching responsibilities at the University of Edinburgh and service to the wider academic community, and was a daily reminder of our identities as scholars and creative professionals when these are threatened with obliteration in attending to the managerial and administrative business our institutions increasingly bestow on us. A flexible working arrangement granted by the University of Edinburgh helped complete this monograph in time for the REF exercise of 2021.

Last, but by no means least, huge thanks to my family: thank you for grounding me, for cheering me on and, most of all, for reminding me that a community of love, praise and labour is the foundation of all that we are and seek to become. This book is dedicated to my father and to the memory of my mother and my parents-in-law who did not live to see its publication. In their different ways, they would have appreciated my work here as an achievement and as a contribution to our conversations.

Introduction

I try to imagine the twenty-three-year-old Dr Sally Daiches, as he was known in 1903, stepping on-board the ship that would take him to Britain. Did he board in Hamburg or Bremerhaven? Where did he alight? Dover, or Southampton, Hull or Grimsby? Or did he dock in Liverpool? His name is not to be found in the shipping lists I have consulted. I see him walking up to the office to complete the formalities preceding embarkation, his suitcase in one hand, his ticket in the other, also holding on to his hat which threatened to blow off and tumble on to the pier. In my mind, the image, though moving, is in the format of an old film reel, black-and-white, our rabbi-to-be and all other people on the pier are moving fast and in the somewhat unnatural way of early films. Salis's face is obscured by the brim of his hat and by the hand which holds it so that I cannot make out his expression. What did he feel as he set foot on to the ship? Was he nervous and apprehensive? Or was he excited, full of hope for the future and calmly confident of a glittering career ahead of him? Perhaps all of these emotions coincided in the young man as he walked up to the large steamer which would deposit him in the south of England before travelling further west to New York. Did Salis travel alone or did his older brother Samuel accompany him? Were they perhaps with a group of friends all set to emigrate westwards? We are unlikely ever to know the answers to these questions.[1] We do know, however, that Salis was part of a large number of young Jewish men who sought their fortune serving Jewish congregations in the anglophone world, men who left behind, at least geographically, the traditions of Eastern European Jewish life.

This monograph adds to a number of recent publications that investigate, or at least presuppose, the mutual influence of Jewish lives across borders during the migrations of Jews in the nineteenth and twentieth centuries. Salis Daiches here exemplifies not only trends in Lithuanian, German and British Jewish Orthodoxy,[2] his life also testifies to an international network of interlocutors in the religious Jewish world: he corresponds with rabbis in Eastern Europe, Germany, and Palestine, and he is headhunted by congregations in South Africa. Not only is Daiches's opinion sought, he is part of a Jewish cultural and intellectual circle that includes the old and the new worlds of Jewish life. Salis Daiches is also part of a movement of religious professionals who cross borders, bringing their specific training, religious practice and ideology to bear on the places in which they live and work. In order to interpret Daiches's professional journey, this book focuses on a specific location, bearing in mind the practices of a transnational historiography 'that is sensitive to local context but also appreciates the interconnections, commonalities, and areas of overlap between communities',[3] such that the local becomes relevant to broader fields of study.

A larger context of inquiry to which this book contributes is that of migration history. As Panikos Panayi demonstrates, British immigration history is composed of a number of different strands of inquiry: in the first place, immigration history was, until recently, primarily written by historians with an immigration background themselves but now is beginning to inform mainstream British national history, thereby diversifying the understanding of the nation and its past. Secondly, a new research focus on the experiences of migrants themselves has developed in the past two decades at the same time as migration narratives and the transmission of the memories of individuals have come to the forefront of the public imagination.[4] As Tony Kushner has shown, much of the energy in the study of immigration to Britain centres on the memory of refugees to the country, particularly refugees from Germany and Nazi-occupied Europe in the 1930s and post-World War II.[5] Within the British Jewish community, as immigration from Eastern Europe soared, interest in the preservation of Jewish heritage arose at the close of the nineteenth century. Heritage, at that time, meant predominantly an engagement with the medieval and early modern contribution of Jews to society and economy, in a drive to keep in the public eye the long-standing and well-established place of Jews in British society. This, along with a programme of 'anglicisation' of recent migrants, were concerted efforts to manage hostility from within and outwith the Jewish community to co-religionists of vastly different cultural and economic backgrounds.

Recent historical approaches to the study of migration differentiate between the investigation of narratives of arrival, narratives of the migrant journey, and narratives of settlement.[6] These approaches are significant in that they allow us to rethink assumptions about the impact of migration by focusing on individual and cumulative biographical research. They are also a consequence of the increasing availability of archives at the points of origin of the Jewish migrants and the various staging posts of the Jewish migrant journey, thus allowing different perspectives on the reasons for, and practices of, leaving one's home to be analysed. The fact that many migrants not only maintained regular exchange with their locations of origin but, following exit from continental Europe, also often migrated more than once to various locations of the anglophone world, is now a feature of research into migration and its effects on individuals, communities and locales.[7] In this book, then, Salis Daiches's life serves as an example that helps us to shine a spotlight on specific aspects of Jewish religious change occasioned by large-scale migration in the early twentieth century. Rabbi Salis Daiches's life thus serves as the focal point for a number of issues relevant to the exploration of religious authority and change and in the understanding of relationships between central and centralising Jewish religious institutions in London – such as the *Chief Rabbi* and the London *Beth Din* – and Jewish life in other cities in the United Kingdom. More specifically, this monograph also contributes to the historiography of British Jewish Orthodoxy by suggesting that a focus on 'provincial' communities can help us better to understand and to interpret religious developments affecting all British Jewry.

Terminology

In the following I use provincial, when referring to Jewish communities outwith London, to indicate their remove from what is generally understood to be the centre of Jewish life in Britain. I indicate with parentheses, however, when there is a need to draw attention to underlying ideological or argumentative assumptions that differentiate centre and periphery and where I suggest that there is a need to (re)-examine these.

I am using British Jewish communities and British Jews or British Jewry throughout to speak about the Jewish population of Britain. This is to signal the geographical location of these Jews and their developing or already established identification with the United Kingdom as a place to settle and call home. More specific identifications of Jews as English, Scottish, Welsh or Irish will be mentioned where appropriate. I do not hyphenate these designations because it seems to me that there is an extent to which these identifications are fluid and adapt to the context in which they are used. For example, Salis Daiches insisted on being a Scottish Jew but he also identified as British Jewish in his loyalty to the state and the Jewish communities across Britain. Earlier studies preferred the term Anglo-Jewry and its derivatives, terminology that has been criticised for its exclusion of Jewish communities of the other nations of the British Isles and for assuming that English Jews, particularly those resident in London, are setting the parameters for the interpretation of Jewish history in Britain.[8]

Orthodox, in the context of this study, refers to Jewish self-descriptions of a particular range of Jewish religious ideologies and practices debated in Germany at the turn of the twentieth century which contrast with other contemporary religious identifications such as Reform and Liberal. The most significant distinguishing feature of all forms of Orthodoxy in this context is the exclusion of the Pentateuch from historical–critical investigation, and the primacy of *halakhah* in the organisation of the life of the individual and a Jewish community. Within Orthodoxy, as we will also observe later in this study, there is a wide spectrum of ideologies and practices, and interpretations of *halakhah*, including the rejection of the designation 'Orthodox' in favour of other descriptors such as 'Conservative', 'traditional' or 'authentic' Judaism. Reform and Liberal Jewish ideologies at the time were not only including the Pentateuch in historical–critical studies, they were also considering the modification of Jewish practice through authorities derived from sources other than *halakhah*.⁹ In Chapter 1 we explore the epithet 'Orthodox' further, specifically in relation to Salis Daiches and the Hildesheimer Seminary, as well as in relation to the United Synagogue and the congregations under the authority of the Chief Rabbi, and those who rejected his leadership. Other Jewish immigrants to the United Kingdom at that time would have eschewed this terminology altogether such that the descriptor 'Orthodox' is better understood as an outsider category. I shall clarify in the text when there is a need to differentiate between insider and outsider use of the epithet 'Orthodox'.

Setting

The comparatively tiny Jewish population of Scotland is well positioned as an example that illustrates major currents in Jewish migration, transnationalism and Orthodox religious authority in the anglophone Jewish world of the early twentieth century. Located at the northernmost Celtic Fringe, Scotland's Jews, even those in the nation's capital city of Edinburgh, were, and are, as far removed from the most populous centre of Jewish life in the London metropolis as is possible on this small island. If, for a moment, we exclude the colonies of the British Empire from our view, in the first half of the twentieth century only the even smaller Jewish population of the Emerald Isle of Éire across the Irish Sea was more difficult to control by the emissaries of the Chief Rabbi of Great Britain and the Empire. During a period characterised by mass migration and massive cultural change, keeping hold of his rabbinical spheres of influence and authority was one of the challenges confronting the Chief Rabbi located in London. While he primarily presided over the largest urban Jewish community of the British Isles and while his office had grown out of the unification of London's *Ashkenazi* synagogues, his jurisdiction encompassed, and encompasses, all British dominions. The centralisation of rabbinical authority under Chief Rabbis Nathan and Hermann Adler has been written about elsewhere and forms the backdrop to the local, regional, national and inter- or transnational analysis of the chapters of this monograph.[10] As will become clear below, one aim of this monograph is to begin to think about local British Jewish religious history within the larger frameworks of Jewish migration and religious organisation across the anglophone world.

As indicated in the preface, Scottish Jewry, along with the Jewish populations of the Celtic Fringe of Ireland and Wales, has, as yet, received little critical scholarly attention. As is true of other regional or 'provincial' Jewish communities, where their history has been written, it has been written largely by local historians who write for a readership principally within their own communities, acting at once as archivists of their community's history and as memory-makers who extend the reservoir of shared narratives.[11] While these local studies are helpful first steps and provide a wealth of information and contextual expertise, little effort has been made to connect the study of Scottish Jewry to similar historiographical work on small Jewish communities in other places, notably in North America, South Africa and Australia.[12] The past decade, however, is characterised by burgeoning scholarship on 'provincial' 'Celtic' Jewish communities in Britain. Here we find historians, literary and film scholars alongside genealogists and statisticians offering new interpretations and extending the conceptual basis for the study of Scottish, Irish, and Welsh Jewry.[13]

The themes Jewish migration, transnationalism and Orthodox religious authority frame the analysis put forward in the four chapters of this book. Thus, the monograph continues modes of inquiry begun in other places, such as Kahn and Mendelsohn's *Transnational Traditions*, and furthers the conversation about what we may learn when we place Jewish history in its own context rather than in that determined by other fields of study. Similar trends in scholarship are observable in the study of Jewish communities in the American south, all of which complement the scholarship on Jews in acknowledged 'Jewish spaces', such as New York and its Lower East Side and London's East End.[14] And scholarship on urban and rural Jewish communities in the American north adds further dimension to the study of the local. I argue for similar attention to be given to Jewish communities in British towns and cities in a manner that eschews both an insider focus on Jewish affairs only and an effort to speak solely in relation to other fields of inquiry by supplying a comparative 'Jewish dimension'. The fact that transnational Jewish history is gathering interest and feeds into the writing of local Jewish history is thus an encouraging sign. In many ways, the current focus on transnational migration studies continues and expands on Sander Gilman's and Milton Shain's 1999 anthology *Jewries at the Frontier*. Here, Gilman proposes the concept of the 'frontier' as a way in which to democratise the study of Jewish history, lifting it out of the binary of an assumed (textual or geographical) centre and a corresponding periphery. Thus, the concept of the frontier allows Jewish history in various places to assume local and international significance without prioritising specific locations. While the notion of 'Jewry at the frontier' primarily speaks to the internal structure of Jewish history, the idea of a transnational Jewish historiography seeks to reflect both inner Jewish historiographical concerns and the relationship of Jewish history to other national histories.

This monograph also touches on how the religious and cultural lives of Jews complicate ideas of identity, in this case of 'Scottishness' and of 'Jewishness'. 'Jewish spaces' are constructed as ethnic, religious and cultural environments as well as real, mappable places. The impression hitherto has been that Jewish migrant communities in Scotland existed in a pattern of transition and acculturation that lies outside major Scottish or Jewish historical narratives of belonging.[15] Studies on larger populations, such as London's East End or New York's Lower East Side, in many ways pave the way for the study of smaller Jewish communities by demonstrating how the perception of 'Jewish space' in specific geographical places is conditioned by historical lives and contemporary narratives that memorialise the people populating these locations in the past.[16] Thus, the distinction between geographic 'place' and Jewish 'space' in Scotland links the development of Scottish Jewish identity formation with a number of factors: urban space, historical memory, cultural production, religious artefacts, religious institutions, texts and documents, all contributing to constructions of belonging. By focusing on the themes of Jewish migration, transnationalism and Orthodox religious authority in a specific local context and 'space', and by discussing them in relation to a particular individual, the monograph adds a new dimension to the study of British Jewish history.

Recent debates in British Jewish historiography

In 2012 Tony Kushner and Hannah Ewence edited the provocatively titled collection *Whatever Happened to British-Jewish Studies?* whose contributions cast a critical eye across the post-war decades of British Jewish historiography.[17] The desire of the editors and several of the contributors was to link the still rather insular work in British Jewish studies with international scholarship in related fields, though achieving this has proven difficult as several of the contributions evidence. For the nineteenth century, we see work on Britain and transnational migration emerge from scholars such as Adam Mendelsohn, and the work of Tobias Brinkmann and Joachim Schloer for the early twentieth century offers a broader view on developments in British Jewish history.[18] Research specifically on Scottish Jews – though the same could be said for research on Welsh and Irish Jews – runs parallel to, rather than in conversation with, research on Scottish (Welsh/Irish) history and migration. Thus, the charge of insularity with regard to Jewish historiography on the Celtic Fringe still stands, yet emerging scholarship on these Jewries, which is utilising the concept of the 'frontier', is set to change this.[19]

This book focuses on a very particular immigrant journey, largely within the United Kingdom, and the analysis presented in the chapters that follow offers an exploration of the themes of migration and acculturation with a still more specific focus on religion, more particularly, Jewish Orthodoxy which is treated here in an international context. In doing so, the book implicitly casts a fresh light on debates in British Jewish historiography. As David Cesarani has outlined, the writing of British Jewish history since the nineteenth century followed, or responded to, particular social and political agendas:

> The study of Anglo-Jewry has been hobbled by an apologetic tendency that has taken two successive forms. The first mode of apologetics was the product of Anglo-Jewry's particular route to modernity and the conditions under which Jews in Britain gained emancipation in the mid-nineteenth century. Jews were accepted not for who and what they

were, but according to terms set by the English majority and cast in the liberal rhetoric of toleration and universalism. Accordingly, Jewish historical research devoted itself to showing that Jews had earned and continued to deserve full civic equality. Research stressed the duration of Jewish settlement in Britain and the contribution of Jews to the 'host' society.[20]

The moves away from the glorification of the medieval Jewish past in Britain, and away from the celebration of British tolerance following readmission under Cromwell, and the move to a critical historiography, occurred with the professionalisation of British Jewish history by a new generation of scholars from the 1960s onwards:

> Prior to the 1960s, Anglo-Jewish studies were almost entirely the preserve of gifted amateurs or part-time historians who combined busy professional lives with research and writing. Cecil Roth was the doyen and virtually sole exponent of professional Jewish Studies in Britain. The monopoly position of enthusiasts in the Jewish Historical Society of England, clustered around Roth, remained virtually unbroken until the welcome intrusion of the American-born and trained Jewish historian Lloyd Gartner. His study *The Jewish Immigrant in England*, published in 1960, catapulted modern Anglo-Jewish history onto a new level of accomplishment and vastly broadened its scope.[21]

Since then, British Jewish history has mainly been written as a contribution to wider British national history, that is as minority history which augments and adds to (and thereby seeks to become relevant to and part of) the mainstream but does not itself set a historiographical agenda.[22] Todd Endelman suggests that, while British Jewish history thus became part of British history, it did not lose its apologetic agenda with regard to its place in British national history or with regard to other historiographical endeavours as the central question remained what the study of Jewish history 'can do for the study of something else'.[23] More positively, he also notes that the insertion of Jewish history into British history helped push the agenda of Jewish historiography away from generalising paradigms and towards more nuance by giving close attention to context and location.[24] And yet, this historiographical trend is only now emerging in regard to Scottish Jewish history and, indeed, in regard to the distinctive histories and identities of 'provincial' Jewry. While there is recent work which seeks to make a wider claim to the relevance of local Scottish Jewish history to the historiography of Jews in Britain and the anglophone world, notably Nathan Abrams's 2009 study of small Jewish communities across Scotland entitled *Caledonian Jews* and the special issue of *Jewish Culture and History* on *Jews in the Celtic Lands*, these exceptions have not yet led to wider historiographical revisionism in 'provincial' Jewish history.[25] There is, then, scope for revisiting local Jewish history in relation to national and international Jewish history and, at the same time, for rethinking the opportunities and limitations of conceptualising minority history in terms of its functionality for other fields of study. Indeed, it needs to be asked whether the hierarchies operating in the construction of national histories obscure more than they enlighten when labelling the local peripheral. Specifically, in relation to Scotland, Edinburgh as the capital city and Glasgow as the then Second City of the British Empire are anything but provincial. Subordinating the national and international significance of these cities to the hierarchy operating in Jewish historiography, which labels Jewish communities outwith London condescendingly 'provincial', limits the possibilities of inquiry into the self-perception of these communities and their leaders. As we will see in the following chapters, Salis Daiches took his 'provincial' communities seriously and invested his activity into them. Hence, we may well question whether today's understanding of 'local' and 'peripheral' versus 'central' accurately captures Daiches's and his contemporaries' perceptions of their location and status.

With the fragmentation of historical inquiry into various subdisciplines from the 1960s onwards, we find a good deal of research on the social and professional transformation of the British Jewish community through and since the large-scale immigration from 1880 to 1914. Here the focus has largely been on the economy and its relationship with the social history of Jews, on issues of culture, food and language, while much less attention has been given to the transformation of the religious life of Jews and the ideological conflicts between British-born and Eastern European religious Jews.[26] Significantly, the pioneering research was carried out by scholars trained in the United States – such as Lloyd P. Gartner, and Todd Endelman – whose perspective on Jewish history was markedly different from that of their British counterparts. Their perception of Jewish history as a national, ethnic, cultural and religious history in its own right, studied across more than two millennia, offered a refreshing vantage point from which to study Jews in Britain. Hence the work of Gartner and Endelman pushed historians in Britain to engage anew with the Jewish history of the twentieth century.

The past two decades have seen a proliferation in the study of British Jewish religious history, first of all through the work of Geoffrey Alderman and, more recently, in the book-length investigations of the British Chief Rabbinate by Miri Freud-Kandel, Benjamin Elton, and Meir Persoff.[27] The focus of these works is on the central religious institutions of Anglo-Jewry, and the authority of the Chief Rabbi located in London. Neither the 'provinces' of the British Isles nor the international anglophone Jewish world are considered as important counterpoints or interlocutors in this research, even though all British Chief Rabbis – with the exception of Hirschell, Brodie, and Sacks – hailed from outwith the United Kingdom and maintained strong relations with rabbis across the Jewish world. Endelman, very reasonably, argues that it would have been helpful had these works included a broader view of Jewish history and indicts what he considers a continuing insular trend even within recent British Jewish historiography.[28]

Another development of the past thirty years is an increased engagement with British Jewish heritage, the archiving of Jewish historical documents and the preservation of artefacts and other items of Jewish material culture, and their academic study. Bill Williams's pioneering study of Manchester Jewry marked not only a broadening of the focus of British Jewish historiography, it also appeared at a time crucial for the preservation of Jewish heritage, architectural, material and documentary. Firstly, Williams put the largest British Jewish community outwith London in the spotlight for the first time. Secondly, Williams also pointed to the failure of the Jewish and wider communities to preserve recent Jewish history at all, allowing the documentary evidence of many defunct communities to disappear into the waste bin of history. In this context, David Cesarani shows convincingly that, even though British Jews did, since Victorian times, have a strong engagement with their heritage in Britain, heritage was deliberately constructed in relation to discourses of British national identity:

> From the 1890s onwards, the construction of an Anglo-Jewish heritage was not merely an exercise in the establishment and perpetuation of Jewish values: it was also part of a continuing struggle with the taxonomy of Englishness. Anglo-Jewish history was part of the weaponry deployed by English Jews in the struggle against exclusionary tendencies in English culture and politics.[29]

As Tony Kushner demonstrates, however, this construction of heritage went together with a (purposeful) neglect, if not destruction, of the documentary, architectural and material culture of contemporary Jewish mass immigration:

> Thus at the same point that the Anti-Demolition Movement was set up to preserve the elite Bevis Marks (the oldest surviving synagogue in Britain with close links to the resettlement of the Jews), establishment Anglo-Jewry was trying [...] to destroy the tiny informal synagogues, or *shtiebls*, which housed the *chevroth* (societies) of the East End. To the elite it was essential to Anglicize the immigrant masses as soon as possible. It was therefore undesirable to preserve for posterity *in any way*, including for the historical record, the immigrants' radical politics or un-English religious habits.[30]

Publications such as *The Making of Manchester Jewry* prompted a turn in the interests of the Jewish Historical Society of England which only as late as the 1980s began to be concerned about the preservation of Jewish heritage and history of the late nineteenth and early twentieth centuries. Since 1990, the University of Southampton has hosted the largest public collection of archival materials relating to Jewish history in Britain complemented by the holdings of the London Metropolitan Archives (LMA), the Jewish Museum London, the Jewish Museum in Manchester and the Scottish Jewish Archives Centre (SJAC).[31]

From the 1960s onwards, British Jewish studies revived with the work of Williams, Endelman, Cesarani and Kushner. Kushner, in particular, pursued migration history alongside local Jewish history, paving the way for studies like the present monograph which seeks to make a contribution to British Jewish history and to migration studies by evaluating the impact of Jewish immigrants on communities outwith London. In this context, Endelman rightly highlights the fruitful preoccupation of a few historians of British Jewry with place, space and locality.[32] Williams and Kushner, in their focus on specific urban and rural communities, and the historians of London's Victorian Jewry, in particular, are mindful of the profound influence of the geographical and architectural contexts in which Jewish lives were, and are, lived. My own monograph works on these themes through the example of Scotland by focusing on Rabbi Salis Daiches's career and a specific geographical and national context. I thereby aim to show the relevance of both place and context for interpreting larger, international currents in Jewish history in the early twentieth century, such as those pertaining to religion and authority in the era of Jewish mass migration. In a sense, this book develops a larger historiographical agenda, taking its cue from Kushner and Ewence and the recent work of Abigail Green, Adam Mendelsohn and David Feldman.

In a 2008 article, Abigail Green called attention to the need to examine the 'encounter between religion and modernity' in an international setting, pointing to the current trend to examine Jewish modernity in national and regional contexts.[33] The focus on analysing Jewish relationships with modernity within national and regional frameworks was understandable, seeing that the social and political conditions across Europe varied as did the moves towards emancipation and as did Jewish responses to these. Green proposes, however, that 'Rethinking the encounter with modernity in terms of a transition from pre-modern Jewish internationality to religious internationalism may help to make good this short-fall.'[34] Green's 2008 article and the subsequent work of Adam Mendelsohn illustrate such reconfigurations of Jewish international networks in the nineteenth century through the examples of Sir Moses Montefiore and emerging networks of migrant religious professionals.[35] This monograph seeks to contribute to the study of Jewish modernity by examining aspects of such Jewish religious internationalism in a local setting through the biography of one migrant religious professional. Further impetus for the exploration of the transnational in the local comes from a 2017 article by David Feldman.[36] Feldman proposes a re-examination of the binary division between Eastern and Western Jewry, taking his cue from Jonathan Frankel who, already in 1992, suggested that, rather than a straightforward opposition between East and West, scholars might be better placed to look out for 'a multiplicity of conflicting forces interacting in unpredictable ways'.[37] Feldman suggests that the following binary account of a straightforward culture clash between Eastern and Western Jews can be found in the works of Alderman, Cesarani and Endelman as well as in his own earlier research:

> With remarkable consistency, we find this history narrated and analyzed as the outcome of interaction between a familiar triad of forces: first, a population of immigrants whose vibrant religious practice and confrontational politics led to conflict with the established communal leaders and institutions; second, an acculturated and decadent community of British-born Jews; and, third, a majority population liable to be hostile to both foreigners and Jews.[38]

As we shall see later on in this monograph as well, however, Bill Williams's 1990 chapter 'East and West'[39] already 'sought to confront the conventional triadic framework of analysis and break from it'.[40]

The history of Jewish migrants and their communities, then, has been, and is being, written from a variety of perspectives, depending on the questions asked by the scholar and the disciplines the writer is at home in. Accordingly, we find national, ethnic and religious approaches to the westward migration of Jews written by archival, social, cultural, and religious historians. These works categorise the subjects of their inquiry in line with the dominant analytical framework of their discipline or the readership they are aiming for. Thus, the ideological and methodological context of scholarship and the intended readership determine the shape of the analysis: are Jews understood as a subgroup which, in some way, needs to be related to the mainstream historiography of a nation, a cultural or a religious context? Or is Jewish history, in the terms of national history, the overarching interpretive framework into which Jewish religious history is inserted as a subcategory? This monograph presents a coherent Jewish historical and religious narrative which seeks to relate its subject to various national, cultural and religious contexts. Migration history and transnational studies appear to be two of the most fruitful frameworks into which to integrate the chapters of this book.[41] Both contexts offer frameworks of inquiry which open the possibility of connecting the history narrated in this book to other contexts of analysis without determining hierarchical relations or dependencies between national, cultural, religious or ethnic histories. Rather, the themes of migration, religious orientation, identity and belonging are explored through the prism of the biography of Rabbi Dr Salis Daiches whose personal story – as far as we are able to piece it together from the sources – offers the opportunity to tap into various discourses without having to pin the analysis into one thematic framework. This approach then reflects on the diversity of experiences and outlooks found within the immigrant and resident Jewish communities which refract and assume a number of, sometimes competing and always coexisting, hierarchies and dependencies. Transnational studies, in particular, allow for the recognition that concepts and experiences identified with the local are of interest not only as contrasts but as features of the transnational framework. While the following analysis is shaped by three overlapping contexts – the life of an individual, the concerns of central Jewish religious institutions in Britain, and the local Scottish scene – the backdrop for the exploration of religious authority is the transnational framework of Jewish migration from Europe to and across the anglophone world.

The sources

The sources available to recover Salis Daiches's biography and his contribution to Jewish life in the United Kingdom are scarce. This is not unusual for his generation of migrants as few documents survived the journey and, until 1987, there was no archive in Scotland dedicated to the preservation of Jewish history.[42] While the collections of some larger Jewish institutions and significant individuals were donated to national and local repositories, the same is not true for the documents of most Jewish organisations and persons of Jewish interest in Scotland. The majority of the papers of the Daiches family, containing mainly those pertaining to Rabbi Dr Salis Daiches, was donated to the National Library of Scotland (NLS) in 2003 by his granddaughter, Jenni Calder, having been with the family for close to sixty years after the death of Salis. It is not possible to reconstruct whether and how the family evaluated and sorted the papers, what was destroyed (accidentally or with purpose), held back or simply lost. For example, it is surprising that we have very little record of extensive correspondence with Daiches from any other well-connected rabbi in the first two decades of the twentieth century. One reason for this might be that Salis Daiches himself may have not kept records from this period though we have no way of knowing whether this was the case. Only from 12 October 1925 to 23 May 1932 did he appear to keep a correspondence book.[43] This book allows the tracing of some correspondence but, crucially, the early years of his residence in the United Kingdom, his work in Hull and Sunderland, as well as the first seven years of his work in Edinburgh are not recorded systematically or at all. It is also not possible to ascertain whether this correspondence book holds all the letters sent during the period in which the book was in use. The correspondence book does not, for example, collect personal letters but is filled solely with letters sent in his capacity as rabbi of the Edinburgh Hebrew Congregation. It is most likely that the rabbi did not systematically keep copies of his own letters nor those addressed to him before and after this period which would have allowed him (and others later on) to trace his professional correspondence; and private correspondence is close to non-existent.[44] Additionally, it is likely that files were lost or destroyed in the family's many moves or not deemed suitable or relevant to be given to the archive.[45] The Daiches family archive at the NLS contains only a few private letters addressed to Salis Daiches. The bulk of the archive consists of a significant collection of handwritten sermons, some manuscript drafts, proofs of publications and an array of syllabus cards and invitations for Salis to speak, legal papers concerning a major court case in the 1920s, the Levison Case, and assorted newspaper cuttings and miscellaneous printed matter.[46]

Casting a wider net, there is no record of rabbinical or other official community correspondence for any of Edinburgh's synagogues nor for the majority of Glasgow's synagogues. Hardly any records of the immigrants' synagogues survive and there are no papers accessible in local or national archives either pertaining to the rabbis serving them. While the SJAC has been collecting all manner of documentation about the Jewish communities in Scotland and continues to receive donations on a weekly basis, papers concerning the religious organisation of the communities and those relating to religious professionals (rabbis, ministers, cantors)[47] are hardly found in the archive. If such papers survive, they would be in the possession of family members many of whom have moved on to different locations in the United Kingdom, Israel or further afield. The records that survive in the SJAC are mainly minute books and even these are far from complete even for the oldest Glaswegian community in Garnethill. This is not an unusual state of affairs seeing that the drive to collect recent Jewish heritage in the United Kingdom post-dates the move to the suburbs, the decline of many synagogues and the resulting loss of real estate which had the consequence that most of the paper documents of abandoned synagogues and community centres were pulped when the land and buildings were repurposed.[48] Scotland is no exception among British nations and regions here, and the absence of materials complicates the reconstruction of the development of national British and Scottish, as well as local, traditions in relation to and extension of the *minhag(im)* brought by migrants.

A source which has hardly been evaluated is the extensive correspondence of the Chief Rabbi's office with communities across Britain and the anglophone world. My own analysis of the correspondence of Daiches and others with the Chief Rabbi's office thus is one of the first forays into a study of the community-related correspondence, promising a fruitful field for further study.[49] Among other things, a detailed evaluation of similar correspondence would allow us to understand more about local religious practices and disputes which arose, for example, with regard to *minhag*. Staff at the Chief Rabbi's office kept a record of incoming correspondence and carbon copies of letters sent. While there is no way of knowing whether the surviving record is complete, the Chief Rabbi's archive having changed locations a number of times in the twentieth century before finding permanent homes in the LMA and in the Anglo-Jewish Archives at the University of Southampton's Hartley Library (HLS), a strong and continuous record does survive. These two archives also hold papers and reports pertaining to the Conference of Anglo-Jewish Ministers (later Preachers) which will play an important part in the discussion in Chapter 2.

Research on Scottish Jewish history to date has made extensive use of the archives of the *Jewish Chronicle* (*JC*), the oldest surviving Jewish weekly newspaper, and the local press in Scotland.[50] Regarding the Scottish Jewish press, hardly anything survives of the *Yiddish* papers,[51] and it is only with the establishment of the English-language *Jewish Echo* in 1928 that an unbroken line of weekly issues is available until its final edition in 1992.[52] The community journal the *Edinburgh Star*, founded in 1989, regularly carries obituaries as well as articles remembering aspects of community life from the early twentieth century.[53] With decreasing opportunities for gathering ethnographic material on Jewish life during Rabbi Salis Daiches's tenure, the *Star* and the memories of Daiches's contemporaries offer some insight into the perception of his work, albeit mainly from the vantage point of those who were small children at the time of Daiches's ministry.

In 1928 Daiches published one volume of essays, *Aspects of Judaism*, in which he gathered a number of philosophical essays and some linguistic works he had developed since his days as a student.[54] He intimates in the introduction that he planned to publish another book of collected essays.[55] Certainly, Daiches had much material from which to craft another anthology. He had many speaking engagements and, unless he spoke freely most of the time, he would have had a mass of notes and perhaps even full speech manuscripts. It seems that Salis Daiches wrote his sermons in longhand for most of his career. While we do not have a complete collection of his sermons, there are enough to allow a detailed evaluation of his preaching.[56] Daiches's obituary in *The Scotsman* also suggests that he planned to publish a collection of his sermons.[57] Furthermore, the syllabus cards and invitations to speak allow a reconstruction of Daiches's status in the wider community and also, when triangulated with his diaries, give a reliable insight into his busy speaking schedule.

How do we evaluate these different sources? We have no 'ego-documents' from Salis, unless we think of letters written in a professional capacity as such, seeing that they project a deliberate public image of the rabbi. The professional correspondence is the largest part of the available written sources and, as such, sets the reader right *in medias res*. Syllabus cards and diaries offer an insight into when something happened and where and sometimes also who was present. Beyond that, we can only infer proceedings from events documented in the press and extrapolate what is likely to have taken place in other venues. Memories of Salis Daiches are prominent in David Daiches's *Two Worlds* because they occupy substantial space in the memoir and because the memories David Daiches has of his father are the most prominent text we have about the rabbi. The status of the text as a memorial and a coming to terms with the death of his father, while David himself was on the other side of the Atlantic and unable to participate directly in the family's mourning, informs what we may glean from the book about Salis and how he was perceived in the community and beyond. Reminiscences in the *Edinburgh Star* and local memoirs, such as Howard Denton's *The Happy Land*, are reflections on childhood perceptions of the rabbi and contemporary Jewish life, and coloured accordingly. Taken together, these sources provide a seedbed for a historical analysis of Rabbi Salis Daiches's work and offer some clues about his personality and the effect he had on others.

The chapters

The career of an immigrant rabbi who came to the United Kingdom in 1903 and ministered in three communities (Hull, Sunderland and Edinburgh) which were composed of British and immigrant Jews, and, indeed, Salis Daiches's own migration journey, his ideology and his leadership ambitions, form the thread linking the four chapters of this book. The rabbi's career path offers an opportunity to evaluate aspects of the contribution made by immigrant rabbis to the structure of the Jewish community in Britain through ideology and leadership (Chapter 1). The early decades of the twentieth century and the growth of the Jewish communities made Jews much more publicly visible in many cities of the United Kingdom. As a result, the relationship with the non-Jewish majority population came to matter enormously to the British Jewish leadership, particularly in the lead-up to both World Wars when 'aliens' were subject to much suspicion. 'Anglicising' rabbis, such as Salis Daiches, who placed a positive relationship with secular society and education at the centre of his ministry, allow us to understand better the efforts of the leadership of the British Jewish community to promote integration without the loss of tradition. At the same time, placing rabbis trained on the Continent in leadership positions across Britain's religious Jewish communities exposed conflicting visions of congregational life and religious authority among immigrants as well as in relation to the central institutions of Jewish religious authority in Britain: the Chief Rabbi and the London Beth Din.

Rabbi Salis Daiches's life, then, also allows a closer investigation of the relationship of the United Kingdom's regional communities to the centralised institutions of the United Synagogue in London, notably the Chief Rabbi and the London Beth Din (Chapter 2). Glasgow, as the Second City of the British Empire since the late nineteenth century, has boasted the largest Jewish community in Scotland: up to 15,000 Jews were resident in Glasgow at the community's largest expansion just before World War I; Edinburgh's community, at its greatest expansion, numbered no more than 2,000 Jews. It was Edinburgh, however – as the Scottish capital closely associated with the intellectual traditions of the Scottish Enlightenment – which first attracted the services of a rabbi of greater public stature: Daiches, trained by both Eastern European rabbis and also trained in the context of the modern Orthodox German Jewish tradition of the Hildesheimer Seminary in Berlin, a combination hitherto unparalleled in Scotland. Hence, while serving the smaller, and thus numerically less significant or impactful, community, Daiches became the public face of Scotland's Jews, able to articulate 'the Jewish contribution' to society and the compatibility (as he saw it) of Orthodox belief, values and practices with full participation in the secular life of the country. Glasgow boasted a number of Eastern European rabbis of excellent stature[58] but it took until the appointment of Reverend I. K. Cosgrove at Garnethill Synagogue in 1935 for a Glaswegian minister to match Daiches's outward-facing disposition with someone who was able to forge a firm relationship with the Scottish churches and other public institutions in the city.

The relationship between the religious Jewish leaders in Edinburgh and Glasgow following World War I allows us to examine the reach of the Chief Rabbi's authority in the United Kingdom's northernmost Jewish population (Chapter 3). While the size of Glasgow's Jewish community rendered Daiches largely irrelevant to local Jewish politics in Glasgow, his unparalleled combination of religious and secular learning, his close relationship with Chief Rabbi Joseph Hertz and his popularity in non-Jewish society made him an ideal 'outpost' of the London Beth Din in Scotland, conveniently positioned to offer a public defence of Jews and Judaism. The friendly relationship Salis Daiches enjoyed with Hertz arguably also had an impact on how he was perceived locally.

Thus, the first three chapters of this monograph evaluate, from different perspectives, the perception of the institution of the Chief Rabbinate and resulting authority structures. Rabbis and other Jewish religious functionaries trained in various locations on the Continent and adhering to, and propagating, a number of religious ideologies faced the question of how to relate to the Chief Rabbi. Here, a transnational perspective is particularly helpful as it is plausible to suggest that the perception of the institution by immigrants was based on their experience of Jewish leadership structures and *halakhic* authority in other countries. For example, was the Chief Rabbinate perceived predominantly as a representation of Jewish leadership to gentiles or was it seen as an institution for resolving differences within the Jewish community? For immigrants who hailed from states in which the authority of chief rabbis and central *batei din* was more extensive, the Chief Rabbi in London might have been perceived as an institution of the state to exert control over the Jewish community and he might have been accepted because of a perceived relative weakness of autonomous religious structures that might seek solutions for Jewish issues independent of the state.[59] For the resident Jewish community, the Chief Rabbi may also have had a function analogous to the relationship enjoyed by the Anglican Church with the monarchy. Indeed, the origins of the Chief Rabbinate, as conceived and implemented during Nathan Adler's tenure from the middle of the nineteenth century onwards, suggest that the office of the Chief Rabbi was directly modelled on that of the Archbishop of Canterbury with the ambition of similar authoritative and representative functions, and a close alignment to the monarchy. It is possible simply to suggest that the key difference between immigrants is their Continental region of origin: those originating in the East had experience of strong Jewish communal autonomy and limited authority granted to state rabbinate, while the mental maps of those having lived in the West relied on small Jewish communities within strong states whose centralising rabbinate reflected the need to work with gentile powers. Perhaps, however, it may be possible to differentiate this picture further and research across different parts of the Russian Empire at different times, and focus on the large city communities of the Habsburg Empire and those in Frankfurt–Berlin–East Prussia who numbered secessionist communities alongside the *Einheitsgemeinde*. Salis Daiches and his brother Samuel probably would naturally have resisted a strong central chief rabbinate model, seeing that they hailed from Vilna and lived in Königsberg and Berlin within the secessionist forms of Orthodoxy. By contrast, as we shall see in Chapters 1 and 2, the transformation of the Chief Rabbinate and the United Synagogue under Nathan Adler also reflect ideas about the safeguarding of the dignity of the Jewish community which can be seen to parallel arguments about the function of the monarch. This monograph proposes that further research into conflicting models of leadership and authority among Jewish immigrants and residents is warranted in the future. Indeed, it may be helpful to complicate the picture roughly outlined above by detailed attention to the diverse cultural factors which affect how Jews in early twentieth-century Britain – long-term residents and recent immigrants – assess the legitimacy and effectiveness of the Chief Rabbi in London.[60]

The book concludes with a chapter on memory, seeking to position the Jewish community of Edinburgh and its most significant rabbi in the twentieth century within the city's and the community's narrative and physical spaces (Chapter 4). Edinburgh's 'Jewish spaces' are created by those who inhabit(ed) them and by the relationship of the current residents of Edinburgh to these spaces, physically and in local memory.[61] Thus, a map of contemporary Edinburgh can be viewed as a palimpsest which enables the reader to view various perspectives on the city's history through the eyes of previous and current inhabitants. The fourth chapter explores David Daiches's memoir *Two Worlds: An Edinburgh Jewish Childhood*, first published in 1957, and a recently created Jewish walking tour of Edinburgh's Southside, 'Jewish Edinburgh on Foot'. I would argue that it is possible that, in the Jewish community and among interested outsiders, we observe community-sustaining local narratives across local cultural, transgenerational and also transnational boundaries. As migrants, Jews are often identified with urban environments. Patterns of Jewish settlement are a way of observing the transformation of city spaces into Jewish spaces. Tony Kushner argues in *Anglo-Jewry since 1066* that

> British Jewish history has been regarded as being of minor importance, and its provincial experiences even more so. Yet the histories revealed in *Anglo-Jewry since 1066* show the richness of previously neglected

Jewish communities from the medieval era onwards. They show that the 'global is everywhere and already, in one way or another, implicated in the local'.[62]

Chapter 4, by mapping changes in the interpretation of parts of the city of Edinburgh by today's resident Jewish population, contributes to a better understanding of the performance of religious and cultural identities of an urban immigrant population in the first half of the twentieth century, and the place historical memories of the Jewish residents have in the local and international imagination of this city. Indeed, with Kushner I would argue that

> Jews were an integral part of the local world, and their subsequent invisibility or problematic, 'alien', representation fails to do justice to the richness of the past. Movement and diversity are not simply products of modernity: heterogeneity is the natural order of things. While rarely acknowledged, the places covered in this study were, I argue, in Ruth Gruber's phrase, 'virtually Jewish'. By acknowledging and accepting that *all* places (and not just the post-Holocaust European continent) are, amongst other things, 'virtually Jewish', we can at least start to challenge the ethnic and racial certainties that are continuing and intensifying in the twenty-first century.[63]

And yet, I would also wish to introduce a different slant: whereas Kushner is highlighting that, in the local, one can helpfully contrast heterogeneity of experience with certainties of ideology about identities, I am also wanting to highlight ways in which performances of authority and religious ideology embed both local and transnational components and thus expose a heterogeneity which need not be used to counter certainties. Starting with the migrant journey of Salis Daiches from Vilna via Königsberg, Berlin and Leipzig to Leeds, and, more than a decade later, to Edinburgh, we begin to explore the location of religious ideology and authority in the Jewish spaces created by early twentieth-century Jewish immigrants in Scotland.

CHAPTER 1

Portrait and Ideology

In the *sukkah* of the Edinburgh Hebrew Congregation there is a display of portraits of the community's rabbis. Whenever I visit this building, perhaps to take my children for an event or to pick up a delivery of *kosher* food from Glasgow, I pause in front of this wall of mostly black-and-white portraits of distinguished-looking gentlemen. There they are, in their best suits, worn for the occasion of taking a portrait; some have donned a *tallit* and all face the viewer with a look of benevolence and slight distance. My five-year-old points at the large frame, situated slightly to the left, and exclaims 'Mama, there is your rabbi!' Indeed, Salis Daiches's portrait stands out as plain and commanding at the same time. He wears all the markers of his status, no *tallit* but a clerical hat and gown and a large Geneva band collar, items which distinguish a religious functionary in the early twentieth century. British rabbis, along with their German counterparts, had long adopted a uniform similar to that of Protestant clergy. In the portrait, Daiches faces to the viewer's left, his eyes look into the distance, as if searching for an acquaintance on the far side of the room. A somewhat austere presence whose sense of humour is just about visible behind a small goatee and the moustache framing his lips. The *sukkah* houses the synagogue's library, an assortment of furniture and bric-a-brac currently not needed in the main building and is infrequently used these days. I wonder what Daiches would think about the assembly of portraits surveying this somewhat chaotic space. Would he set about energetically to rearrange the room and instil some of the decorum he so favoured? Would he feel even a little at home in the synagogue building he initiated, whose completion he oversaw, and into which he processed alongside Chief Rabbi Joseph Hertz and Edinburgh city dignitaries at its inauguration in 1932? What would he have to say about that much-discussed topic: the decline of the community which now has only one full-time employee, the rabbi, and whose membership has been shrinking for decades? How would he relate to the other Jewish congregation in town, Sukkat Shalom – Edinburgh Liberal Jewish Community – which as yet has no building of its own? More than seven decades have passed since Daiches's death in office in 1945, and the Jewish landscape of Edinburgh has been completely transformed; the uninitiated observer will notice little of the Jewish life once teeming in parts of the city. There are identifiable structures of Jewish history in a few corners across the city but the synagogue, built to reflect the aspirations of Daiches for the Jewish community of the Scottish capital, is the most obvious Jewish feature of the city. For this reason, and for others too, the life and work of Rabbi Dr Salis Daiches remains intimately connected to the history of the Jewish community in Edinburgh, indeed with Scotland's Jewish history. That he is hailed as its most significant religious leader in the twentieth century speaks to his role in serving the community when it was most populous and to his impact in creating a model for a Scottish Jewish symbiosis which, decades later, is still associated with Daiches by Jews in Edinburgh.

Salis Daiches's life personalises and exemplifies the migration from Eastern Europe to the United Kingdom taken by more than 120,000 Jews between 1880 and 1914. His journey, in many ways, paralleled that of others caught up in the mass migration to the West, escaping poverty and lack of economic prospects, and sometimes also persecution. Among those seeking their fortunes in Western Europe and the anglophone world of the British colonies and of North America were also religious functionaries, cantors and rabbis, teachers of Hebrew, Bible and *Talmud*, who sought employment in Jewish congregations. The large-scale migration from the late nineteenth century onwards presented challenges to existing community organisation, and propelled the creation of new structures of authority as migrants had to reconfigure their position in Jewish and non-Jewish society following the upheaval of international and often intercontinental moves. Central to Jewish religious developments in the anglophone world was the Chief Rabbi of Great Britain and the Empire. It was Nathan Adler who configured this office so that, from the middle of the nineteenth century, he exerted authority not only over the congregations of the United Synagogue in London but also over all Ashkenazi Orthodox communities in the United Kingdom and over colonial congregations, in an effort to establish a more homogenous Orthodoxy throughout the Empire.[1] Adler, as Chief Rabbi, presided over the London Beth Din which functioned, among other things, as arbiter in all *halakhic* matters, particularly those concerning Jewish status, and the appointment of religious functionaries. While congregations in the United States were not formally under Adler's jurisdiction, his authority was sought by migrants en route to America and by American congregations looking to employ religious officials.[2] In the emerging 'international ministerial marketplace', fluency in English offered 'opportunities for personal and financial advancement'.[3] Salis Daiches was one such migrant who sought his religious and economic fortunes in Britain, having been educated in the Lithuanian part of the Russian Empire, and then in Germany, at both religious and secular institutions at which he gained the highest academic qualifications.

Daiches's religious qualifications were obtained in the 'old world' but he brought with him the modern Orthodox outlook cultivated at the Hildesheimer Rabbinical Seminary of Berlin and, with this, an ideology of *Torah u'maddah*, a combination of traditional religious with secular learning which had grown in German-speaking lands since the middle of the nineteenth century. The post-Enlightenment generation, which included scholars such as the Seminary's founder Esriel Hildesheimer, Samson Raphael Hirsch, Zacharias Frankel, Leopold Zunz and Abraham Geiger, came of age in a world in which many Jews had the opportunity to engage with vastly different models of education. Exposed to various social, scientific and religious discourses, these rabbis, and others alongside them, sought to develop, for the first time, a modern Jewish curriculum to educate a new generation of rabbis. At the same time, these scholars furthered historical scholarship on Jewish texts through *Wissenschaft des Judentums*. All embraced a secular curriculum, though they did so with varying rationale and enthusiasm. They also had to formulate a response to one another's approach to the study of Jewish textual history and the implications such academic pursuit had for Jewish religious thought and practice. Marc Shapiro succinctly summarises Esriel Hildesheimer's interpretation of *Torah u'maddah* as follows:

> Hildesheimer's approach was to establish a rabbinical seminary, for he believed that Orthodoxy would only survive in modern times if there were spiritual leaders who were thoroughly conversant with the era they were living in. [. . .]
>
> Hildesheimer's seminary was the only institution under Orthodox auspices in which students were required to have a significant secular education before they were admitted. It was expected that they would also continue their general education at the university level.[4]

Hildesheimer's colleagues – Zacharias Frankel at the rabbinical seminary in Breslau and Abraham Geiger at the (Liberal) *Hochschule für die Wissenschaft des Judentums* in Berlin – agreed on the need for a secular curriculum alongside a religious one, and all agreed on the necessity of the academic study of Judaism as part of the religious education of rabbis.[5] Indeed, as Elton argues, 'Hildesheimer was convinced that the use of the methods of *Wissenschaft* would reveal more of the truth, which was the object of all study and a sacred undertaking.'[6] Where they differed was in the approach such academic inquiry should take in relation to the Pentateuch and the historical development of *halakhah*. Frankel and Geiger, to different degrees, were willing to incorporate biblical texts, including the Pentateuch, in their historical inquiry. Hildesheimer and his Orthodox colleagues either refrained from doing so or qualified their approach with a set of presuppositions about the divine origin of the text of the Torah (*Torah min hashamayim*) which precluded the texts' historicisation.[7]

The simultaneous pursuit of religious and secular learning decisively influenced the American East Coast, notably the rabbinical seminaries in New York, such as the Jewish Theological Seminary (JTS). JTS was founded and staffed by graduates of the Hildesheimer and Breslau rabbinical seminaries and modelled, in the words of Bernard Drachman, on 'the fundamental harmony of the basic concepts of Traditional Judaism and its adjustment to modern conditions' as espoused by both Berlin and Breslau.[8] Indeed, JTS and its more traditional counterpart, the Rabbi Isaac Elchanan Theological Seminary, the rabbinical training college of Yeshiva University, formed the main educational centres which supported the establishment of rabbinical associations and authority structures of American Orthodoxy in the early twentieth century. In contrast to the centralised organisation of rabbinical authority in Imperial Britain with London's Chief Rabbi at its head – a position which placed the British Chief Rabbi at the helm of all anglophone congregations of the Empire – American Orthodoxy did not adopt this model, opting instead for a non-centralised administration in which various rabbinical and educational institutions exist side by side, if not always in harmony.[9]

JTS was alma mater to Joseph Hertz who was its first graduate and who later became Chief Rabbi of Great Britain and the Empire, a position he held from 1913 until his death in January 1946. While Hildesheimer graduates who migrated in the years before World War I and in the interwar years in the majority flocked to the opportunities offered by the United States, some, like Salis Daiches, by deliberation or accident, made their lives in the United Kingdom. In this chapter we shall explore aspects of Daiches's life as an example of an immigrant's journey which illustrates major themes in the history of early twentieth-century British Jewish religious communities. While the specifics of Daiches's biography are not shared by the majority of religious functionaries who immigrated to Britain in the early twentieth century, his employment journey saw him serving different congregations in the United Kingdom, and his religious ideology helps us to understand better the transformation of British Jewry in the first half of the twentieth century. In short, this rabbi's life and work allow us to explore seminal issues regarding the changes within British Jewry in the years of, and following, the great migration. Through focusing on religion and tracing one immigrant's career, we shall thus gain a deeper understanding of the migrant journeys of elite religious professionals to, and particularly within, the United Kingdom.[10] Daiches is well placed to serve as an example of the journey from Eastern European to modern Orthodoxy and acculturation to Britain. His published writings and the range of his public-speaking engagements evidence a clear mission to demonstrate the compatibility of traditional Jewish life with the opportunities open to Jews in a modern society, such as Britain, which did not discriminate by law against minorities.

This chapter, then, has a number of aims: by embedding Salis Daiches's biography in research on Jewish migration at the end of the long nineteenth century, I seek to focus particularly on the transformation of the religious character of the United Synagogue during the tenure of Chief Rabbis Hermann Adler (1891–1911) and Joseph Hertz (1913–46).[11] Such an approach is necessary for understanding the transnational context in which local debates about religious authority were carried out: to understand these debates we need to be sensitive to the cultural, religious and educational background of the participants. Most research in this field concentrates on the office of the Chief Rabbi and the London-based United Synagogue.[12] The already condescendingly named 'provinces' do not receive much attention in these accounts and, if they do, only in relation to the concerns of the centralising United Synagogue.[13] Social history research in this field rightly highlights the Eastern European religious traditions of Jewish immigrants and the clashes with the British-born Jewish population across the United Kingdom.[14] Yet, to date, other than for the Chief Rabbis, there is no study of the contribution made by individual Jewish religious leaders in the transformation of Jewish communities in the wake of the mass migration which overwhelmed small resident communities with co-religionists of very different cultures.[15] Salis Daiches is one such leader: while he originated in Eastern Europe, he was educated in Berlin and developed there a modern Orthodox ideology which he used to suggest to immigrants the possibility of becoming fully British without losing what he perceived to be the 'essence' of Judaism. The only British figures with a similar educational background and ideological orientation to have been examined in some detail are the Chief Rabbis, from the Adlers through to Jacobovits, with a strong focus in the existing literature on Hertz himself.[16] I shall argue here that an analysis of the life's work of one 'provincial' rabbi, who was trained in Germany at the Orthodox Rabbinical Seminary of Berlin, sheds new light on the relationship between the 'provinces' and London. Indeed, I suggest that a focus on the leadership of religious congregations is a topic which needs greater scholarly attention.[17] Even where social histories observe a declining interest in religious observance and community affiliation among immigrants, the leadership is worth examining in its own right for its perception of the context the leaders are working in. The case looked at here may add substantial detail to our understanding of a strategy used already by Chief Rabbi Hermann Adler but particularly employed by Joseph Hertz to ensure the Orthodoxy of congregations at the same time as mediating between British Jewish and immigrant religious traditions: committing a rabbi, such as Salis Daiches, whose training satisfied the religious standards and expectations of both immigrants and residents, to act as a de facto representative of the London Beth Din in the region in which he was appointed, complemented the co-opting of traditionally trained immigrant rabbis on to the London Beth Din.[18] Most rabbis emigrating to the United Kingdom from Germany in the years prior to World War I were of Eastern European origin. At that time Eastern European students constituted between 24 and 50 per cent of the student body of the Hildesheimer Seminary,[19] the number of German-born and German-trained rabbis being small in the first place and those emigrating subsequent to completing their rabbinical education even fewer.[20] Hungarian graduates of the Hildesheimer scored the most desirable rabbinical positions in Germany whereas Russians had considerably lesser odds in accessing pulpits in big cities.[21] Hence British Jewish communities could have been in a good position to employ rabbis who matched the London Beth Din's desire for standards of secular education among Jewish religious professionals while, at the same time, satisfying the traditional religious expectations sought after in the communities which, by the early twentieth century, were predominantly formed by migrants from Eastern Europe.

In Chapter 2 we shall see that Salis Daiches, who had Eastern European rabbinical ordination as well as Western certification by the Hildesheimer Rabbinical Seminary, was immensely useful to the Chief Rabbi. An impressive line-up of Eastern and Western rabbinical endorsement placed Salis Daiches in the position of being a religious professional able to bridge the gap between both worlds, being equally conversant in the traditional religious, modern Orthodox, and secular cultures.[22] In all his correspondence and public statements, definitely since his appointment in Sunderland in 1908, Daiches insisted on the title 'rabbi', that is, in his understanding, someone who has the authority to make *halakhic* rulings, in contrast to colleagues who lacked rabbinical ordination and had to defer to a *beth din* or at least to a qualified rabbi.[23] In many ways, Salis Daiches was 'overqualified' for the job specification of a minister of the United Hebrew Congregations of the British Empire.[24] The Chief Rabbi's Office took a close interest in the hire of Jewish clergy, particularly those seeking to serve in larger congregations or as a *rav* to the entire community of a city. As in other cities with a growing Jewish population – such as Manchester and Leeds – Glasgow's fragmented Jewish communities for a long time were held together by a single authority figure (*rav*) approved of by all: Rabbi Samuel Hillman. Hillman's departure for London in 1914 to serve as *dayan* on the London Beth Din led to a flurry of correspondence by various congregations about appointments of rabbis who may fit the brief of a *rav* for the entire city.[25] Hillman was the first appointment to the London Beth Din from Scotland; indeed, the first from the 'provinces'. Later appointments, particularly those of Chaikin and Schonfeld, hailed predominantly from the East End of London.[26]

Rabbi Daiches arrived in Edinburgh in 1919. He could not fulfil the position of *rav* in Glasgow, owing to his own ideological position which favoured a modern presentation in language and appearance, and thus would have rebuffed the majority of the immigrants who hailed from *Yiddish*-speaking, traditionally Orthodox Jewish cultures. Further against him was the distance between the cities, and the different community structures, and the general perception of rivalry between Scotland's two major cities.[27] As we shall see in Chapters 2 and 3, however, appointing Daiches as minister to the Edinburgh Hebrew Congregation was significant for Scottish Jewry as a whole: firstly, the Chief Rabbi explicitly affirmed Daiches as a rabbinical authority in Scotland, often conferring with him about questions concerning Jewish status in relation to possible irregularities in conversions or marriages in Scotland.[28] Secondly, as we shall see, Daiches had already established a reputation as an orator who would do well in uniting the fragmented community in Edinburgh and in making Jewish religious life accessible to wider society. As such, Daiches was useful to the Chief Rabbi by furthering his mission to demonstrate the possibility of a harmonious relationship between Jewish religious ideology and life in a secular society. At the same time, when necessary, Daiches was able to act decisively in matters of *halakhah*, thus commanding the respect of the Glasgow Jewish community without being in a position to assume its formal headship. This was useful as the departure of Rabbi Hillman to the London Beth Din had left a gap in the city's religious Jewish leadership which had not been filled by a man of similar stature. The Glasgow weekly, the *Jewish Echo*, not without criticism of local leaders and initiatives, had no critical word to say about Rabbi Salis Daiches in any of its pages. To be sure, the obituaries penned for Daiches were not numerous and nor were eulogies printed in honour of Daiches when he died prematurely in the spring of 1945, aged only sixty-five but, understandably, other historical events that spring took priority in people's minds. There is not a single article in the *Echo* which suggests anything other than outright admiration for the Edinburgh rabbi.

Biography and migration

Salis Daiches was born Bezalel Daiches in 1880 near Vilna, Lithuania, then part of the Russian Empire. He was one of ten children born to Rabbi Israel Hayyim Daiches and his wife Bella Bielitzki who both migrated to Leeds in 1901. Following an early education with his father, Salis completed a transitional qualification at the *Kneiphöfisches Gymnasium* in Königsberg, East Prussia, studied philosophy for one semester at the Alberts University in Königsberg and then matriculated at the Hildesheimer Rabbinical Seminary and the *Königliche Friedrich-Wilhelms Universität zu Berlin*.[29] While his older brother, Samuel, chose doctoral work in the field of ancient history and philology alongside his rabbinical studies, Salis gained his doctorate in philosophy at the University of Leipzig with a dissertation on the relationship of historiography to practical philosophy in the works of David Hume (1903).[30] We can trace his acquisition of English to his engagement with Hume, and he does not seem to have had any difficulty in gaining fluency in English soon after arrival in Leeds in 1903. Salis occupied positions as minister first in Hull and then in Sunderland, interrupted only briefly by a year as a locum in Hammersmith. In 1919 he moved to Edinburgh where he remained rabbi to the Edinburgh Hebrew Congregation until his untimely death in the spring of 1945.

This brief overview of the main staging posts of Salis Daiches's life belies the cultural and religious journey that accompanied the physical movement of this rabbi across Europe. Born into a *Litvak* rabbinical dynasty and growing up speaking *Yiddish* as *mameloshn*, Israel Hayyim Daiches, notwithstanding – or even because of – his rabbinical standing, chose to supplement his sons' traditional education with instruction in a German grammar school, rendering both Salis and his older brother Samuel fluent in at least three languages: *Yiddish*, Hebrew (and Aramaic) and German. The decision to add education in secular subjects set Salis and Samuel Daiches on a seemingly inevitable journey westwards. As far as we can determine, Daiches senior seems to have remained within the traditional world of Eastern European Judaism, even following his move to Leeds in 1901 as rabbi of Beth Hamedrash Hagadol Synagogue.[31] He appears, however, to have encouraged his sons to seek their fortunes in the West by supporting their secular education while ensuring that they both also completed rabbinical training worthy of an Eastern European *rav*.[32] In contrast to their German-born contemporaries, the Daiches brothers thus were part of the last generation of rabbis to unite these two educational systems within their own biographies. Many of their contemporaries lacked one or other form of training; rabbinical training was in flux at the turn of the twentieth century, being subject to both ideological conflicts and massive population movements.[33] Salis Daiches and his older brother, Samuel, thus were perhaps in the rather exceptional position of bringing the 'old world' with them into the 'new', their children already no longer able fully to access these worlds, having grown up in a very different society and culture.[34] Salis Daiches's generation was also the last before the Holocaust to have been able to migrate West without being displaced by war. Daiches took part fully in the educational opportunities offered by both his native culture and by the cultures he migrated into. Bearing in mind the transnational framework of this book, it is helpful to pause briefly and reflect that the Daiches brothers' journey troubles some of the stereotypes all too easily implied when referring to a contrast between East European and German Jewish habitus in the late nineteenth century. At the time, Vilna was a cosmopolitan city, as was Königsberg in East Prussia, places which thrived economically and where Jews and non-Jews mixed. Young Jews had educational and cultural opportunities removed from the impoverished *shtetls* and their *yeshivot* in the *Pale of Settlement*. An echo of this tolerant and outward–looking environment can be detected in the life of Immanuel Jacobovits who hailed from Königsberg and was Britain's Chief Rabbi from 1967 to 1991.

The educational and linguistic journey westwards was complemented by a matching cultural journey. How much the cultural change which then influenced the religious ideology of Salis Daiches was through gradual acculturation or premeditated intellectual choice is hard to tell because we do not have enough evidence to piece together the student life of the Daiches brothers in Berlin and Leipzig. Outwith David Daiches's memoir *Two Worlds*, which includes reflections on his father's journey, and Salis's university matriculation books, we can gain circumstantial evidence from Jack Wertheimer's study *Unwelcome Strangers: East European Jews in Imperial Germany*. Wertheimer argues that at German universities Jewish students from Russia did not overlap much with German students,

Jewish or not. This finding persists, notwithstanding the fact that the ethos of the *Rabbinerseminar*, founded in 1873 by Rabbi Esriel Hildesheimer, demanded that its students matriculate simultaneously at a secular university. Rabbinical students from Eastern Europe dominated the seminary's student body owing to the fact that few German Jewish students aimed for a career as religious professionals. For this reason, Eastern European students stood a good chance of employment in German congregations, particularly within congregations in urban areas.[35] Before World War I, 24 per cent of those matriculated at the Hildesheimer were Eastern European, far surpassing their German contemporaries in traditional learning.[36] Wertheimer also finds, however, that, even though they constituted a significant proportion of the student body, rather than their traditional ethos influencing the seminary, the 'Eastern students were thoroughly Germanized' because the institution 'shaped their students by demanding linguistic proficiency in German'.[37] Whether already on their way to Westernisation and the valuing of secular knowledge alongside traditional learning, certainly their years in Berlin must have transformed the Daiches brothers' outlook and ideology. The long physical journey from Vilna via Königsberg to Berlin was also a linguistic and cultural journey begun in East Prussia under the influence of the local Russian Jewish aspirations to become 'German' in habitus and emulate the cultural aspirations of the educated middle class.[38]

Education at the Hildesheimer Seminary was designed to create a new type of rabbi. While the traditional *yeshiva* equipped Jewish men to interpret Jewish law and navigate through the vast legal and narrative literature of the *Talmud* and its commentaries, it did not aspire to make its graduates into community rabbis with a host of other, pastoral responsibilities and with the task of representing the Jewish community to the non-Jewish majority society. Instead, learning and traditional scholarship could be perceived and pursued as ends in themselves, fulfilling the commandment of *talmud torah* for its own sake, incumbent on all Jewish men.[39] The challenges of modernity and emancipation which paved the way for the integration of Jews in the public life of mainstream society in all European states also brought about a process of transformation of the rabbinate. From the middle of the nineteenth century new institutions for the education of Jewish clergy developed across Western and Central Europe. These responded to the demands for community leaders trained in religious as well as secular subjects which corresponded to the changed expectations of Jewish congregations, mainstream society and secular authorities. No longer was a rabbi someone whose academic education had the sole focus on extensive and detailed knowledge of Jewish law. Rather, a rabbi trained at the Hildesheimer Seminary was supposed to show a balance of religious and secular learning. The secular component of the curriculum was carried out at a secular university and had an impact on the amount of traditional Jewish learning students could accomplish during the course of their degree. Those students, who did not arrive at the seminary already with a strong and complete traditional Jewish education, had no hope of 'catching up' with their thus educated peers. Hence rabbinical students of East European origin might perceive their German Jewish fellow students as sorely lacking in learning and 'astonishingly ignorant; their knowledge was about equal to that of a *cheder* boy at home, in his second or third term'.[40] The 'modern Orthodox' rabbi, graduating from the Hildesheimer Seminary, was supposed to be able to relate well to both the Orthodox Jewish community they ministered to and the secular municipality to which they represented their community. This required, in particular, a high degree of concentration on the challenges of outward-looking representation of Jewish interests in the cultural idiom of non-Jewish Germans. Graduates thus had to balance their Jewish with their secular education. The secular curriculum varied according to the interest of the student and could encompass philosophy as much as ancient history and philology. These fields of study were popular among candidates for the rabbinate and many achieved a doctorate, the highest qualification available at German universities to those not entering the academy as full-time scholars.[41] Most graduates did leave the Seminary as ministers (preachers), falling short of full rabbinical ordination.[42] Some sought ordination elsewhere, however, as Salis Daiches did; afterwards, much later, he even returned to the Seminary to gain authorisation as a rabbi there as well. It is unclear whether the lack of full rabbinical ordination of most graduates was due to their inability to achieve the required standard of learning or whether there were other reasons. Depending on where employment was sought, ordination from other individual rabbis may have been preferable. In addition, many communities may not have been able to afford employment of a rabbi and could only guarantee the salary of a minister.[43] Full ordination from the Hildesheimer Seminary was conditional on never taking a pulpit in a congregation following non-Orthodox practices; should such a position be obtained, the graduate would lose their *semicha*.[44] Yet, some Hildesheimer graduates went on to serve Reform congregations in Germany and Conservative congregations in the United States.[45] In Germany, most communities were those of the *Einheitsgemeinde* which united Jews of various practices and religious ideologies. Some privileged Orthodox practices while, in others, a non-Orthodox majority set the tone. Hildesheimer himself was not strictly opposed to this model and remained in conversation with non-Orthodox leaders. Yet, he also served as rabbi at Agudath Israel, a secessionist community of strict Orthodoxy of the same ideology as the *Austrittsgemeinde* of Samson Raphael Hirsch in Frankfurt. The predominance of the *Einheitsgemeinde* could have deterred many from seeking the status of rabbi, graduates preferring to be flexible in seeking employment and not to make promises that may have become impossible to keep. Suffice it to conclude that the '*Rabbiner*' or minister graduating from the Hildesheimer Seminary often also had obtained a doctorate at a secular university and had the skills to represent a local Jewish community in relation to the municipality and the wider public.[46] Thus equipped, a career as a Jewish religious professional was a respectable role, often taken, as observed by Wertheimer, by Eastern European immigrants to Germany.

Why Salis and his brother Samuel chose to emigrate from Germany further West to the United Kingdom is unclear. If Wertheimer is correct in his assessment, there would have been ample opportunities for employment for both these gifted and highly educated young men. It may be that their parents' location in Leeds prompted both to join them and seek employment in the United Kingdom. The draw of Scotland and particularly Edinburgh as the home of David Hume and the Scottish Enlightenment, which David Daiches suggested was the pull factor for bringing his father to the Scottish capital, is less easy to detect.[47] It was, after all, a long haul from arrival in Leeds in 1903 as newly minted Dr Daiches to the position of Minister and Headmaster of the Hebrew Classes[48] in Edinburgh in 1919. The journey in the United Kingdom was taken exclusively in congregations composed of British-born Jews struggling with rising numbers of recent immigrants and, by all accounts, Salis Daiches's skills as a mediator were necessary to keep the peace and then even to unite the cities' divided congregations.[49]

Education and ideology

It is evident that, right from the start of his career in the United Kingdom, Salis Daiches identified strongly with what we may, in retrospect, recognise as a version of modern Orthodoxy, that is, the ability to appreciate and enjoy secular learning while maintaining traditional religious practice, and set himself on a mission to promote the acculturation of immigrant Jews. As we shall see below, Daiches's version of the relationship between religious and secular learning approximated to that of a harmonious synthesis where the religious provides the all-encompassing foundation on which all other knowledge rests. Thus, scientific discovery, particularly that of the natural sciences, is seen as confirmation of the divine foundation of life rather than perceived as a challenge to Jewish traditional ideology. We can hear the echoes of the Hildesheimer Seminary in this presentation, particularly the teachings of Hildesheimer's successor at the *Rabbinerseminar*, David Zvi Hoffmann. By extension, in the appreciation of philosophical thought, Daiches anchors all explications of morality and ethics in Jewish tradition, seeing the philosophers discovering only what he saw had already been included in the divine plan. Chief Rabbi Hermann Adler, in office when Daiches arrived in Britain, shared the same religious ideology, following closely in the footsteps of Hildesheimer and colleagues.[50]

The Chief Rabbi under whose leadership Daiches's career in Britain flourished, Joseph Hertz, presented himself as a bridge between Eastern European and modern Orthodoxy, the latter enabling a pragmatic full integration into secular society while eschewing assimilation. Hertz's and

Daiches's religious ideologies were close, seeing that they were both influenced by Hildesheimer's approach to Jewish tradition and modernity, but they were not identical. Hertz showed more of a defensive strategy, desiring to 'defend the traditional belief in its [the Torah's] origin', valuing secular learning only when it did not appear to threaten or undermine traditional belief.[51] Indeed, according to Elton, Hertz, while valuing *Wissenschaft*, approached it more pragmatically along the lines of Samson Raphael Hirsch's concept *Torah im derekh erets*, and limited any notions of a synthesis between the religious and the secular.[52] Hirsch, with whom the contemporary use of *Torah im derekh erets* originates, used this phrase to promote an approach to secular culture that enabled Jews to participate in the social and economic life of non-Jewish society while remaining fully within the bounds of Jewish tradition and without assimilating.[53] This presented a more utilitarian approach to secular culture and limited the opportunity for an engagement with *Wissenschaft* and philosophy along the lines suggested by Hildesheimer and Frankel. While Hertz built bridges between resident and immigrant Jews, Daiches placed himself firmly on the side of a modern Orthodoxy which sought to cast off all vestiges in habitus that could be associated with his Eastern European background. Visually, this difference in approach may, perhaps, be seen in Hertz's self-presentation which emulated that of the Eastern European rabbi, with a full beard, contrasting with Daiches's clean-shaven face with a small, fashionable, moustache.[54] The fact that Hertz's and Daiches's self-presentation to the immigrant community differed radically was probably also conditioned by their positions in the community and their temperaments. Hertz's position as Chief Rabbi relied on diplomacy and the ability to hold together a potentially strongly divided constituency of religious leaders. Daiches as a local leader, on the other hand, while ministering to congregations of British-born Jews and recent migrants, stated his ideology clearly in his appearance, thus appealing to the leadership of the religious and secular communities alike. As we shall see in the next chapter, in his ministry he sought to bring on board the immigrant community by relying on his Eastern European rabbinical pedigree and strong, authoritative and outward-facing leadership; after all, he was an immigrant himself and his personal and professional life could be seen as evidence of the possibility of transformation without sacrificing religious commitments.

Daiches's entire public and private output on the future of the Jewish community in the United Kingdom promoted the fusion of traditional Jewish and secular life, enriching both parts without finding contradictions. Throughout his life in Britain, Salis Daiches promoted his ideology in flamboyant speeches and in writings that mirrored his talents as an orator. We should remember that English was his fourth vernacular following *Yiddish*, Hebrew and German. Daiches's ideology may be the key to his career trajectory in the United Kingdom. His employment in Hull, Sunderland and Edinburgh matches well with his ideological mission to promote a full fusion between traditional Jewish values, Orthodox observance and participation in secular society. The choice to work in communities which were divided between residents and newcomers whose cultures could be seen to clash may be seen as a direct application of his ideology, expressed in practical ways by facilitating the acculturation of immigrants and their integration with residents.

The very same skills and forceful personality, however, were also likely to contribute to tensions with the London Beth Din who claimed *halakhic* authority across the United Kingdom and the British Empire. This ambitious and gifted rabbi needed to be integrated into the London Beth Din's strategy for achieving community cohesion following large-scale immigration. Chief Rabbi Hertz and Rabbi Dr Salis Daiches were on friendly terms, as can be gleaned from their correspondence, the occasional tension notwithstanding.[55] As we shall see in the next two chapters, however, Hertz may have played a significant part in ensuring that Daiches stayed in distant Scotland rather than occupy a position closer to the Beth Din. Salis's older brother Samuel, by contrast, seemed a lot less interested in community leadership and excelled academically at Jews' College and as a barrister,[56] after Hermann Adler's death removing himself from many of the debates about the relationship of the provincial communities to the London Beth Din in the early twentieth century.[57]

Salis Daiches's threefold education, which spanned traditional Jewish, modern Orthodox and secular learning, was largely unmatched by his colleagues in the United Kingdom. His British-born colleagues could not compete with his Jewish education while his fellow Eastern European immigrants could not show comparable secular learning. Ministers, *shochetim* and rabbis were bound by the authority of the Chief Rabbi, and their religious knowledge was subject to regular tests under the auspices of Jews' College.[58] London's Jews' College, founded in 1855 by the then Chief Rabbi Nathan Adler, sought to improve the standard of religious education of the leadership of British Jewry. Like the Chief Rabbinate itself, Jews' College was a centralising institution with its focus on the United Synagogue. 'Adlerism' extended its force across the Jewish congregations of the United Kingdom (and the British Empire) through the creation of 'a strong, centralized rabbinical establishment, with supreme authority over the public religious and educational life of the community [. . .] to preserve traditional Judaism'.[59] From 1847, Adler's *Laws and Regulations for All the Ashkenazi Synagogues in the United Kingdom* purported to determine the organisation, liturgy and education of all Orthodox Jewish congregations across Britain. This move, according to Todd Endelman, was akin to 'an authoritarian episcopal system that swept away congregational autonomy and rabbinical independence'.[60] Since its inception, Jews' College functioned to educate future leaders of the religious Jewish communities with a strong emphasis on the pastoral side of leadership and the ability to preach a good sermon. Until the early twentieth century, Jews' College did not offer rabbinical ordination in the traditional sense, and its graduates were not learned or authorised in *halakhic* decision-making.[61] Those who graduated from Jews' College in the majority had the status of 'minister' or 'reverend' who had to defer in *halakhic* questions to the authority of the Chief Rabbi and the London Beth Din: 'Anglo-Jewish ministers were not ordained rabbis but rather well-mannered, sweet-voiced clergymen who preached and led services'.[62] The majority of candidates who were serious about their studies went to Central and Eastern Europe to be educated and to achieve rabbinical ordination as even the Chief Rabbi's son, Hermann Adler, did. Jews' College was not able to attract large-scale enrolment of students at school and college level. Candidates for the ministry were neither attracted by the curriculum nor the social standing conferred by the status of 'minister', the remuneration for which ranked alongside lower middle-class professionals on a mediocre salary.[63] The situation had not changed at the turn of the twentieth century and, as we shall see in Chapter 2, the conflicting needs of the established and immigrant communities, as well as the perception of the Chief Rabbinate in general, were cause for a great deal of religious turmoil in the years leading up to World War I.

Daiches's entire self-presentation thrived on appealing simultaneously to the established and to the immigrant Jewish communities, as well as to a non-Jewish community, addressing all three interest groups with the aim of presenting Jewish life and culture as positive social forces in the United Kingdom, and particularly so in local contexts. The immigrant Jewish community, as we shall see in the following chapters, was supposed to be pulled along the path to acculturation on account of Rabbi Daiches's traditional learning which would satisfy their religious needs without sanctioning the perpetuation of an East European, inward-looking Jewish habitus. With Jewish community membership in the United Kingdom being entirely voluntary, the religious leadership was extremely concerned about retaining and perpetuating subscriptions. The decline of affiliation 'on the way to the suburbs'[64] occupied congregations and much activity concentrated on promoting *sabbath* observance and offering religiously acceptable socialising occasions for younger generations. As congregations had to raise enough income to maintain their buildings, clergy and other communal institutions, loss of income through declining religious affiliation was (and remains) a real existential concern. Rabbis, such as Salis Daiches, acted from the conviction that they had the opportunity to make a difference in this situation and to boost community allegiance and membership by offering an intellectually satisfying religious alternative compatible with professional and intellectual aspirations in secular society.[65] Regarding his work in Scotland, David Daiches identifies the following aim at the heart of his father's efforts:

> Indeed, one of my father's great aims in life was to bring the two worlds – the Scottish and the Jewish – into intimate association, to demon-

strate, by his way of life and that of his community, that Orthodox Jewish communities could thrive in Scotland, true to their own traditions yet at the same time a respected part of the Scottish social and cultural scene.[66]

To achieve this, Salis Daiches embarked on a programme of preaching, teaching and publication, practically demonstrating to the Jewish and non-Jewish worlds the synthesis he promoted.

Accordingly, Daiches sought to propagate his views in three ways. Firstly, he preached every *shabbat*, sometimes more than one sermon. At the beginning of his appointment in Edinburgh, he would preach morning and afternoon in two different locations to the two main constituencies of his not-yet united community: in the '*Englishe shul*' in English and then in *Yiddish* in the '*Russisher*' or '*Griner shul*' dominated by recent immigrants. The message, as I argue below, will most likely have been the same, just expressed in a different idiom.[67] Addressing each in the language of the community – English for the Edinburgh Hebrew Congregation, mainly comprising established residents who worshipped in Graham Street, and *Yiddish* for the worshippers in the other *shul* in Roxburgh Place which served mainly recent immigrants – Daiches worked from a verse of the week's *parashah* and its context in Jewish history and tradition to the message he wanted to convey to his audience. This was sometimes a point of Jewish doctrine but was just as likely to have been about relations with the non-Jewish population, about Zionism or about defence against Christian missionaries.[68] Daiches's approach to sermons reflected a new and modern strategy of exposition developed during the nineteenth century. Here, the sermon was seen as a major educational tool, designed to influence the religious, social and political outlook of the communities, such that 'the biblical verse becomes a springboard catapulting the preacher into the central logic of his own address'.[69]

Secondly, Daiches was frequently invited to speak to gatherings of various Jewish and non-Jewish social groups.[70] He quickly gained a reputation for being an excellent public speaker and was sought after in a variety of venues and by different institutions and groups. His speeches, as well as his sermons, were reported on in the local press, thus reaching an audience beyond that of the Jewish community. Daiches also wrote letters to newspapers and offered articles for publication, particularly in the Jewish press. As such, his ideology had a ready-made audience, specifically within the Jewish community, but, through the secular press, he reached out also to a wider local constituency. Daiches not only sought to present the public with a positive image of Judaism,[71] he also intervened frequently in local political debates, advocating for the concerns of religious and cultural minorities.[72] Daiches's interventions in political debates during his tenure in Edinburgh, such as his letters to newspapers opposing moves to ban *shechitah*, his involvement in discussions about religious education in

Scotland following the 1918 Education Act, his championing of Zionism in the secular press, and also combating missionary activities, were presented as stemming from his commitment to equal rights for all citizens.[73] These interventions also express his conviction that Judaism, properly understood by both Jew and gentile, not only can, but should, be seen as a valuable contribution to the political and social life of Scottish society.[74] Daiches's strategy of public engagement with Jews and non-Jews resonated with Chief Rabbi Joseph Hertz's approach who used his sermons and publications to set out the religious agenda of his Chief Rabbinate to the congregations, thus seeking to educate about core Jewish values and practices.[75] Indeed, Daiches and his colleagues emulated the mobilisation of the Jewish press as harnessed by migrant Jewish religious professionals since the middle of the nineteenth century and now extended this to non-Jewish publications:

> All of these men recognized the potential of the press to reach and teach the dispersed Jewish communities of England and the United States. Moreover, the press provided a vehicle to advance their ambitions as educators, preachers, and self-publicists. The press would amplify their sermons across America and the British Empire and provide them with a huge new audience. The *Jewish Chronicle*, the *Voice of Jacob*, and the *Occident* routinely publicized, recorded, summarized, and critiqued sermons delivered by a variety of preachers.[76]

Thirdly, then, Daiches wrote a number of articles on Jewish topics and published them in 1928 in a small volume entitled *Aspects of Judaism*. It would be fair to characterise this publication as a kind of ideological manifesto, demonstrating, through the form of the essay, his way of uniting Jewish with secular learning and presenting the reader with an erudite and elegantly argued synthesis. His obituary in the *Scotsman* suggested that Daiches also planned to publish a volume of his sermons.[77] He certainly kept scripts of his sermons and seemed to continue this practice throughout his career even though he was very well able to extemporise without notes on a given text or subject.

Throughout his career, Salis Daiches sought to articulate a consistent approach to Orthodox Jewish values and practice which stands in harmony with scientific discoveries and not only enables full participation in the life of secular society but offers Jewish values as an important corrective to a purely secular value system. Not only was there no contradiction for Daiches between Orthodox Jewish life and science, values propagated by *Torah* and embodied in Jewish practice, as we shall see below, he also suggested that non-Jewish society would profit from a Jewish Orthodox presence as a consistent reminder of the origin of all morality in the divine. He was circumspect about his audience, careful to publicise the same message in different ways to Jewish and non-Jewish audiences, addressing each in their specific medium and idiom. While we have no documentation about his sermons given in *Yiddish*, and have been able to consult only a few examples from his early career in Hull and Sunderland,[78] we can risk an educated guess and suggest that it is likely that he preached the same message to his *Yiddish*-speaking listeners as he did to his anglicised congregants and to a non-Jewish audience. Alternatively, one could argue that he preached in *Yiddish* in the way in which his listeners wanted to be addressed and without challenging them to change their ways and their language, fully expecting their children to move out of what he in Scotland perceived to be a self-inflicted ghetto.[79] I think the latter is unlikely because Salis Daiches believed strongly in an extensive Jewish religious education being made available so that his congregants could observe the positive message of *Torah u'maddah* he preached. Thus, I would argue that he adjusted the idiom while keeping his message consistent. The sermons I was able to access while researching this book expound Salis Daiches's message of acculturation on the basis of *halakhah* through an explication of the weekly *parashah*; his speeches on Jewish history, on important Jewish thinkers of the past, generally addressed to an overwhelmingly Jewish audience, do so for Jews but keep an eye out for the non-Jewish listener. Many of Daiches's sermons and speeches for the literary societies were reported on by the secular press or church papers so it was likely that he expected non-Jews to be in the audience. While we do not have much written evidence from Salis Daiches himself about the content of the speeches, the newspaper reports in the Jewish and non-Jewish press give a good account of their arguments.[80]

Placing philosophy in relation to modern Orthodox Jewish thought

Our main source of direct evidence on the above topic is the small volume, *Aspects of Judaism*, that Salis Daiches published in 1928. This unites seminal essays collected since his early years as a minister and scholar, the themes replicating those predominant in his speeches but also those repeatedly appearing in his sermons throughout his professional career. Addressed primarily to Jewish readers, but having a non-Jewish readership in mind as well, Daiches approached each of the fourteen essays in a similar way. The object of each, except the penultimate one concerned with philology and, by his own admission, an odd choice for inclusion in the volume,[81] is to demonstrate the inherent ability of Judaism to support and augment any modern philosophical and scientific discovery. Because of its divine origin, Judaism, correctly understood, argued Salis Daiches, contains already all that human beings may ever discover and learn about the world. Therefore, no scientific novelty, nor any philosophical system, not even those seeking to sever the ties of human reason from those of the divine, can possibly contradict or seriously challenge Jewish Orthodoxy. In these essays, Daiches joined Jewish Orthodoxy with Kant's philosophy and argued that Kant, had he only known anything about Judaism, would doubtlessly agree with Daiches's own assessment of a coincidence of Jewish with Kantian thought.[82]

The following paragraphs focus on Daiches's essay 'Kant and Judaism' as a key example of his approach linking his Jewish religious ideology with a prominent Western philosophical tradition. In this essay Daiches set out to explain the complete compatibility of Kant's philosophy with Orthodox Jewish thought and practice.[83] He opens by acknowledging that Kant had an ambivalent, if not outrightly hostile, attitude towards Jews and Judaism. Daiches is ready to excuse this as a product of ignorance:

> Kant's inability to understand and appreciate the tenets of Judaism has never prevented Jews from understanding and appreciating the philosophy of Kant, and to-day it is admitted by those who combine in themselves a thorough knowledge of Jewish teachings with a full appreciation of Kant's philosophical theories that there is no religious system which is so compatible with that of the philosopher's epistemology as well as with his ethical doctrines and postulates as the system embodied in Judaism.[84]

Daiches concludes that it was only Kant's ignorance of Jewish teaching and thought that led to his anti-Jewish stance:

> Had he known where to look for it Kant would, indeed, have found that his ethical theories, so far as they are practical and are applicable to human nature as it is, have been anticipated by the Rabbis, just as his epistemological doctrines have been foreseen – if only dimly and vaguely – by the Jewish thinkers of the Middle Ages.[85]

Consequently, Daiches finds that

> the absoluteness and binding force of the moral law, termed by Kant 'the Categorical Imperative', finds nowhere a more eloquent expression, and is given nowhere a more prominent position, than in the Torah – as understood and interpreted by its Jewish exponents of all ages.[86]

While Kant would have objected to claims that ethical principles originate with God, Daiches transforms this criticism into an explanation of the advantages Judaism derives from the attribution of ethical law to the divine:

> The plea that submission to external authority deprives man of his moral freedom and his actions of their ethical value [. . .] has been indirectly refuted by the Jewish religious philosophers, who have identified moral freedom with readiness to obey the Divine Law – even when it is contrary to one's own physical impulses and desires – and discovered the ethical value of an action in the approval which religious teaching gives to that action. This does not mean, however, that Judaism denies the existence of an absolute moral law as a principle which is good in itself and therefore *ought* to be binding for the ideal man, irrespective of the fact that it is part of the teaching of the Torah.[87]

The principle of assimilating non-Jewish to Jewish philosophy rests on Daiches's understanding of the divine origin of the Torah. For Daiches, no serious and well-reasoned thought can arise which cannot already be found in the foundational Jewish text. By extension any moral and ethical value found in the secular world needs to be anchored in the Torah because, in Daiches's school of thought, the origin of all values, morality and ethics is with God.

This strategy of argument places Daiches firmly in the tradition of Orthodox *Wissenschaft des Judentums*. To enable Orthodox scholars to engage in *Wissenschaft*-related research, traditional approaches to the Torah needed to be squared with the principles of the scientific study of history. One way to accomplish this was to argue that all research rests on presuppositions held by the scholar and hence Orthodox scholars can participate in the scientific community by stating these clearly and exposing such presuppositions in others.[88] Though Daiches did not work in fields such as biblical studies where such justification was, strictly speaking, needed, he effectively adapted the stance he was familiar with from his studies at the *Rabbinerseminar* to his philosophical writings and his politics in the United Kingdom. In a sense, Daiches modelled a position of modern Orthodoxy, the combination of traditional learning with secular, scientific knowledge – *Torah u'maddah* – existing not only side by side but intertwined in perfect harmony. Indeed, Daiches's PhD on Hume's approach to historiography placed him in a Hildesheimer tradition that drew on Kant rather than on the then dominant German historicists who were more inclined towards a Hegelian approach to history. Indeed, Hume was a clear influence on Kant, waking Kant up from his dogmatic slumber through his sceptical approach to causation, allowing a divergence between experience and reason. Hildesheimer graduates who followed the ideal of *Torah u'maddah*, such as Daiches, were more likely to be influenced by Kant, rather than Hegel, and thus were more likely to view social and political conflicts as the backdrop to a move towards truer knowledge, morality and political peace. In this view, Jewish and non-Jewish law and knowledge could be understood to be at core an expression of the same truth, the expression of which was in need of refinement. This Kantian view could afford the idea that differences between bodies of knowledge exist without this troubling the essence of civilisation. *Torah u'maddah* in a Hildesheimer version, then, placed Salis Daiches in a position to advocate for the vital contribution to be made by observant Jews to contemporary society.

Conclusion

As we step out of the *sukkah* into the courtyard of the synagogue of the Edinburgh Hebrew Congregation in Salisbury Road, we return to a quiet side street linking two of the city's main southern arteries. Exiting the synagogue in the 1930s would not have been very different, the street remains flanked by residential buildings. Already in the 1930s the synagogue was not located in the part of the city populated most densely with Jews. The less affluent remained further north in the St Leonard's area, though the short distance to the new synagogue could easily be covered in a brisk walk of five to ten minutes. Those of greater economic status moved across the Meadows into Marchment and the Grange, still within comfortable walking distance of the original area of Jewish settlement but, as we will see in Chapter 4, perceived as removed to the 'suburbs'. The community's residential areas quickly fragmented 'on the way to the suburbs' although, to this day, the core of the community remains resolutely in the south of the city. Salisbury Road Synagogue survives as *the* Jewish architectural landmark in Edinburgh and stands also as a memorial to Salis Daiches's efforts at uniting the community. United in one building, the community thrived until the second half of the twentieth century, Salisbury Road Synagogue functioning as the hub for the congregation's religious activities and also for many of the community's social events and societies. Fondly remembered, but also recalled as distant and aloof, Rabbi Daiches is present in the memory of Jewish residents of Edinburgh and is still a well-known name in the non-Jewish society of the city, not least because of the prominence of his two sons, Advocate Lionel Daiches and the literary critic, David Daiches, as well as his granddaughter, the writer Jenni Calder.

Salis Daiches's journey as presented in this chapter is as exemplary of an immigrant's life as it is exceptional. His educational background made him stand out from his fellow travellers on the great migration but his career trajectory, which led to a comfortable middle-class existence in the Scottish capital – his children enjoying the benefits of a university education and all moving into the higher professions – is something he shared with many other migrants. Salis Daiches came to Britain at a crucial time during the religious transformation of British Jewry. His was a voice, alongside that of the Chief Rabbi, that sought to instil religious pride in the generation of Jews born to immigrants, and he made every effort to disseminate his message in his sermons, his lectures and his writings, in his latter days also contributing to a new Zionist programme of education for Jewish youth.[89] And yet, as we shall see in Chapter 3, Daiches's ideology did not sufficiently inspire the next generation. Even Daiches's own children were not able to maintain the carefully calibrated synthesis of Jewish and secular culture Salis proposed and sought to live. Of the 'two worlds' of David Daiches's childhood, he chose the secular one, leaving behind (though not abandoning) his Orthodox Jewish inheritance.[90] The moment of forging such a synthesis had gone, the conditions for recreating the educational opportunities Salis Daiches had enjoyed were irretrievably destroyed in the Holocaust. Yet, for the first two decades of the twentieth century, a window was open in British Jewish history to effect a religious transformation of an entire generation. At least, that appeared to be the opportunity perceived by Salis Daiches, and it was what he worked for in the Jewish communities in Hull, Sunderland and Edinburgh. He did so in close contact with the Chief Rabbis, first with Herman Adler and then with Joseph Hertz.

Chief Rabbi Hertz and Salis Daiches worked well together; as we shall see in Chapter 3, there is ample evidence of religious agreement in their exchanges of letters. Daiches sought Hertz's opinion on his own professional ambitions, and appears to have been content to submit to the authority of the Chief Rabbi, particularly as Hertz's ideology and religious policy closely matched his own. And yet, there is a tension between Daiches's ambition for regional rabbinic leadership and Chief Rabbi Hertz's centralising approach designed to maintain the hegemonic position of the United Synagogue and his Beth Din. Scotland offered what Daiches perceived as a significant sphere of influence and leadership, with some *halakhic* decision-making involved. As we shall see in the next chapter – which explores the relationship Daiches had with the Chief Rabbis under whose authority he worked – by 'sending' Daiches north, Hertz also ensured that this rabbi would not become a threat to his own leadership.

CHAPTER 2

The Chief Rabbi, the London Beth Din and the Battle for Leadership in the 'Provinces'

The first two speeches on 'The Functions, Titles and Status of the Jewish Ministry and the Jewish Minister' had been delivered to a packed and slightly overheated auditorium at Jews' College, London on a frosty morning at the end of December 1909. Reverends A. A. Green and J. Raffalovitch had taken their seats on the top podium during a thundering ovation. Now the Chair of the First Conference of Anglo-Jewish Ministers raised his hand and waited until the room had fallen completely silent. From his elevated position, he overlooked a sea of black suits encasing white shirts, and ties in muted colours. The front row's gaze followed the tips of their polished black leather shoes which were pointing upwards at the podium. In the middle of the auditorium, twenty-nine-year-old Reverend Doctor Salis Daiches glanced at his notes which were stuck to his hands, moist with nervous sweat, while his face did not show any signs of stage fright. He fidgeted in his chair, eager to register his intention to contribute to the discussion that was to follow. This was *his* topic; he held strong views formed during his journey from Vilna to Sunderland where he occupied the pulpit of the Sunderland Hebrew Congregation. His earlier service as a minister in Hull and in Hammersmith, he estimated, had provided him with enough experience and authority now to speak out. The chair motioned for him to make his contribution. Salis gently cleared his throat and fixed his eyes to the wall behind the podium. He took a deep breath and began his intervention, only occasionally glancing down at the sticky pile of papers in his hands.

The *JC* reported Salis Daiches's passionate contribution seemingly verbatim so that we can almost hear him addressing the assembled conference delegates. He argued

> that the present state of the ministry was so chaotic and so confused that if some radical way of remedying the position was not found the ministry in England would soon lose its entire significance, and there would be nothing left but their title of reverend and their clerical clothes. [...] Perhaps it was not possible to find a more adequate term [than 'minister'] for the simple reason that there were not men forthcoming qualified to occupy the high position of Rabbi in a Jewish

congregation. The Jewish community in England during the last thirty or forty years had grown to such an extent that they were capable of introducing the Continental system into this country, and unless they did it now the time would come when they would find nothing but chaos and confusion.[1]

Dr Daiches was not short of opinions and, with characteristic directness, appears to have had no qualms about openly addressing the situation as he saw it. Identifying the state of affairs of the religious leadership of the Jewish communities outwith London early on in his career, Daiches placed himself on the Standing Committee of the Conference of Anglo-Jewish Ministers which set out to influence the Chief Rabbi and the leadership of the United Synagogue to reform the authority structures of congregations in the 'provinces'. The documentary evidence suggests that the status of Jewish clergy and the establishment of regional *batei din* appear to have been a lifelong quest for Daiches, most clearly seen in his interwar service in Edinburgh when he had become an established figure within British Jewry. Before we examine Daiches's ambitions for a local Scottish Beth Din in the next chapter, however, we need to place the rabbi's designs into the wider context of the religious crisis of British Jewry at the beginning of the twentieth century.

From 1909 until 1911, and then intermittently until the early 1930s, a vigorous and repetitive debate occurred in the United Synagogue about the best way in which to deliver Orthodox religious leadership in the communities. The inaugural Conference of Anglo-Jewish Ministers in 1909 first suggested the establishment of regional *batei din*, under the broad supervision of the London Beth Din, in order to address the needs of the local communities in matters of *kashrut*, *shechita*, marriage and divorce, Jewish status and religious education. While a few ministers and rabbis argued for the complete devolution of *halakhic* decision-making and the abolition of the Chief Rabbinate, proposing an Eastern European devolved government of Jewish congregations outwith the auspices of the state, the majority favoured a middle way of maintaining the Chief Rabbi and the London Beth Din as the central *halakhic* authorities which supported regional *halakhic* institutions. Local *batei din* were understood as a measure for ensuring that basic *halakhic* standards were upheld by appropriately trained clergy and as a means of facilitating the integration of immigrant *rabbonim* with the established community leadership in the United Kingdom.[2] They were never seen as a means of completely devolving rabbinical authority away from the London Beth Din. Rather, the discussions about local *batei din* were a way in which to negotiate perceptions of religious authority and power, forging a means for the London Beth Din to establish and maintain its hegemony in relation to the immigrant majority. Aside from the negotiations about the lines of religious authority which played out in these discussions, the establishment of regional *batei din* implied a programme in the congregations to bring about the acculturation of immigrants and was also a means by which to control the public image of Jews in British society.[3]

Regional *batei din* with the oversight of the London Beth Din never came to fruition in the way that had been envisaged by these ministers throughout the first decade of the twentieth century. Only three *batei din*, with powers confined mainly to issues of *kashrut* and *shechita*, were established outwith London in the three numerically strongest Jewish communities of Manchester (1902), Leeds (1913) and Glasgow (1929). The debates surrounding various models of devolution of rabbinic authority, however, and the resulting vision of changes to the status of the London Beth Din offer a useful perspective on the impact of large-scale immigration on the religious life of British Jewry. The first two decades of the twentieth century and the interwar years were times of consolidation as immigration was slowing down owing to the 1905 Aliens Act and World War I. The end of Chief Rabbi Hermann Adler's tenure and the interval before the appointment of Joseph Hertz in 1913 are crucial years in which different visions for the future structure of Orthodox congregations in Britain were discussed. Salis Daiches's career, as leader of three provincial communities – Hull, Sunderland and Edinburgh – illustrates aspects of this consolidation process. As an immigrant rabbi, he had the opportunity to observe and facilitate the integration of newcomers and to make his views on the future of the Orthodox communities in Britain heard. Daiches, as we shall see, was a prominent advocate of regional *batei din* long before he arrived in Edinburgh and even after the subject had been abandoned by the Conference of Jewish Ministers in the aftermath of the appointment of Joseph Hertz as Chief Rabbi. In Scotland Daiches particularly favoured the establishment of a Scottish Beth Din, and, while ideologically largely aligned with Chief Rabbi Hertz, he thereby also set himself in renewed tension with the centralised established leadership of the United Synagogue and the London Beth Din. While other Eastern European rabbis were co-opted to the London Beth Din as *dayanim*, Daiches, whose name was floated once in the late 1930s for a position as *dayan* to replace the recently retired Dayan Feldman,[4] remained committed to decentralising the power of the London Beth Din through the establishment of a Scottish Beth Din. A Scottish Beth Din, as envisaged by Daiches, would have had greater *halakhic* powers than those granted to the Manchester and Leeds *batei din* (and previously the Glasgow Beth Din) and would have included the mandate to arbitrate on marriages, divorces and issues of Jewish status. As we shall see, Salis Daiches was simultaneously in ideological agreement and organisational conflict with the London Beth Din.

An examination of the movement for regional rabbinic authorities and Daiches's role therein will contribute to a better understanding of the ways in which the religious integration of the new immigrants was perceived and managed in London and among religious leaders across Britain. Particularly significant, as we shall see in Chapter 3, is the local, in this case mainly Scottish, context in which the debate about regional religious leadership played out. In many ways, the Edinburgh rabbi's strong advocacy for a Scottish Beth Din, with himself as *av beth din*, challenged the hegemony of the numerically more significant Scottish Jewish community of Glasgow which exhibited more disunity, factionalism and strife between the world wars than the Jewish community of the Scottish capital.[5] Before we can address the Scottish context, however, we need to focus on the relationship between Daiches and the two Chief Rabbis during whose tenure he served. We will pay close attention to the career ambitions of Daiches, and to the institutional leadership of Adler and Hertz, seeking to account for Daiches's position within the wider British Jewish religious context. Daiches here serves as an example illustrating the tension and convergence in outlook and approach of a modern Orthodox immigrant rabbi and that of the Chief Rabbi who needed to mediate between a number of different constituencies. The context in which these explorations take place is that of the adjustment of British Jewry to the large-scale and permanent immigration of Jews from Eastern Europe, specifically the *Pale of Settlement* under Russian rule, to the United Kingdom. This immigration, which began in the late nineteenth century and continued until 1914, in many cases was a transmigration with the United Kingdom being a stepping stone in the movement of individuals and groups to a more permanent new place of residence.[6] Only with the beginning of World War I did the communities stabilise and proceed towards an accommodation between British-born and recently arrived Jews.

Immigration and religious leadership: British Jewry at the turn of the twentieth century

> Between 1881 and 1914, 120,000 to 150,000 East European Jews settled permanently in Great Britain, effecting a radical transformation in the character of Anglo-Jewry. Their poverty, occupations, and foreignness drew unwanted attention to them and native-born Jews alike, fueling the fires of xenophobia and antisemitism. By virtue of their numbers, they swamped the established community and gave Anglo-Jewry, once again, a foreign-born, lower-class cast, which disappeared only in the mid-twentieth century.[7]

Todd Endelman's succinct summary recalls the result of mass migration which saw the Jewish population not only of London but also of northern cities, such as Manchester, Leeds and Glasgow, quickly grow so that, at the turn of the twentieth century, the Eastern European migrants constituted the majority of the Jewish population. The issues arising from this massive influx of newcomers, coming from very different cultures to that of most of the resident Jewish population, not only affected the social and economic make-up of the communities but also posed challenges for integration into the existing religious community structures. The religious outlook of first-generation immigrants tended to favour the authority of immigrant rabbis over that of British Jewish ministers. Geoffrey Alderman characterises the clash between immigrant religious sensibilities and those of the established Jewish community as a *Kulturkampf*, diagnosing that 'the authority and legitimacy of [. . .] [the Chief Rabbi's] office within British Jewry was subject to unprecedented challenge'.[8] He continues, in characteristically polemic fashion, to argue that

> [. . .] it was during Hertz's tenure of office that the suzerainty of the Chief Rabbinate came under serious and sustained attack, in the course of which the weakness of the claim of one man, and of one office, to be able to embody and represent within himself and itself all the varieties of Judaism to be found in Britain – let alone the Empire – was fatally exposed. The attack was mounted largely from within the orthodox community [. . .][9]

In the following, we shall turn to an assessment of aspects of this 'attack'. For now, we need to establish how the cultural landscape of British Jewry changed irrevocably through the influx of a large number of immigrants from Eastern Europe. The ways in which this change was negotiated in the area of religious practice and authority are closely bound up with the changing leadership styles and their ideological foundations in the final years of the Chief Rabbinate of Hermann Adler and the tenure of Joseph Hertz and their impact on the integrating communities. Miri Freud-Kandel's and Ben Elton's research on the development of the Chief Rabbinate and its incumbents since the middle of the nineteenth century to the present has helped to provide a detailed account of the Chief Rabbi's office and the United Synagogue that underpins the following argument.

For the local level, Bill Williams's research on the development of Manchester Jewry sheds light on the way in which resident and immigrant Jews negotiated local economic, social and religious leadership in the decades since the middle of the nineteenth century. Williams's assessment challenges the categorical assessment of a simple culture clash and offers a more nuanced account of the ways in which residents and newcomers learned to work together. Williams demonstrates such a pattern for Manchester:

> It was out of the social chemistry of [. . .] triangular encounters – between the elite, the alrightniks [see Glossary] and the immigrant masses – that a 'new community' was created and a new communal leadership was forged. So, for example, although it is true that in the battles over *shechita* no *chevra* or immigrant synagogue won lasting autonomy, important concessions were won from the elite, if only to ensure their overall control. Most notable were the setting up in 1892 of a communal Shechita Board, on which immigrant rabbis were rep-

resented as supervisors and alrightniks as members, and in 1902 of a Beth Din on which Eastern European rabbis like Coffey and Dagutski sat in judgement alongside Dr Salomon of the Great Synagogue.[10]

While perhaps only a minority among the immigrants, those who were seeking religious advice and who asked *halakhic* questions, unsurprisingly drew on the expertise of rabbis who shared not only their own cultural and religious background and outlook but also their recent experience of migration.[11] Furthermore, liturgical traditions, religious customs and ritual expectations and needs were significantly different from those of the resident community.[12] Language barriers with the resident Jewish population and its leadership also contributed to the division between immigrant and British Jews. In short, the lack of acceptance of the existing structures of community leadership and religious authority caused rifts between residents and incomers.[13] As Israel Finestein argued, 'in provincial eyes the Chief Rabbi was essentially a London personality with predominantly London interests'.[14] At the beginning of the twentieth century, this division gave rise, from within the British Jewish community, to calls for separate *batei din* in the regions to ensure that issues affecting the status of individuals and the practice of entire communities were regulated properly. How such institutions should relate to the Chief Rabbinate was a matter for debate.[15]

The religious crisis in British Jewry 1880–1939

At the turn of the twentieth century, the religious infrastructure of British Jewry was in a state of crisis. The increasing number of immigrants with a religious outlook and with needs diverging from that of the resident community challenged the hegemony of the Chief Rabbi which both Adlers, father and son, had cultivated so carefully for the past five decades.[16] Irregularities in the practice of *kashrut*, the regularisation of marriages, and the determination of Jewish status exercised Jewish communities across the United Kingdom and worried the Chief Rabbi at regular intervals. In the early twentieth century, rows, particularly about *shechita*, were frequently covered in the national and local Jewish press. A small but vocal and significant minority among the recent immigrants, namely that of the observant, the religious professionals and those strongly attached culturally to Jewish religious tradition, more or less openly challenged the authority of the Chief Rabbi in matters of religious law and practice.[17] In London a group of synagogues under the leadership of Samuel Montague declared independence from the United Synagogue in 1887, intending to offer a more traditional and strict religious alternative in an effort to emulate the spiritual style of the immigrant communities. The resulting Federation of Synagogues, mainly based in London, expanded from an initial sixteen congregations to fifty-one by the time of Montague's death in 1911.[18] And other independent congregations, notably the community in Gateshead, had to negotiate their status with the Chief Rabbi. While today, formally accepting the authority of the Chief Rabbi, the Federation continues to exist in some tension with the practices of the United Synagogue which are understood to be more lenient than the stricter observance promoted by Federation communities. Another set of challenges arose from the gathering momentum of the Reform Movement in London which then also touched communities elsewhere.[19] Compounding these primarily religious issues was a growing lack of interest among the younger generations to participate in, and have their lives shaped by, the religious authorities of their communities.[20] We find frequent exhortations to young men in particular to attend religious services, and Sabbath Observance Societies were founded in virtually every community. The London Beth Din actively had to pressure Jewish clergy across the United Kingdom to ensure that marriages were conducted in accordance with *halakhah* and civil law, and that conversions of non-Jewish spouses were carried out with the appropriate formality and firmly within the bounds of Jewish law. The *halakhic* hegemony of the London Beth Din was threatened by these challenges to the authority of the Chief Rabbi and to his ability to control central community services – such as *shechita*, the appointment of ministers and other religious functionaries, marriage, divorce and conversion – and, if this was true in London, it was even more so across the rest of Britain.

Since Nathan Adler's installation as Chief Rabbi of Great Britain and the Empire in 1844, the religious authority associated with this office expanded outwards from the London congregations it originated in. The London Beth Din, with the Chief Rabbi as its head, assumed *halakhic* leadership across the Ashkenazi Orthodox Jewish congregations in the United Kingdom and the British Empire.[21] Since its constitution in 1870 by an Act of Parliament, the United Synagogue's London Beth Din had become the sole arbiter of the Jewish religious practice of Ashkenazi Jews with a Chief Rabbi as its supreme authority.[22] With expanding numbers of congregations across the United Kingdom as a result of immigration, the Chief Rabbi extended his influence across the nation and also included under his authority the congregations of the entire Empire.[23] In the presentation of his office, the Chief Rabbi emulated the organisation of the Anglican Church and the Archbishop of Canterbury, constituting thus a version of state-approved Jewish authority with appropriate representational facilities to match.[24] De facto, the United Synagogue, through its satellite organisation, the United Hebrew Congregations of the British Empire, centrally controlled (or sought to control) all matters relating to Jewish religious affairs and the conduct of these within the law of the United Kingdom and the British Empire.[25] The Chief Rabbinate of Nathan Adler, in particular, is associated with this drive to centralisation of religious and specifically of *halakhic* authority, a movement supported strongly by the lay leadership of the United Synagogue.²⁶ As a result, Jewish clergy across the Empire – ministers, *shochetim*, and *hazzanim* – received their authorisation to occupy religious offices from the Chief Rabbi. Most of the British-born and locally educated clergy either never reached the qualification of rabbi or were unable to lay claim to the authority derived from the title, not least because all *halakhic* decision-making was concentrated in the hands of the Chief Rabbi.²⁷ Even when Jews' College began ordaining individuals as rabbis, their ability to exercise any *halakhic* authority remained tied to their relationship to the London Beth Din.²⁸ The British Chief Rabbinate was, then, truly a transnational institution, binding congregations to the capital of the Empire by seeking to exert religious control over communities across the dominions. This leadership model stands in contrast to developments in other parts of the anglophone world, notably North America, where a more pluralistic and decentred leadership structure grew since the late nineteenth century. Through a plurality of institutions which sought to respond to the needs of religious functionaries and their congregations, the Union of Orthodox Rabbis of the United States and Canada supported rabbis, their communities and educational institutions to sustain Orthodox Jewish life and adapt it to the New World.²⁹

Hermann Adler, Chief Rabbi from 1891 following his father's death in 1890 until his own death in 1911, in some ways, was a 'caretaker' Chief Rabbi, following closely in the footsteps of his father and continuing his legacy of holding on to the supremacy of the Chief Rabbinate. As traditionally educated Jewish men, however, who were also ordained rabbis, arrived in large numbers from Eastern Europe, a gap opened between immigrant and indigenous religious functionaries, with the British-born men offering no match for the *halakhic* knowledge of their Continental brethren. To make matters worse for them, Jewish ministers and their colleagues were poorly paid, making religious office an unpopular career choice.³⁰ As a result, the leaders of the established Jewish communities, overwhelmed with recent Eastern European immigrants, struggled to communicate the religious authority of the Chief Rabbi and his Beth Din to the newly arrived migrants who, if they cared about religious observance at all, in any case preferred religious officials from their own cultural context.

When Adler died in 1911, the United Synagogue needed to find a replacement who would be able to integrate the immigrant community.³¹ The election process ending with the installation of Joseph Hertz as Chief Rabbi in 1913 offers an insight into the power structures of the United Synagogue. Here we find the anglicised lay establishment claiming the majority of the votes in the 1912 Chief Rabbinate Conference by limiting the eligibility of provincial congregations to those who had paid their dues to the Chief Rabbinate Fund. As a result, the Chief Rabbi was elected primarily by the London-based United Synagogue, effectively excluding a meaningful representation of congregations outwith London, and inside London prohibiting the Federation of Synagogues from voting.³² As we shall see in the next section, the structures of the United Synagogue were such that the efforts of provincial ministers and rabbis to challenge the Office of the Chief Rabbi were repelled as part of the election of Hertz. Nevertheless, Hertz had to address the challenges to the authority of his office emanating from 'the provinces'.

Joseph Hertz, installed after a long and protracted election process in 1913, was seen as having the appropriate talents to provide a bridge between 'East and West', between immigrant and resident. Practising firmly within the bounds of tradition, but intellectually broad-minded enough to appreciate the need for adjustment to modern society, he bridged traditional Orthodox practice and a commitment to the revealed authority of the Pentateuch with an appreciation of the values of *Wissenschaft*, and he endorsed the necessity for secular learning.[33] In practice, it is apparent that he followed a combination of Hirsch's *Torah im derekh erets* and Hildesheimer's ideal of *Torah u'maddah* and worked hard to preserve traditional Jewish values through scrupulous ritual practice, such that Eastern European rabbis were able to accept his leadership.[34] In addition to ordination from JTS, Hertz had also been given *semicha* by six traditional rabbis, thus gaining approval from rabbis across the breadth of Jewish Orthodoxy, including those who did not approve of intellectual engagement with secular learning and sought to shield Jewish tradition from *Wissenschaft*-related study.[35] Hertz's secular qualifications were attested through a doctorate in philosophy from Columbia University. He served a number of Orthodox congregations in the United States and South Africa. In Witwatersrand, Hertz ministered to a particularly diverse community and this tested for the first time his abilities as a bridge builder and mediator between *Yiddish*-speaking recent immigrants and the established community. The much less clear division between Orthodoxy and other forms of Jewish religious practice in America at that time led him to look for opportunities in the United Kingdom which, Elton suggests, 'may have been based, in part at least, on an understanding that his theological position was ideally suited to Anglo-Jewry'.[36]

Once installed, Hertz needed to capitalise on the support he had received from all parts of the Jewish community in Britain. He needed the *rabbonim* to respect him and to contribute to the running of the United Synagogue and the wider community of the United Hebrew Congregations of the British Empire and its institutions while also retaining the British Jewish character of the communities. To this end, Hertz continued and expanded a strategy that Hermann Adler had previously begun to adopt, namely the appointment of *rabbonim* on to the London Beth Din:[37] when he took office, the London Beth Din consisted of only two permanent *dayanim*, relying on the Chief Rabbi to complete the court which needs three judges to be quorate; Hertz increased not only the number of permanently employed *dayanim* from two to five, he also appointed Eastern European rabbis to positions becoming vacant or newly formed.[38] Hertz's first appointment to the Beth Din was the confirmation of Glaswegian Rabbi Hillman who had already been co-opted on to the London Beth Din in 1911 by Hermann Adler but did not actually take up the position until 1914.[39]

Hertz needed all his diplomatic skills to unify a dividing and divisive religious leadership at least as much as necessary to enable co-operation on maintaining religious Jewish life in accordance with *halakhah*, British law, and British Jewish established forms of communal organisation and authority structures. It is no mean feat that he was able to transform the institutions of British Jewry from within to make room for the religious needs of immigrants without wavering in his commitment to the established anglicised forms of religious decorum. Hertz enabled the integration of immigrants by allowing the stricter *halakhic* needs of the *rabbonim* to take priority over the far more lenient and permissive ways of British Jewish ministers while, at the same time, insisting that the immigrant rabbis had to assimilate to the customs of British Jewry.[40]

Right at the beginning of his term of office, Hertz had to address the schismatic challenge to the Chief Rabbinate coming from the only recently established Conference of Anglo-Jewish Ministers which, at its first two meetings in 1909 and 1911, had proposed and accepted a scheme for the reorganisation of the administration of the Jewish communities. This scheme included a significant devolution of *halakhic* decision-making from the London Beth Din and the Chief Rabbi to provincial religious institutions. While not without opposition from their own ranks, the Conference also challenged the election process of the Chief Rabbi, claiming that the concerns of ministers and rabbis across the United Kingdom were not able to be heard by the consortium of those mandated to vote.[41] The proposal on its own was a challenge to the authority of the Chief Rabbi but, when combined with the separatist tendencies of the Federation and a group of immigrant *rabbonim* in the 'provinces' who queried the desirability of a Chief Rabbi in the first place,[42] the threat of a split within the Orthodox communities in the United Kingdom was palpable. As we shall see in the following section, Hertz understood these issues well and skilfully steered a diplomatic course of maintaining the status quo at a national level while sanctioning devolution of some authority to *batei din* in Manchester, Leeds and Glasgow.

Regional *batei din* and the authority of the London Beth Din: a diplomatic journey

Towards the end of Chief Rabbi Hermann Adler's tenure, emotions among those serving as religious functionaries in the Jewish communities across Britain were running high.[43] Religious officials from resident and recently immigrated stock were both equally exercised about the state of the rabbinate in Britain: those trained in the United Kingdom because of their lack of authority and the challenges to their skills to fill rabbinical shoes; and those who had immigrated because of the apparent lack of recognition afforded them by the religious establishment of their new home country.

The fact that the Chief Rabbi was aged and ailing presented an opportunity to review the governance of the Ashkenazi Orthodox congregations and the role of the Chief Rabbi and the London Beth Din within the religious institutional structures of British Jewry. Thus we can observe the venting of a valve of built-up tension in the years following the slowing of immigration in the wake of the Aliens Act of 1905 and the halting of the same with the beginning of World War I in 1914. Crucial dates are the conferences of rabbis and ministers held in 1909, 1910 and 1911 in London and Leeds, each bringing together a number of different religious constituencies to air their concerns and push for change.

The conference which perhaps had least influence but which was a clear indicator of the strength of feeling among the immigrant *rabbonim* was held in Leeds in 1910, convened by none other than Rabbi Israel Hayyim Daiches, Salis Daiches's father. Israel Hayyim Daiches, rabbi at Leeds's Beth Hamedrash Hagadol Synagogue since 1901, was a Lithuanian *halakhic* authority who had published widely on the Jerusalem Talmud and also authored *responsa*. He was known as lenient in his desire to integrate innovative technology with traditional religious observance, an approach mirrored by his son Salis who, for example, sanctioned the active use of electrical lights on *shabbat*.[44] In Britain, Israel Hayyim had founded the Union of Orthodox Rabbis[45] and he remained committed to the traditional religious practice of his home rather than seek cultural adaptation in his habitus to his new surroundings. The Leeds conference of Orthodox immigrant rabbis sought to establish a platform for the concerns of Eastern European rabbis and their congregations and propose a process for configuring a link with the Chief Rabbi. Such a link would have needed to acknowledge the *halakhic* competence of the rabbis while respecting the authority of the Chief Rabbi and the status of the civil law of the United Kingdom. Key to the success of this endeavour, argued the *rabbonim*, was the mutual recognition of *halakhic* authority and a clear indication of the relevance of the immigrant rabbis' traditional outlook and expertise. Commentators at the time and in retrospect classed the 1910 conference in Leeds as a failure, the Eastern European rabbis merely displaying their irrelevance even to the communities they served. Evidence for this assessment was the close attention displayed in conference debates to the details of *halakhah* on topics of apparently little concern to the majority of immigrant Jews; the conference language being *Yiddish* rather than English which demonstrated a lack of understanding of the social, economic and cultural aspirations of the younger migrants and the second generation already born in the United Kingdom.[46] The challenge, however, from immigrant rabbis addressed to the authority of the Chief Rabbi touched on an important issue in the relationship of the immigrant *rabbonim* to the London Beth Din: the immigrant religious leaders spoke as *rabbis* and invoked the authority of this status thereby drawing our attention to competing models of religious authority among immigrant and resident Jews.

Chief Rabbi Hermann Adler had been invited by Samuel Hillman, then the *rav* of Glasgow, to attend the conference in Leeds but was unable to travel because of ill health.[47] Hence, while the conference challenged the Chief Rabbi's authority, the desire to have him present also signalled a willingness for co-operation with the leadership of the British Jewish community.[48] Hillman is an interesting figure in this context because he clearly commanded authority owing to his learning while he also sought to further the integration of immigrant rabbis with the Chief Rabbi's claim to authority. Thus, Hillman promoted Adler's views and directives regarding *shechita* among his peers and thereby perhaps sought to build a bridge between immigrant and resident Jewish religious practice.[49] But what about Hermann Adler himself? Elton argues that Adler followed an 'expansive-hegemonic approach to religious leadership',[50] which tolerated a degree of religious pluralism within the Orthodox congregations under his jurisdiction, while centralising authority in the office of the Chief Rabbi.[51] This approach rested on not recognising those ordained to the rabbinate as rabbis but could tolerate the activities of non-conforming *rabbonim* as long as they did not publicly violate the authorised standards of religious practice and did not at any point come into conflict with civil law when dealing with the religious aspects of life-cycle events such as marriages.[52] Adler, we see, was charting a diplomatic course that relied on just the right amount of silence and only so much interference as absolutely necessary to maintain the status quo of the Chief Rabbi's authority and promote a positive image of the Jewish community within British society.[53] His overall concern was perhaps not so much the conversation about the standards of religious observance as it was about the safeguarding of the place of Jews in British society. Adler, a social conservative, enjoyed a respectful and sometimes friendly relationship with individual immigrant rabbis but, overall, these instances of friendship could not detract from Adler's generally discouraging attitude towards immigrants.[54] Hermann Adler's approach to the religious challenges of large-scale immigration appeared simply to extend the distancing and appeasing approach taken by his father Nathan who had established and cemented the supreme authority of the Chief Rabbi in Ashkenazi Orthodox affairs in Britain. The conference of immigrant rabbis in 1910, however, and the 1909 and 1911 Conferences of Anglo-Jewish Ministers challenged the viability of such a centralised and hegemonic form of religious leadership.[55]

The Conferences of Anglo-Jewish Ministers 1909–11

From the first conference in 1909 onwards, the topic of the regional reorganisation of Jewish religious communities was on the agenda. A subcommittee was formed specifically with the brief to address the issue and develop a proposal that could be discussed at the conference. Salis Daiches was part of this subcommittee and he and his brother Samuel were outspoken about the dismal state of authoritative leadership in the 'provincial' communities, largely blaming the London Beth Din for a failure to institute proper authority structures between ministers, the Chief Rabbi, and London Beth Din. The solution advocated by the conference's subcommittee was to devolve some authority to the 'provinces' while suggesting that London should retain overall control by sanctioning which aspects of community regulation were to be taken care of locally and in what way. The subcommittee presented a detailed proposal in 1909 and appeared to continue its meetings for further conference preparation until 1913 when, following the installation of Joseph Hertz as Chief Rabbi, the reorganisation of Jewish communities, particularly outwith London, no longer appeared on the agenda.

Trouble had been brewing in the East End of London and in the regions for some time before the 1909 conference and there are indications that, across the country, immigrant rabbis were increasingly frustrated with the government of congregations and the religious officials occupying key positions. In 1907, Rabbi Dr Samuel Daiches, then the minister to the Sunderland Hebrew Congregation, on the occasion of a *bar mitzvah*, thundered from his pulpit about the state of England's congregations and their ministers as follows:

> How will English Jewry look in fifty years' time? And I feel: unspeakable grief fills me, and my life-nerves are as cut. The whole hopelessness and lifelessness of the present state of Judaism here is vividly brought before me, and nothing seems to be left but despair. A gloomy landscape. Devastated fields. Trees uprooted. A leaden sky. Thunder and lightning. A sweeping storm. No life. No sunshine. The end seems to be near. Thus English Judaism looks. [. . .] There is no country where the Jews are so leaderless, so masterless as in England.[56]

It might be that we could imagine the *bar mitzvah* boy and members of his family – some of whom may have travelled from quite some distance – expected a less accusatory, gloom-filled address on the occasion of his thirteenth birthday, though perhaps not. The rabbi was clearly both passionate and deeply serious about his charge, and he continued:

> A man cannot sit in London and rule Judaism in Manchester or Edinburgh. Every Jewish community must have its own independent religious guide. Otherwise the general leadership is only used in order to make the individual heads of the congregations powerless. Ministry in English Jewry is now in a state that no self-respecting and intelligent man can join or remain in it. Slave-natures are wanted. And what for are they wanted altogether? They really are not. But what will our neighbours say? We keep our Synagogues and the officials for the sake of the Gentiles.[57]

In concluding, Daiches sought to gesture towards a silver lining and offered a glimpse of his vision of the thriving future of Judaism and its clergy in Britain:

> A new spirit must come over English Judaism. The gloom must disappear. Knowledge must increase. Understanding and love for Judaism must grow. [...] The Ministers must be for our inner wants and not for appearance sake, for the living and not for the dead. [...] The present state cannot continue. It is unbearable. It can make one fall under the burden of slavery. Every Jewish community in England will have to have its absolutely independent religious guide. And then men of talent, of knowledge will come to you.[58]

Samuel Daiches had this sermon printed and distributed, meaning that, already at the point of delivery to his own congregation in Sunderland, the words of the address were aimed at a wider readership. The rhetorical flourishes help us to imagine the rabbi in the moment of giving the sermon and we may imagine some part of the force of his speech was a matter of his accustomed style. But there were also serious ramifications to his passionate call for change which went far beyond the hall: the sermon presented an indictment of, and a challenge to, the leadership of the Chief Rabbi, ascribing to him a deliberate unwillingness to devolve any authority away from himself and from his *Beth Din* and a failure to imagine for Britain a different form of religious authority. Indeed, at that time Samuel Daiches was one of the most vocal spokespersons for abolishing the Chief Rabbi's office altogether.[59] His younger brother Salis, in 1907 serving in Hull, was largely in agreement with Samuel although he spoke in more deferential tones about the Chief Rabbi's authority. Indeed, Salis Daiches was radical in his wishes for reform of the institutional structure of British Jewry and argued forcefully for a devolution of authority but he did not suggest that the Chief Rabbi and his *Beth Din* were obsolete. In the Daiches brothers, then, we may see the spectrum of possibilities for the reorganisation of the United Hebrew Congregations of the British Empire: Samuel, in emulation of the autonomous congregations of the *Pale of Settlement*, would have done away with the existing authority structures in their entirety by abolishing key institutions and offices. By contrast, during his tenure as a member of the Conference's subcommittee, Salis sought a compromise and suggested the deliberate concession of some authority away from London while, overall, retaining the established British institutional authority structures with the Chief Rabbi as the head. Surprisingly, perhaps, following the 1911 Conference of Anglo-Jewish Ministers, we see Samuel, since 1908 ensconced in the faculty of Jews' College, ceasing to challenge the Chief Rabbi so openly. Salis, on the other hand, congratulated Joseph Hertz on his appointment as Chief Rabbi and, in the same breath, called for a reorganisation of 'provincial' communities.[60] This is a stance Salis held throughout his service in Sunderland and Edinburgh where, as we shall see, he strongly advocated the establishment of a Scottish Beth Din with *halakhic* decision-making powers.

The meetings of the Conferences of Anglo-Jewish Ministers in 1909 and 1911 took place under the auspices of Hermann Adler. Without deviating from his centralising approach, Adler welcomed the efforts of the ministers who worked on subjects such as unifying the standards of Jewish education, expressed concerns over issues of Jewish status and Jewish marriages, and made concrete proposals for the establishment of regional *batei din* with greater powers than the supervision of *shechita* and other matters of *kashrut*.[61] The religious officials employed by congregations under the authority of the London Beth Din vigorously advocated the need to establish an appropriate status for ministers as well as the recognition of some within their ranks as rabbis. In short, the conferences tried to persuade the Chief Rabbi and the leadership of the United Synagogue to elevate the status of all religious officials in the congregations. The ministers were concerned with the education of religious functionaries, pushing for reform that would also enhance their position in the community and vis-à-vis the immigrant *rabbonim*. While never discouraging the ministers' efforts, Adler remained characteristically non-committal on actually devolving authority away from himself.[62]

In 1909, the conference heard speeches about the role of ministers and their educational brief and facilitated a discussion of the general social and economic situation of ministers and preachers in congregations across Britain. Also included in the proceedings of this first gathering were two papers on the 'District Organisation of Provincial Congregations', both favourably disposed towards a change in the organisational structure of the United Hebrew Congregations.[63] Reverend S. Friedeberg, following Reverend M. Abrahams, argued, forcefully, as follows:

> [London's] United Synagogue is practically a District Organisation of Metropolitan Congregations. I am not suggesting that we should take the United Synagogue as our model. We want something less narrow in scope, less parochial in spirit, more elastic, more comprehensive, more ecclesiastical, dare I say more spiritual in character and constitution.[64]

While nine separate district organisations outwith London were envisaged, all were intended to be configured to work alongside, and under the authority of, the Chief Rabbi. The topic of district organisations remained on the agenda for the second conference in 1911 at which the 'Sub-Committee on the District Organisation of Provincial Congregations' presented its report and made concrete suggestions for the reorganisation of the United Kingdom's Jewish communities which were adopted by the conference.[65] Reverend Dr Salis Daiches is listed as a member of this subcommittee as are two immigrant rabbis from Scotland, Rabbi Hillman of Glasgow and Rabbi Rabinowitz, then rabbi at the Edinburgh New Hebrew Congregation.[66]

The subcommittee recommended the establishment of 'District Councils' on to which 'English' and 'Foreign' rabbis would be co-opted as equals as long their congregations were recognised by the Conference of Anglo-Jewish Ministers. The recommendations of the subcommittee intended this joining of native-born and immigrant religious functionaries as a counterpoint to the frequent conflicts within communities divided along religious ideologies:

> The Committee was unanimous as to the inclusion of the Rabbis (as distinct from Preachers or 'Ministers' in the accepted sense of the term), in the proposed Council. They felt that the English Ministers and the foreign rabbis have much to teach and learn from each other. Moreover, the very large *clientèle* of the foreign Rabbis and the distinct line of cleavage that is noticeable in too many places between 'English' and 'Foreign' sections of the community, make it most essential, in the view of the Committee that, in the highest interests of Judaism in this country, there should be as much co-operation and understanding between all sections of clerical workers as it is possible to obtain.[67]

The proposal suggested that District Councils were to remain under the authority of the Chief Rabbi and the London Beth Din and that they should deal with immediate and local *halakhic* concerns for which the Chief Rabbi would delegate authority to qualified local rabbis. Furthermore, these councils would safeguard standards of Jewish ministry and education, co-ordinate the charitable work of the communities, arbitrate between communities and their clergy and recommend to the authorities in London whether and how newly established congregations should be recognised. The subcommittee proposed a regional confederation of communities under the jurisdiction of the Chief Rabbi to facilitate the integration of immigrant communities and their rabbis with the British Jewish congregations and the safeguarding of standards in Jewish religious leadership, *kashrut, shechita,* religious education and welfare. Delegation of authority in questions of Jewish status was not proposed but District Councils would be in a position to offer guidance on matters for which a decision had to be sought from the Chief Rabbi and to keep an eye on the compliance of marriages and divorces with civil law:[68]

> This recommendation in no way involves any interference with, or usurpation of, the function of the ecclesiastical authorities in London. It is contemplated, however, that the Councils will always contain a sufficient number of qualified rabbis to enable them to deal, through them, with such questions as the Chief Rabbi may see fit, by previous arrangement, to delegate to them. Generally, in framing this recommendation, the Committee had in mind questions of a purely local character which can be dealt with quickly and efficiently in the districts in which they may arise.[69]

Taken at face value, these proposals do not threaten the authority structure of the United Synagogue nor do they appear to question the position of the Chief Rabbi and his Beth Din. These remain in the position of being the final arbiter of *halakhah* in the British Isles and the Empire. The discussion surrounding these proposals, however, which was reported on and extended in the press, suggests other interpretations surrounded the succession of conferences.[70]

The Conferences of Anglo-Jewish Ministers in 1909 and 1911, and the 1910 conference of immigrant rabbis in Leeds, all heard contributions by rabbis and ministers who argued for the abolition of the Chief Rabbinate altogether. These clergy were naturally in favour of the proposals for a devolution of *halakhic* decision-making through the establishment of regional authorities. By contrast, members of the British Jewish establishment who participated in the Conferences of Ministers, particularly *dayanim* Hyamson and Feldman, were opposed to the level of devolution proposed when the scheme was adopted for implementation by the 1911 Conference. When a delegation of ministers pushed for a delay in electing a new Chief Rabbi following the death of Hermann Adler, querying the entire process of election, and, in letters made public in the *JC*, asked specifically for more British regional representation among the electorate, Hyamson and Feldman strongly voiced their opposition to the ministers' proposals in the press.[71] Salis Daiches had not only been part of the subcommittee authoring the proposals for institutional reform but he was also a member of the Standing Committee of the Conference. In this latter capacity, he attended the Rabbinate Conference as member of a delegation of four aiming (but failing) to ensure that the views of the Conference of Ministers would be considered during the election process of the new Chief Rabbi.[72]

The heated discussions among members of the Conference and their fallout in the press demonstrate the need of ministers and other religious officials, in particular outwith London, to vent their frustration with the centralised and authoritarian administration of ritual and *halakhah*. The two pre-war conferences also offer a snapshot of the situation Jewish communities across Britain found themselves in with regard to central themes of religious life, the authority of Jewish clergy and the status of the synagogue in the life of the Jewish community: papers were read and discussion was had on the status, title, education, payment and pension of their officials, as well as the education of children, *sabbath* observance, mixed marriages and the district organisation of 'provincial' congregations.[73] The level of an actual threat to the authority structure of the British Jewish community is debatable. Indeed, Samuel Daiches's advocacy of the abolition of the Chief Rabbinate after the death of Hermann Adler surely sounded like a call to revolution but it was not, in fact, supported by his ministerial and rabbinical colleagues.[74] In terms of actual 'real power', it is unclear whether immigrant rabbis posed a threat which could have toppled the Chief Rabbinate and the London Beth Din. The debates in the Conferences, however, and their echo in the Jewish press expose competing ideologies about the authority and legitimacy of Jewish leadership in Britain and were a space in which battle lines over the influence of particular positions were drawn. That Hermann Adler was already very much an outgoing Chief Rabbi in 1909 perhaps made these debates more confrontational and contributed to the choice of Joseph Hertz – a fellow migrant with a wide education and experience of divided communities – as his successor. The debates also point to the volatile situation surrounding Jewish religious life across Britain and the diminishing pull exerted by the synagogue on the younger generations. Thus, in a situation in which the social and religious hegemony of British Jewry was already outnumbered by Eastern European immigrants, the proposals for a devolution of organisation and authority may have exacerbated the perception of the threat. It is clear, then, that, on the one hand, old structures had weaknesses and were not reaching immigrants effectively while immigrant rabbis could operate without formal recognition. On the other hand, old structures had state recognition and thus the stable support of the majority of the British Jewish establishment and, thus, ultimately were able to withstand the turmoil brewing just before World War I.[75]

The death of Hermann Adler in 1911 appeared to create a real opportunity to debate the organisational and authority structures of the United Synagogue and the role of the Chief Rabbi and his *Beth Din* in relation to the Ashkenazi Orthodox congregations in the United Kingdom and the Empire as a whole. Delegations from the Conference of Anglo-Jewish Ministers continued to make their frustration with the status quo heard and actively sought opportunities for meaningful engagement in the election process of a new Chief Rabbi. By stealth and closing of ranks, however, the drawn-out election of Joseph Hertz provided a way for the British Jewish establishment, that is, the lay leadership of the United Synagogue who determined the process of election, to sideline their ministers and quietly to 'forget' about the plan for devolution.[76] No conferences took place in 1912 or 1913. Following his installation as Chief Rabbi, Joseph Hertz was invited to become president of the Conference and, from 1914, the newly formed Organising Committee of the Conference of Anglo-Jewish Ministers took place at his residence in Hamilton Terrace. In July 1913 Salis Daiches asked that the Standing Committee raise the scheme to establish district organisations with *halakhic* decision-making powers as per the conference resolution with Chief Rabbi Hertz.[77] This motion was not seconded, however, nor was the topic of devolution taken up by Hertz himself. Thereafter, this topic no longer appeared on the agenda of the Standing Committee. From 1914 onwards, there was no further mention of devolution of rabbinical authority through regional *batei din* during the conferences which, under their new title of Conference of Anglo-Jewish Preachers, met at irregular intervals from 1923. The topic surfaced again only in 1948 in the planning of the first post-war Conference of Anglo-Jewish Preachers.[78] In 1913, the minutes of the Organising/Standing Committee are silent about the details of the change in attitude towards the devolution of rabbinic authority among its members. And Rabbi Dr Salis Daiches ceased to be a member of the Standing Committee.

While the devolution of rabbinic authority was no longer part of the discussions of the Conferences of Anglo-Jewish Preachers, Hertz continued to face individual calls for regional *batei din* following World War I. These calls came particularly from one interlocutor who repeatedly brought his perspective to the Chief Rabbi's attention: Salis Daiches, now located in Edinburgh.

Conclusion

We leave the debating floor of the 1909 conference having sampled the excitement and passion of the moment at which rabbis, ministers and *hazzanim* debated the future of the religious organisation of British Jewry. Called at a crucial moment, the early twentieth-century conferences allow us a glimpse into the emotionally charged atmosphere of the time and give us an insight into the challenges felt by religious officials across the Jewish congregations of the United Kingdom, aware that newcomers were outnumbering the established congregations. The very real frustration of the underpaid and powerless ministers and the even more lowly placed *hazzanim* are palpable in the conference reports in the *JC*. No concrete action appears to have been taken as a result of the proposals for the reorganisation of provincial communities which were debated and accepted at these conferences. Rather, the passage of time worked in favour of the Chief Rabbi and the London Beth Din, and the concerns raised disappeared within one generation. What we read in the *JC* and the minute books of the Standing Committee, however, allows us an intimate insight into the status quo of Jewish communities across Britain on the eve of World War I.

Hermann Adler, as patron of the first Conference of Anglo-Jewish Ministers, had shown himself to be empathetic to the ministers' plans and had given the go-ahead for stronger and more focused proposals.[79] This policy of at least seeming to offer an 'open ear' to those serving in the 'provinces' enabled both Daiches brothers to voice their strong views on the centralised religious authority and to push for change from the pulpit, in the press and by participation in the relevant committees of the Conference of Anglo-Jewish Ministers. Joseph Hertz, when taking over as chair and patron of the conference at its third gathering in 1914, equally signalled his empathy to the concerns of the ministers and drew attention to the challenging times in which the community found itself.[80] And yet, on this issue Hertz was a master of diplomacy, never relinquishing the central ties of authority connected to his office. Thus, Hertz made supportive noises about any number of initiatives without actually ever giving any one of them firm support nor encouraging local agitation for their implementation. Hertz seemed to strategise his involvement in the movement for semi-autonomous provincial *batei din* by suggesting his willingness to hear proposals, to schedule meetings and to listen to representations but, when it came to the point of taking concrete action, he, more or less gracefully, simply bowed out, citing other commitments, not enough support from the ground and the prematurity of the proposals as reasons to stall any further action which could have brought the realisation of some of the suggestions.

It seems fair to conclude, then, that the Chief Rabbi, by playing the long game, won the power struggles between his office and the *rabbonim* in the 'provinces'. Hertz found different ways of binding immigrant *rabbonim* to the London Beth Din. By appointing rabbis respected in immigrant communities to the Beth Din, Hertz secured not only the rabbis' loyalty but also that of their constituencies. During the 1930s, some wanted to revive the discussion about regional *batei din*, not least in Scotland, as we shall see in the next chapter. It is likely, however, that discussion subsided, on the one hand, owing to the worsening situation of Jews on the European continent which called for united action across the United Kingdom, and on the other hand, because the bridge between religious and secular life promoted by the Chief Rabbi and the explicit synthesis of these two realms offered by provincial rabbis, such as Salis Daiches, proved unattractive to the next generation.

Is it possible that Salis Daiches, a modern Orthodox rabbi, was perceived as a greater threat to the authority of the Chief Rabbinate than the Eastern European *rabbonim* who made no direct appeal to the value of secular culture to religious Jews? It can be argued that the *rabbonim* presented the lesser problem because their status was more transient: the younger immigrant and British-born generations were not so interested in the intellectual foundations for, and the maintenance of, religious observance; indeed, the rise of Sabbath Observance Societies suggests that it was a struggle to sustain an appropriate level of synagogue memberships to fund essential religious institutions, such as the upkeep of synagogue buildings, a minister, a *hazzan* and a *shochet*, even when sometimes two of these functions were combined within one person. What was troublesome to the Chief Rabbi about the *rabbonim* was perhaps not so much their religious difference, vis-à-vis the normative practices of British Jewry, but their ignorance of British civil law which opened the possibility for effecting illegal marriages. Similarly troublesome was their sidelining of the London Beth Din – through ignorance or ideological opposition – in conducting religious affairs and the very real possibility of individual communities splitting along cultural and generational lines. On the other hand, modern Orthodox rabbis, such as the Daiches brothers, while ideologically close to the Chief Rabbi and culturally integrating, could have seemed the greater challenge to the aim of maintaining the hegemony of the London Beth Din in religious affairs in Britain. Such rabbis could claim *halakhic* authority by virtue of their ordination from both Eastern European *ravs* and modern institutions in Europe, and this gave them resources that undermined the Chief Rabbi's status where they chose to take up independent decision-making or arbitration. In reality, the number of such educated rabbis in Britain was insignificantly small – Hildesheimer graduates, who migrated West, predominantly did so towards North America. Of more immediate concern to the Chief Rabbi, then, were the inward-facing *rabbonim.*

As will become apparent in the next chapter, the discussion about a Scottish Beth Din predated Salis Daiches's arrival but was taken up among the Edinburgh communities with renewed force in the 1920s at Daiches's instigation. Across the 1930s community efforts were absorbed in concern for the worsening situation for Jews on the European Continent and in activities to provide assistance for refugees. The 1920s, however, which are the focus of the next chapter, are instructive for understanding Daiches's ambition and his vision for a semi-autonomous Scottish Jewish community whose affairs would be regulated in Edinburgh rather than remotely controlled by London. The next chapter, then, will use Salis Daiches's work in Scotland as a case study that allows a more detailed understanding of Jewish religious acculturation in the context of migration from the perspective of a religious official. How Daiches, in his new national context of Scotland and as religious head of the Jewish community of the Scottish capital, interpreted his relationship to the Chief Rabbi will allow us to understand better the development of ideas of leadership and authority among immigrant religious functionaries during the interwar years.

CHAPTER 3

Scotland: Local Leaders, Local Communities

'He was a towering figure. You knew that he was a man of great importance and learning just when you saw him sitting in *shul* during the service. And he was very kind, a very kind man.' I am in conversation with a gentleman in his eighties, walking from what was Salis Daiches's house in Millerfield Place towards the synagogue in Salisbury Road. Michael remembers Rabbi Daiches from his youth in the late 1930s, a kind but distant and powerful figure. Towering to a child, perhaps, but Salis was not a tall man; his stature derived from his position in the community and his own sense of worth. When Michael was a child, Daiches had served the Edinburgh community for almost two decades. He was at the height of his career and his success in bringing the divided congregations together under one roof in Salisbury Road Synagogue was visible to all. World War II had not yet begun and the extent of the impending genocide of Jews on the European Continent was still in the future. Salis Daiches died only six years later, aged barely sixty-five, on the eve of peace in Europe and in full knowledge of the irreparable loss of European Jewish lives and cultures. However far Daiches had moved away from the cultural contexts of the Eastern Europe of his formative years, the violent destruction of his people and their culture broke his heart and spirit and, to a large degree, can be seen as contributing to his early death. Gone also was the dream of a synthesis of Jewish with secular culture which the rabbi had championed since his student days. It was not only the reality that few sought the kind of Jewish education which would enable such a synthesis, it was rather that already since the rise of the Nazis to power, for Daiches, such a synthesis lacked all intellectual foundations, based as it was on the trust that gentile society would accept Jews as equals.

By contrast, the early twentieth century was full of promise for the young, energetic Daiches. We have seen his interventions in the debates about the reorganisation of regional Jewish communities during the tenure of Chief Rabbi Hermann Adler. While consistently interested in the work of the leadership of the British Jewish community, Salis Daiches's primary interest and field of activity were the local communities he served, first in Hull and then in Sunderland and, finally, in Edinburgh. Each community signified further status and achievement to Daiches. The 'call' to Edinburgh, in particular, he thought of as a great career advancement and a step towards realising his ambition of creating a significant sphere of influence for himself. An important part of this career strategy, even after World War I, was the creation of a local *beth din* in Scotland. Establishing local *batei din* had failed in England but, as we shall see, when he arrived in Edinburgh in 1919, Daiches continued to emphasise the importance of this project for the future of Scottish Jewry.

This chapter, then, turns the spotlight on to Scotland to understand better what Salis Daiches aimed for and how his ambitions for Scottish Jewry sat with Chief Rabbi Hertz in London and with Daiches's colleagues in Glasgow. At the heart of this chapter is an exploration of Salis Daiches's relationship with the Chief Rabbi and of his *halakhic* work on the Chief Rabbi's behalf. Daiches's *halakhic* activity had an impact on Scottish Jewry and, in particular, affected his relationship with Jewish clergy in Glasgow. He was also useful to his local community and to the Chief Rabbi because he was acculturated and articulate, being liked as a speaker in a great variety of settings. Hence, to set the scene, we shall first draw a brief picture of Daiches's ministry in Edinburgh and consider some of the issues shaping his local religious leadership. Thereafter, we shall look across the central belt of Scotland to Glasgow and examine, as much as the sources allow, how Daiches related to his colleagues in the larger city to the West. Key to understanding Daiches's position in Scotland, however, is his relationship with the Chief Rabbi which influenced Daiches's relations with his colleagues in Glasgow and which had an impact on his ambitions for a devolution of rabbinic leadership in this northernmost British nation.

Rabbi Salis Daiches and Edinburgh's Jews

A settled Jewish community in Edinburgh can be traced to the second decade of the nineteenth century mainly through the acquisition of space to house a synagogue, the subsequent appointment of religious officials, and the purchase of a communal burial ground in the Sciennes district of the city.[1] But it was only with the wave of emigration from Tsarist Russia in the last two decades of the same century that the community experienced significant growth such that it needed to find new premises for worship and expand the congregation's staff. The influx of large numbers of Eastern European Jews saw the number of Jews in the city swell to *c.*2,000 people, equalling approximately 400 households; thus the Jewish population of Edinburgh had quadrupled within thirty years.[2] The resulting overwhelming majority of Jews of Eastern European origin in the religious community caused rifts within the congregation largely between anglicised residents and 'foreign' newcomers and, to a lesser extent as the numbers were small, between different Eastern European Jewish forms of spirituality and worship. As a result, the synagogue community split into smaller units who worshipped in a number of different locations in the city. The first such division occurred in 1879 when the Edinburgh Hebrew

Congregation was joined by a new synagogue established by Hasidic Jews from Manchester who had come to work in the Caledonian Rubber Works on Fountainbridge in the Dalry area in the west of the city.[3] A second *shul* was consecrated in Dalry in 1892 by the Chief Rabbi, again largely serving those employed in the nearby factory.[4] Additional smaller congregations were formed by groups distinctive in origin and religious custom moving to Edinburgh from other parts of the United Kingdom, and as splits from the Edinburgh Hebrew Congregation such that, in 1892, Chief Rabbi Adler reported his concern about these divisions in the *JC*.[5] At the turn of the century the majority of the Jewish community originated mainly in the Lithuanian part of the Russian Empire. These first-generation immigrants were mainly small artisans and craftsmen in traditional Jewish occupations, selling cloth and clothes, furriers, picture framing, tailoring.[6] Religiously, the Jewish population of Edinburgh was divided between anglicised residents who had arrived in the first half of the nineteenth century, recent immigrants from Russia with distinctive religious customs, and Hasidic groups from Manchester and Leeds who worshipped in a different style again. The 'culture clash' between the groups was such that a series of conflicts ensued that gained the Edinburgh community the reputation of being particularly divided and troublesome. In the summer of 1911, the *JC* characterised the Edinburgh community as follows:

> Today the Edinburgh community is comparatively a small one, but it is, to quote Kipling, a terror for its size. [. . .] The Edinburgh Jews, comprising some two thousand souls, pray in four synagogues. [. . .] But synagogual dynasties in Edinburgh have such a knack of being suddenly overthrown, and communal revolutions are so frequent, that by the time these words appear in print there may be no synagogues in Edinburgh, or there may be half a dozen.[7]

Mark Gilfillan helpfully points out that the fee-paying membership of the congregation encompassed only a small proportion of the Jews resident in Edinburgh.[8] Accordingly, the actual size of the worshipping community is difficult to assess but we must consider that a large number of Jews was unable to afford seat rents while still frequenting the synagogue and making use of its social and religious services. Indeed, the Minute Books of the Edinburgh Hebrew Congregation until the middle of the twentieth century suggest that the congregation was struggling financially.[9] Edinburgh's Jews, in the majority, were situated at the lower end of the economic and social scale, themselves often hard up and not easily able to support their religious institutions but rather relying on these institutions to make ends meet.[10] The Edinburgh Board of Guardians and other welfare organisations were frequently called upon.[11]

In 1918, the Edinburgh Hebrew Congregation, based in the Graham Street Synagogue, and the Central Edinburgh Hebrew Congregation, worshipping in Roxburgh Place, had come together on paper to form one congregation but the old factions dividing the congregants were still very apparent.[12] When Salis Daiches arrived in Edinburgh in early 1919 to take up his position as the minister of the Edinburgh Hebrew Congregation, he found a community that seemed to be eagerly awaiting to unite under his charismatic leadership. As we shall see, however, the path towards unity was not straightforward. Daiches had accepted the offer made by an Edinburgh delegation who had travelled to his Sunderland home in 1918.[13] To the Sunderland community he explained his decision to move to Edinburgh as 'the desire to secure a larger scope for his activities',[14] thus highlighting his career ambitions. The Chief Rabbi had encouraged Daiches to consider the vacancy in Edinburgh as an opportunity to serve in a more significant position than Salis had occupied thus far. Chief Rabbi Hertz probably also felt that he would benefit directly from Daiches's appointment: on the one hand, he now had someone installed in the United Kingdom's nation furthest from London with whom he largely agreed ideologically and whom he trusted *halakhically*, and this would mean that he had a greater purchase on local affairs in Scotland; on the other hand, he had moved someone who was not afraid to challenge the Chief Rabbi's organisation of the Ashkenazi Orthodox congregations outwith London far away from the daily rhythm of his office and from his immediate sphere of influence. The relationship between Hertz and Daiches can be traced in part through the record of their correspondence. As we shall see, the relationship showed much mutual respect, collegiality and trust while we can also observe that the relationship was never completely free from tension.

By the end of World War I, Daiches had acquired a solid reputation in the British Jewish community. He had served on the Standing Committee of the Conference of Anglo-Jewish Ministers since its inception in 1909; he lectured frequently around the country; and he was a regular contributor to the *JC*, often having letters to the editor published and featuring in reports from events and meetings around the country.[15] Thus, Salis Daiches was known to the Edinburgh community as a Jewish public figure who could enhance the community's standing. This reputation was a significant reason for the Edinburgh communities to extend a 'call' to Daiches in 1918 to come to Edinburgh and to unite the divided community.[16] While unity was a condition Daiches set as fundamental to him agreeing to move to Edinburgh, rabbi and congregation knew full well that real unity was quite some way off. Daiches's strategy, however, of encouraging acculturation and anglicisation while respecting the traditions of first-generation migrants had paid off in both the communities he had served prior to his appointment in Edinburgh: the Jewish communities in Hull and Sunderland, equally composed of an occasionally explosive mix of anglicised and newly arrived Jews, had thrived under Salis Daiches's leadership.[17] In Edinburgh, Daiches set to work straight away, preaching every *shabbat* in two locations – in *Yiddish* for the recent immigrants and in English for the established community.[18] Daiches not only preached unity in English and *Yiddish* but he sought to set an example through his own practice. As we have seen in Chapter 1, he wanted to demonstrate that a union of traditional Jewish practice and life in a modern secular society was achievable without the loss of Orthodox Jewish religious integrity. To this end he got himself involved in all matter of things that had an impact on the Jewish community: countering missionary societies that targeted recent immigrants at the bottom of the economic and social scale; engaging with challenges raised by religious education in state schools; or by Scottish marriage legislation, to name but a few. He quickly gained a visible public profile which led to invitations to address a host of learned societies, social gatherings and interest groups.[19] In Scotland, Daiches rose to public prominence as an eloquent advocate for Zionism, making the case for the necessity and desirability of the Zionist enterprise not only in the Jewish but also in the local non-Jewish press.[20] In 1938 Daiches and the Reverend Magnus Nicholson of Fountainbridge Church founded a local Jewish–Christian Fellowship Movement, an organisation of Jewish–Christian dialogue, seeking solidarity and understanding as the genocide of Jews was about to unfold on the European continent.[21]

What we can trace about Daiches's work in the Edinburgh Jewish community and in the city of Edinburgh falls into three categories. Firstly, he worked hard to unite his congregation by leading the recent immigrants into a union with the anglicised Jewish establishment. Within the Jewish community, initial scepticism from the *Yiddish*-speaking congregations notwithstanding, Daiches established himself as a firm Jewish Orthodox authority who also had the ability to present a positive image of Jewish life to the non-Jewish public. In the community he was quickly known as the 'Chief Rabbi of Scotland', a sign of how highly communities across Scotland valued his unofficial leadership. While not without the possibility of a tinge of irony, suggesting that Daiches was perhaps attributed with carrying more authority than his position mandated, even the *JC* referred to Daiches as the 'de facto Chief Rabbi of Scotland'.[22] There is a good measure of esteem in this designation. When Rabbi Isadore Goodman was inducted at Queen's Park Synagogue, Glasgow in 1933, the arrangements were made so late that there was no time for a representative of Chief Rabbi Hertz to be invited. Goodman informed the Chief Rabbi that the Queen's Park congregation had instead invited Salis Daiches to represent the Chief Rabbi.[23] Secondly, he became a spokesman for all things Jewish in Edinburgh and in wider Scottish circles, effectively advocating on behalf of the community to the non-Jewish majority. This paved the way for Daiches's long-term work with non-Jewish Scottish society. Thus, thirdly, as a significant public figure, Daiches also made a strong contribution to Scottish life by participating in many public events and eloquently representing the views of a significant religious minority to the local authorities and in the press. In addition, Daiches's collaboration with a Christian minister in writing a Hebrew Grammar[24] and his role in establishing a Scottish society for Christian–Jewish relations ensured him a lasting place in the memory of the city.

Salis Daiches – spokesman for all things Jewish in Scotland

Daiches entered a range of public discussions in Edinburgh on topics of concern to Jewish residents. We shall select three aspects of his advocacy here which allow us to visualise the rabbi's style and stature in public discourse. Firstly, Daiches advocated on behalf of Jewish concerns when these came into conflict with the practices of the most dominant religious tradition in Scotland at the time, Presbyterian Christianity. He spoke out publicly against the Jewish missions that preyed on vulnerable and poor Jewish immigrants by offering medical and social services as part of attempts to convert them to Christianity. Operating at close quarters to areas in which Jews lived and maintained their religious and other institutions, these missions were frequently discussed in the Jewish press, nationally in the *JC*, as well as locally in the *Jewish Echo*. Among British Jews in touch with community institutions, therefore, Edinburgh was well known as a city with significant missionary activity directed at Jews.[25] Their success or otherwise in actually converting Jews has not yet been fully explored. In any case, these missionary establishments were a constant cause for concern, and Daiches used his position among the city's public figures and his access to the media to call on the right of Jews to live undisturbed by unwanted Christian attention.[26] Indeed, among the reasons Daiches set out for building Salisbury Road Synagogue was his belief that it was necessary not only to demonstrate Jewish unity and to establish a representative landmark that would put Jews on the religious map of the Scottish capital but also to provide a religious presence that would diminish the space in which Christian missions to the Jews represented themselves as addressing an unfulfilled religious and humanitarian need.[27]

Another concern raised by Daiches was the religious education of Jewish children. In his advocacy work, he placed this concern on a par with a concern for the religious education of all Scottish children, highlighting his understanding of the need to assert both Jewish integration and equality: as he saw it, this was a matter of right in a 'secular' nation state, with Jews being able to assert their needs and interests in the same way as the dominant religious tradition can.[28] He intervened decisively in the discussion about religious instruction in state schools and he advocated equality in the marriage laws, arguing that Jews ought not to have to comply with the practice of calling the banns in the church of the parish within which the couple intended to marry. Daiches was successful in both campaigns: the City of Edinburgh made Sciennes Primary School available for Hebrew classes on four weekday afternoons, free of charge, and the reading of the banns was changed in accordance with the rabbi's wishes.[29]

What brought Daiches to much public prominence in Edinburgh and further afield in Scotland, however, and what cemented his religious leadership in the Scottish Jewish community was a court case fought by the rabbi and the *JC* in a defence against the indictment levelled against Daiches and Leopold Greenberg, then editor of the paper, by one Alexander Levison.[30] The Levison Case in 1924 was not only a public test for the Jewish community in Edinburgh and a key stepping stone on its way to unity but also a significant event in 'provincial' Jewish life, establishing the supremacy of the Chief Rabbi in London in all matters to do with the verification of rabbinic ordination and status. Alexander Levison had arrived in Edinburgh in 1922 as minister to the recently formed Independent Edinburgh Hebrew Congregation, a splinter group opposed to the unification of Edinburgh's Jewish congregations. Alexander, brother of Leon Levison, a convert active locally as a missionary to the Jews, had remained faithful to his Jewish origins but played fast and loose with the facts of his biography and qualifications. Salis Daiches investigated Alexander Levison's credentials and found that Levison had invented both a rabbinical ordination from Chief Rabbi Kook of Palestine and authorisation to practise *shechita* from Chief Rabbi Hertz. When Levison refused to show documentary evidence of his qualifications, Daiches turned to Leopold Greenberg, editor of the *JC*, and, in a series of letters, warned the Jewish public against Levison's imposturing. Levison responded by suing Daiches and the *JC*. The case was concluded in favour of Daiches and the *JC* in late 1924 with the main documents being exposed as forgeries. Levison, unable to produce any further evidence to support his claims, absconded and the *JC* stepped up and covered all legal expenses incurred by Rabbi Daiches. Daiches had won the case by sheer tenacity: without his industry and effort, the documentation regarding Levison's fabrications of qualifications and experience would probably not have come to light. Thus, Daiches's position in the Scottish capital was bolstered by the Levison Case irrespective of the fact that this court case cost a lot of time, energy, and money to fight and, for a while, left little energy for other matters of community concern.

Salis Daiches – towering figure of the Edinburgh Hebrew Congregation

The 1920s saw a lot of Daiches's energy expended on uniting the Jewish religious congregations of Edinburgh, particularly through responding to the divergent needs of the congregants. As he had stated in an interview for the *JC* on 14 July 1922, his goal was 'to unite the different sections of the community, and to do away with the distinction between foreign and English which prevails in practically every community in this country'.[31] Daiches made substantial gains in support early on because of his previous reputation and his ability to represent Jewish interests to the wider public and, after the Levison Case, Daiches's leadership was unopposed.

Issues that caused friction in other communities appear to have had little impact in Edinburgh. Thus, we see that Daiches seemed to have been less concerned within his own community about matters such as *shechita* which exercised many Jewish communities in Britain at the time.[32] The *shechita* disputes over who had licence to provide the community with *kosher* meat took up a lot of column space in the Glasgow *Jewish Echo*, for example, and, on occasion, also took place in Edinburgh. These do not seem to have hampered Daiches's efforts in uniting the community, however. His voice on this matter is infrequently reported in the Minute Books of the Edinburgh Hebrew Congregation and Edinburgh appears to have experienced far fewer challenges from rival butchers than, for example, Glasgow.[33]

Daiches's involvement with the City of Edinburgh, which agreed to locate the Hebrew classes to Sciennes Primary School on the Southside of the city in a modern school building proved somewhat controversial in his own community. Holding Hebrew classes in a state school, Daiches argued, would not only place Jewish religious instruction on a par with the religious education offered to Christian children, it would also allow all Jewish children in the city to be educated together and thus contribute to the construction of a united Jewish community.[34] For this to happen, children from the St Leonard's district, in which most recent immigrants lived, needed to travel for 15 to 20 minutes on foot south to Sciennes, a more middle-class district situated beyond the Meadows which divided the city centre from the residential areas of south Edinburgh. The area south of the Meadows was considered suburban at the time and signified a deep social divide in the Jewish community. Daiches's educational programme seems likely to have been controversial because it removed the Jewish children from teachers associated with the smaller, rival Jewish congregations in the district populated by recent immigrants and encouraged mixing with the children of the anglicised congregation.[35] Indeed, Daiches's unification of the Hebrew classes appears to have given rise to the appointment of Alexander Levison, the reason being that he would educate the children on the premises of the Independent Edinburgh Hebrew Congregation rather than send them across town to Sciennes. With the court case surrounding Alexander Levison, however, the opposition to Daiches collapsed and the Independent Hebrew Congregation agreed to unite with the Edinburgh Hebrew Congregation.

Daiches's unifying efforts culminated after 1928 in the fundraising campaign for the building of the synagogue in Salisbury Road which was opened by the Chief Rabbi in 1932. To facilitate this building project, the Edinburgh Hebrew Congregation needed all smaller congregations to join them and, at the same time, to raise substantial new funds. At a time when the community numbered no more than 400 families, when the economic situation was difficult for many and when religious observance was waning, taking on a £20,000 project was a daunting enterprise.[36] Salisbury Road Synagogue's seating for *c*.1,000 people was far too great for the actual worshipping community of Jews in Edinburgh, even at its inception, and filled up only for the *High Holidays* and on festivals and special occasions.

The Minute Books of the Edinburgh Hebrew Congregation demonstrate efforts to fundraise and underwrite the costs but it is clear that the many small contributions left a substantial shortfall and the community ended up borrowing £6,000 to complete the project.[37]

How much of a unifying figure was Rabbi Dr Daiches? It seems from the previous chapters that he was not necessarily a diplomat but more a conviction leader who wore his religious (and other) ideology quite prominently on his sleeve. Arguably, he was hired in Edinburgh because he would be able to represent immigrant and British-born congregants or at least would be able to talk with both parts of the community in their own languages, *Yiddish* or English. Edinburgh Jews, however, had been struggling religiously for a while. Already throughout the 1920s, there was a consistent lack of religious engagement among the younger generations, and the finances of the community were strained, not least owing to a lack of people purchasing *shul* membership. While the community formally united under Daiches's leadership, it is unlikely that the chief reason was the appeal of his religious ideology, a somewhat highbrow modern Orthodox synthesis with secular life. More likely, the reason for such unity was the realisation that the religious Jewish population of Edinburgh could support only one congregation with its religious functionaries.[38] Indeed, as David Cesarani has demonstrated, the interwar and early post-World War II years were years of generational change with a resultant loss of community cohesion and the abandoning of tradition, language and religious commitments.[39] Being the community of the Scottish capital was an additional incentive to hire clergy who would be able to represent the community to the wider Scottish public. The appointment of Salis Daiches certainly offered the opportunity to set the congregation on the right footing with regard to future maintenance and public image.

Salis Daiches was a community leader who established his authority through his educational background and his gifted public oratory. This assessment can be supported by Daiches's successes in unifying the Jewish communities in Edinburgh under his leadership, thus overcoming the challenges for the anglicising community brought by an increase in traditional Orthodox immigrants. It appears that his origin, and being an immigrant himself, gave him much cultural and symbolic capital negotiating a settlement between the immigrant and resident communities. As the only rabbi in Scotland at the time who held these qualifications and characteristics, Daiches was ideally positioned, at least in his own estimation, to fulfil the brief of a 'Chief Rabbi of Scotland' under whose oversight the immigrant *rabbonim* and the leaders of the anglicised communities could make common cause for a Jewish future in Scotland. We next need to examine how Daiches's ambitions sat with Glasgow's Jewish religious leaders who were at home in Scotland's largest city with a more numerous and diverse Jewish community. Thereafter we shall ask how Daiches's drive for a Scottish Beth Din was received by the Chief Rabbi who had cut

A triangle of concerns: Salis Daiches – Chief Rabbi Hertz – Glasgow's Jewish leaders

Salis Daiches had ambitions for the establishment of a Scottish Beth Din, with himself as *av beth din*, and a complete reorganisation of Scottish Jewry. It is unclear why Daiches thought such a venture would be a possibility north of the border long after the proposals for a reorganisation of Jewish regional communities had failed in England and particularly in the face of known opposition from Chief Rabbi Hertz to any such reorganisation of British Jewish congregations. And yet, reading between the lines of his letter notifying the Chief Rabbi of his acceptance of the 'call' to Edinburgh, and pondering on how Daiches understood Hertz's note of congratulations, it seems that Daiches thought that the assurance 'of my utmost sympathy in any direction in which I can be of assistance to you'[40] included support for the establishment of a Beth Din for Scotland. Already in 1919, soon after Daiches's arrival in Edinburgh, he had raised the subject of a Beth Din with the Edinburgh Hebrew Congregation and lobbied Chief Rabbi Hertz with a view to the Chief Rabbi promoting the idea to Glasgow's Jewish leadership. The Chief Rabbi, however, did not take the bait and put off any steps to support a reorganisation of Scottish Jewry. Glasgow's Jews were in a continual state of religious disunity for much of the time between 1880 and 1939.[41] Various attempts at unifying the religious community were made, not least the establishment of a United Synagogue of Glasgow (1898),[42] a Glasgow Board of Shechita (1916)[43] and the founding of the Glasgow Beth Din (1929).[44] Meanwhile, the Glasgow Jewish Representative Council, founded in 1914,[45] sought to regulate affairs concerning the entire Jewish community, including education and welfare. Yet, as we shall see, personal status negotiations and cases of irregular marriages in Glasgow and elsewhere in Scotland were brought to the attention of Daiches in Edinburgh by the Chief Rabbi along with the forceful directive to regularise matters immediately. In what follows, we shall see that an understanding of the interplay between Edinburgh's rabbi and Glasgow's Jewish leadership is an important first step for further understanding of the relationship between British Jewry's religious authorities in London and their official or de facto representatives in Scotland.

We lack primary sources to illustrate this relationship directly. We therefore need to rely on secondary evidence, gathered mainly from newspapers, such as the *JC* and the Glasgow-based *Jewish Echo* (first published in 1928), as well as correspondence between Daiches and Jewish leaders in Edinburgh and Chief Rabbi Hertz, and between Glasgow's leaders and the Chief Rabbi. There is no evidence of correspondence or other close communication between Daiches and the three well-known rabbis active in Glasgow at the same time as Daiches: Rabbis Atlas at South Portland Street Synagogue, Rabbi Lurie at Chevra Kadisha Synagogue and Rabbi Balkin at New Central Synagogue;[46] and there is little direct evidence to be found of Daiches's impact on Jewish life or even Jewish leadership in Glasgow. There are several reasons for this lack of evidence. Firstly, as with many British Jewish communities, not much survives of the records of the Jewish communities in Glasgow in the interwar years, least of all personal or professional correspondence between religious officials. At present, we do not have access to any letters Glasgow *rabbonim* and Jewish clergy exchanged with Daiches, nor do any papers from previous Edinburgh rabbis appear to have survived that might have given evidence of their relationship with Glasgow's Jewish ministers. Secondly, it is plausible that Daiches may have been speaking with Glasgow's rabbis on the telephone, the technology being widespread enough in the interwar years to assume that rabbis in Glasgow either had a telephone installed in their residence or at their synagogue, or at least had regular access to one. We do, however have some limited evidence of Daiches being in touch with community leaders in Glasgow through letters and telegrams.[47] Daiches was regularly mentioned in the *Jewish Echo*, not particularly through his own regular contributions, but because he received invitations to speak at events, notably those of literary societies, which were then reported on in the *Echo*. By contrast, Glasgow's religious leaders used the pages of the *Jewish Echo* to spread their interpretations of Jewish beliefs and religious ideology to their congregations.[48] Daiches was also present in Glasgow for rabbinical installations, retirals and other celebrations, as well as for some of the activities of the Zionist organisations.[49] We can conclude that Daiches was well known in Glasgow and that he appeared to be respected for what he offered to the wider Jewish community of Scotland with regard to the public representation of Jews. It is unclear from these sources how much this respect extended to his work with, and for, the London Beth Din – whose *halakhic* representative he effectively was – and how much he was seen locally as a person to consult on matters affecting Jewish life in Scotland beyond Edinburgh.

Daiches's close relationship with the Chief Rabbi would have had an impact on how he was perceived locally. His standing in relation to London was probably an asset in Edinburgh as it increased the significance of the comparatively small community. In relation to his rabbinical colleagues in Glasgow, Daiches's constant contact with London may have been less welcome. When Daiches arrived in Edinburgh, Garnethill Synagogue, Glasgow's oldest congregation, was waning in significance. As we have observed elsewhere, the majority of recent immigrants sought advice from immigrant rabbis rather than from the city's anglicised establishment. Built in 1879 by the established and well-integrated community in the west of the city centre, Garnethill Synagogue was a symbol of the community having arrived and settled firmly into Scottish life. Garnethill predates the city centre communities of the Gorbals which have become symbolic of early twentieth-century Jewish immigrant life in Glasgow, the largest of which was South Portland Street Synagogue, led from the late 1920s by Rabbi Atlas. Before World War I, the Jewish population had swelled to such numbers that additional synagogues were founded to serve the needs of the immigrants according to their traditions. Located mainly in the Gorbals area, the rabbis serving these communities were immigrants themselves, often recruited specifically to serve the newly arrived Jewish residents of Glasgow.[50] Some were rabbis by training and held qualifications from prestigious *yeshivot* on the Continent,[51] their qualifications often outranking locally established Jewish ministers, such as Revd E. P. Phillips who served at Garnethill from 1879 to 1929. But the immigrant rabbis and ministers lacked familiarity with British civil law and did not always respect the authority structures of the United Hebrew Congregations of Great Britain and the Empire which required all religious appointments and all decisions affecting the Jewish status of congregants (conversion, marriage and divorce) to be administered only with the approval of the Chief Rabbi and the London Beth Din. The correspondence of the Chief Rabbi's office with congregations in Glasgow since the departure of Rabbi Hillman to serve on the London Beth Din was, to a significant degree, concerned with the possibility of appointing a *rav* who would be able to function as a Jewish religious guide for the whole city and bring some form of unity to the various independent congregations; no agreement was reached during World War I but it appears that Rabbi Lurie was trusted by Chief Rabbi Hertz.[52] The Glasgow Beth Din, formed in 1929, oversaw matters of *kashrut* (though *shechita* was devolved to the Glasgow Board of Shechita) and offered advice on *halakhic* matters but lacked the powers to execute any *halakhic* decisions without the permission of the Chief Rabbi.[53] Likewise, *shochetim* had to be licensed by the Chief Rabbi, so that the Board of Shechita was really concerned with the upkeep of agreed standards of *kashrut*, and with local economic relationships, overseeing the market of *kosher* meat, and seeing that civil law regarding the slaughter of animals was observed.[54]

Daiches in Edinburgh was not only remote from the Glaswegian scene, he did not necessarily have the authority that would have been recognised by his rabbinical colleagues in the Empire's Second City. Soon after his arrival in Edinburgh in 1919, Daiches had lobbied privately for the Chief Rabbi to support a Scottish Beth Din and, as we shall see below, he returned to the subject of devolution of *halakhic* authority in correspondence with Hertz throughout the 1920s. In 1928 he went public in the first editions of Glasgow's new weekly, the *Jewish Echo*, and authored a series of three articles on the need for a Scottish Beth Din entitled 'The Need for the Religious Re-organisation of Scottish Jewry'.[55] He argued for a Beth Din for Scotland which would regulate *kashrut*, *shechita*, the issuing of a *get* and performance of *chalitzah*, things the London Beth Din had trouble controlling at such a distance, and which would safeguard Jewish education for children. He bemoaned the inertia of the community in failing to push for a united synagogue for Scotland and hoped that these articles would stimulate debate to such an extent that decisive action would be forthcoming. These articles sparked a discussion in the paper. Two of the three Glaswegian rabbis asked their opinion by the editor (Lurie and Balkin) appeared to support the idea of a Scottish Beth Din, including a leading role for Salis Daiches; the third (Rabbi Atlas) did not or was, at best, lukewarm about the prospect:[56]

> I don't see why Dr. Daiches thought it opportune to bring out now, in the Press, the question of a *Beth Din*. [...] What have we to do with other congregations? Surely, a *Kehilla* like Edinburgh could easily manage its own affairs. We are in Glasgow and we must concern ourselves about Glasgow matters only. [...][57]

Atlas also affirmed that he would recognise the authority of the Chief Rabbi in all *halakhic* matters: 'The Chief Rabbi's authority must remain integral. [...] I am now a staunch supporter of the idea of recognising the Chief Rabbi as the highest authority.'[58] The subject of a Scottish Beth Din was quickly dropped from public discussion, the Glasgow Beth Din was formed the following year and, after 1928, Daiches did not mention the subject publically again either. His energies were then largely absorbed by his work in Edinburgh where the communities were still not fully united even though the massive building project of Salisbury Road Synagogue was underway and which required communal unity, not least in the form of firm financial commitment. From the 1930s onwards, Daiches's attention was increasingly absorbed by events on the European Continent and he committed himself to work for Jewish refugees from Nazi persecution.

And yet, throughout the 1920s, developments in Glasgow notwithstanding, it was Daiches, as the highest qualified rabbi in Scotland, loyal to the Chief Rabbi and his court, who effectively was able to guarantee the Chief Rabbi that *halakhic* processes of concern to the whole British Jewish community were carried out with due diligence and professionalism. Daiches, as we shall see in the next section, thus not only oversaw conversions, marriages and divorces in Edinburgh, he was also consulted by congregations further north (Dundee, Aberdeen, Inverness) and acted as a '*halakhic* firefighter' when irregularities in these areas were brought to the attention of Chief Rabbi Hertz. Levison, the impostor, had been made an example of by Daiches but his was an extreme case of deception. Daiches's colleagues in Glasgow were bona fide rabbis who simply did not always seek permission from the Chief Rabbi in matters of *halakhah*. Some, however, were mindful of the problems associated with rabbis offering *halakhic* services outwith the supervision and authorisation of the London Beth Din. Thus, in 1936, Rabbi Atlas published in the *Jewish Echo* a warning against speedy conversions offered by rabbis acting on their own authority alone.[59] Yet, when he acted alone without prior authorisation from Hertz, Daiches could find himself in conflict with the Chief Rabbi not dissimilar in tone to that experienced by his Glaswegian colleagues. Daiches's actions caused discord with London, for example, when he insisted on his competence to deal with *halakhic* matters, such as divorce, and did so swiftly and on his own accord without first consulting Hertz. In general, Hertz was content with Daiches's actions so long as authorisation was sought from himself. When Daiches assumed the Chief Rabbi's consent, Hertz complained about a lack of respect for the proper chain of authority but approved of his actions all the same.[60] Helpfully, we do have the record of these interactions and can thus see the Daiches–Hertz relationship in sharper relief than that of Hertz (or Daiches) with Glasgow's Jewish religious officials.

Salis Daiches and Joseph Hertz: a relationship in letters

As we have observed, Daiches saw his appointment in Edinburgh as a decisive step up in his career, imagining himself, it appears, with a lot more rabbinic responsibility than he had held in his previous employments. Edinburgh, the Scottish capital, though home only to a small Jewish community, promised greater status and recognition, not least because Daiches seemed to think that his move north would bring about a reorganisation of Scottish Jewish congregations and establish him formally as 'Chief Rabbi of Scotland'. Already in 1919, still within the first year of his ministry in Edinburgh, Daiches was courted by the community in Cape Town and, in 1920, Pretoria Hebrew Congregation also headhunted him. Daiches deliberated whether to move to South Africa: the conditions of employment were markedly better than those in Edinburgh, not least because of the generous salary offered.[61] Yet, he decided to stay in Edinburgh, a decision he made in consultation with Chief Rabbi Hertz and which he explains thus:

> Dear Chief Rabbi
> I thank you for your reply to my last letter re Cape Town which I have just received. Since my return to town I have had the opportunity of discussing the matter with several friends and also relatives. They all are of the opinion that at the present time there ought to be no need for one in my position to emigrate to South Africa in order to find an adequate scope for work and to secure a position of importance in the Community. It ought to be at least as easy – they argue – to organise a District Rabbinate for Scotland as it would be in the Cape Province. [. . .]
>   I was glad to hear from Mr S. S. Stungo, J.P. [treasurer of the Edinburgh Hebrew Congregation] who has given me an account of the interview he has had with you, that you view with favour the proposed formation of a District Rabbinate for Scotland.
>   It seems to me that the first step in that direction ought to be the formation of a United Synagogue for Scotland with a Council to which all Synagogues should send delegates. [. . .][62]

While Cape Town would have been financially more lucrative for Daiches, he accepted what he considered a rather unsatisfactory salary of £350 a year because he hoped for a clear leadership position in Scotland.[63] The Chief Rabbi, however, played a diplomatic card to Abel Phillips, Honorary Secretary of the Edinburgh Hebrew Congregation in September 1919, effectively denying that he ever was supportive of Daiches' ambitions:

> Dear Sir,
> I am in receipt of your letter of September 8th, and note that the movement for a District Rabbinate for Scotland is at present confined to the Edinburgh Hebrew Congregation. The views of the Glasgow community have not yet been ascertained, and it is for me to take the initiative in this direction.
>
> This renders the plan of action far different from what it would have been if Glasgow were as united and as anxious on this question as Edinburgh.
> [...][64]

Daiches, on the other hand, persisted and continually brought evidence to substantiate his claim that a Scottish Beth Din would not only be desirable for his own ambitions but necessary because of the repeated violations of *halakhah* and civil law by inadequately trained rabbis and ad hoc *batei din* in matters of personal status, marriage and divorce, and *kashrut*. In December 1919, just before Chief Rabbi Hertz's visit to Scotland, Daiches writes

> [...] I spent last weekend in Glasgow and came in contact with the leading men of practically all sections of the community. All seem to realise that things in Glasgow are in a very bad state and that the prevailing confusion is mainly due to the lack of proper organisation and the absence of a religious authority whom all would respect and who would be able to bridge over the awful gulf that separates the West End from the Southside and vice versa and the young generation from the old even in the Southside. The *rabbonim* themselves admit that they have no influence, no standing, and no religious authority in the Community and that the sooner a Rabbinate for Scotland is established the sooner the hope of putting a stop to the present confusion and communal deterioration can be realised. Whether the South Portland Synagogue will engage the services of a Rav for themselves or not – this question does not in the least affect the question of a Rabbinate for Scotland. In fact, if such a fourth *rav* is appointed in Glasgow the confusion will be greater than ever, unless at the same time a religious representative is appointed who shall preside over a United Beth Din (giving all the *rabbonim* an official standing) and shall act as the representative of all sections of Jews in Scotland both inside and outside our Community. [...] I think that if you were to call a conference of representatives of all Synagogues in Scotland [...] it

would greatly facilitate matters, and the Community would realise that something important is being done, and that the matter of communal organisation is being tackled in earnest with the view of giving Anglo-Jewry a new lease of life.[65]

The most significant evidence of his *halakhic* work among Jews in Scotland in the interwar years stems from Daiches's correspondence with Chief Rabbi Hertz regarding marriages and conversions, as well as the occasional divorce. When irregularities in the process of marriage and conversion were discovered, Daiches was often asked to deal with matters locally because the affected parties could not be prevailed upon to travel to London nor did the Chief Rabbi appear to be able directly to control the immigrant *rabbonim* in Glasgow. Thus, in 1922, London advised the Aberdeen community to turn to Daiches in Edinburgh for the authorisation of marriages to be conducted via the London Beth Din.[66] There was a stream of prospective converts asking for admission to Judaism via Daiches and, not infrequently, requests originated with the non-Jewish partner of an intermarried couple. In the first year of his service in Edinburgh, Daiches was called upon to register and administer four conversions and, from 1925 to 1933, the records reveal a further six instances of individuals seeking conversion whose eventual reception into the Jewish faith was presided over by Daiches.[67] Recognising the rather high numbers of non-Jews seeking to convert via the Edinburgh Hebrew Congregation, the London Beth Din, while sanctioning the instruction of one prospective proselyte, closed their letter of 24 March 1927 by stating that 'they hope that no further application from your community will be received in the future'.[68] This concern may have been occasioned by the fact that the majority of converts coming forward in the Edinburgh region at that time were already married to a Jew and could be understood as seeking to convert because of their existing relationship rather than of their own accord as required by *halakhah*. A few months later, however, a further application followed and the line of prospective Scottish proselytes continued.[69] The theme of devolution of *halakhic* authority in Daiches's correspondence with Chief Rabbi Hertz on matters of Scottish Jewish communal reorganisation surfaces repeatedly throughout the 1920s until 1932. As we have seen, Hertz sought verification of events from Daiches on matters such as suspected '*shtille chuppe*' and he also instructed him occasionally to legalise the status of converts who had been admitted to Judaism by unauthorised rabbis through a local ad hoc *beth din* presided over by Daiches. In response, Daiches consistently brought up the need for a Scottish Beth Din in his correspondence with the Chief Rabbi.[70] The topics raised by Daiches mostly concerned issues of Jewish status in relation to marriages and conversions undertaken by rabbis in Glasgow without authorisation from the Chief Rabbi and the conversion of individuals seeking admission to the

Jewish faith by appealing to the London Beth Din or to Rabbi Daiches directly.

In all his endeavours, Daiches continued to stress the loyalty of a potential Scottish Beth Din to the London Beth Din, indeed, its submission to the Chief Rabbi's authority. What Daiches seemed to have argued for was an outpost of the London Beth Din that enforced the Chief Rabbi's authority in Scotland. He, Rabbi Dr Salis Daiches, could be entrusted with being the local emissary of the Chief Rabbi because he would make sure that the Chief Rabbi's position became the standard to which a Scottish Beth Din would rule. While the conference Daiches had suggested for the end of December 1919 did not come to pass, he picked up the correspondence on this matter again in early February 1920. Having been approached by Mr Speculant, the President of Garnethill Synagogue in Glasgow, Daiches now asked Hertz to authorise him to call a conference in Glasgow.[71] Hertz, however, continued to stall. On 22 February 1920, Hertz replied as follows:

> Dear Dr. Daiches,
> After very careful consideration and consultation concerning your letter, we feel that it would be inadvisable at this state [sic] for me to direct the convening of the representatives of the Scottish Synagogues you have in mind. Let the movement in this instance come 'from below'.[72]

The letters written to Daiches in response to his pressure for a Scottish Beth Din or for some other authoritative community leadership in Scotland were framed in a non-committal fashion, suggesting that he wait longer, that there was no unified push in the communities in Glasgow and Edinburgh, that his initiative appeared a little one-sided or premature. In short, Hertz was having none of it, in the nicest possible way. These glimpses into his dealings with Edinburgh, Glasgow, and with Scotland as a whole are pertinent examples to have in mind when evaluating the Chief Rabbi's strategy of maintaining overall *halakhic* control over the 'provinces'. Hertz insisted that power would not be devolved and brushed aside and silenced the proposals for the reorganisation of British Jewry made by the Conference of Jewish Ministers just before his appointment as Chief Rabbi. Yet Hertz did, de facto, devolve *halakhic* powers to individuals he trusted, such as Salis Daiches, and thus pursued the continued centralisation of rabbinic authority, and coupled this with actual delegation of *halakhic* decision-making. Daiches, was annoying and persistent enough regularly to push Hertz to give in and formalise the de facto devolution of powers and establish a Scottish Beth Din. Hertz, of course, was successful with his long-term strategy of maintaining *halakhic* hegemony. Historical events on the Continent, and their repercussions for British Jews, overshadow the 1930s and 1940s and only well after World War II do we find another ideological struggle of much greater repercussions between one rabbi and his followers and the Chief Rabbi and his court.[73]

Conclusion

As Michael and I enter the synagogue at the conclusion of our walk in Edinburgh's Southside, we step into a space that physically links the Jewish history of the city with its Jewish present. In the 1980s, the floor of the sanctuary built in 1932 was raised to create a community centre on the building's ground floor. The resulting large function room is bustling with activity, tables are being set and decorated with purple and pink balloons for a *bat mitzvah* party later that day. Facing the room, an exhibition details the history of 'Edinburgh Jews'; various rabbis and dignitaries depicted on screens look out on the scene which celebrates the Jewish present and which promises a Jewish future in the city. I suspect that the Jewish youth of today are no more and no less committed to the study of Hebrew and of classic Jewish texts than was Michael's generation who sat in *cheder* some seventy years ago. Then, Michael recalls, the Hebrew teacher restored order to his classroom by promising that those who read a page of Hebrew without a mistake could go home immediately. But reading Hebrew all boys and girls learned, and the boys also studied their *bar mitzvah* portion and made a speech. And today, as in the past, rabbis, teachers, parents and grandparents are rightly taking pride as they watch the younger generation make these same achievements and mark their first steps into adulthood. At the cusp of maturity, much remains unknown and unknowable about where the teenagers are headed in life and what interests they may be passionate about as adults. Rabbi Daiches saw his sons *bar mizvah*-ed in Graham Street Synagogue. His daughters' steps into adulthood at the time had no comparable ceremony as is available to girls today. But all his children grew up with a sure-footed knowledge of Hebrew, all were well versed in Orthodox Jewish tradition and all drew on this foundation in their adult lives even if, for all four, their intellectual passions were located in the non-Jewish secular world. The synthesis advocated for, and lived by, Salis Daiches could not be replicated in this diaspora city, just as the secular education and freedoms associated with democracies were not enjoyed in the 'old world' left behind by Salis.[74] Salis's life was characterised by a unique set of circumstances that saw the opportunities of secular society and equal rights for all citizens added to a rich traditional Jewish education. Both worlds were transformed into a joint universe in the person of Salis Daiches and those who shared similar experiences and ideology. His children's different experiences joined together the Jewish and secular worlds in yet other creative syntheses. These syntheses could not replicate that created by their father but had to stride out into new territory. Was Daiches disappointed that his children's lives took radically different turns from his own? Perhaps. David Daiches hinted as much in his memoir.[75] But Rabbi Daiches also understood the need for change and adaptation into a new world; and, rather than disappointment, he may have mourned his own hopes and expectations, as his children made their way in the world, while appreciating their talents and visions.

Rabbi Daiches's ideology and style of leadership closely corresponded to that of the Chief Rabbi, and he actively promoted the Chief Rabbi's authority and educational agenda. Daiches sought to occupy a position of leadership commensurate with his educational attainments and the status of his rabbinical ancestry. It is debatable whether his position in Edinburgh and his relationship with the Chief Rabbi amounted to the position of prominence he had aspired to. What is clear from the sources is the *expectation* that a Scottish Beth Din under his leadership would come to pass soon after his appointment in Edinburgh at the conclusion of World War I. While this expectation was not fulfilled, Daiches nevertheless remained in Edinburgh. Daiches, however, became a respected public representative of the Scottish Jewish community. When Reverend Cosgrove came on to the Glasgow scene in 1935, he took on a comparable role in publicly representing the Jewish community to their Christian neighbours and offering erudition on Jewish-related topics in many different venues.[76]

Since 1914, immigration to the United Kingdom had slowed and the communities stabilised. The years leading up to World War I had been characterised by cultural and religious conflict arising from clashes between the habitus of resident and incoming Jewish populations, the immigrants numerically overwhelming the residents.[77] With World War I, the Jewish population, also in Scotland, saw more settlement and less turnover through transmigration. As a result of this settlement, questions of community organisation could be addressed through a longer-term strategy. For Salis Daiches, this involved lobbying for regional authority structures organised around local *batei din*. As we have seen, Chief Rabbi Hertz adopted a different strategy by leaving things as they were while co-opting immigrant rabbis on to the Beth Din and thereby establishing authority figures recognised by immigrants at the heart of the British Jewish religious leadership. With a declining 'provincial' Jewish population – a trend apparent from the late 1920s onwards – and a decline in synagogue attendance and community membership, the strategy of the Chief Rabbi paid off. Rather than devolve authority, he dealt with *halakhic* irregularities on a case-by-case basis, often working through particular trusted rabbis such as Salis Daiches. In time, 'provincial' practices were sufficiently bound to the London Beth Din; indeed, it can be argued that the diminishing Jewish populations outwith London were more receptive to guidance from the Chief Rabbi than when their communities were swelling through immigration. While some regional *batei din* had been established, their jurisdiction concerned mainly *kashrut* and *shechita* and did not extend to status issues on a regular basis. After 1945 these regional *batei din* declined or were dissolved so that, today, only Manchester Jewry survives as a thriving and sometimes rebellious 'provincial' community with its own *beth din*. But, even in the case of

Manchester, status issues are firmly delegated to London, and the majority of *halakhic* issues dealt with by the Manchester Beth Din – as with other provincial *batei din* such as that of Leeds previously – concern matters of *kashrut* and *shechita*.[78]

The discussions and plans for regional Jewish authority structures to work in conjunction with the London Beth Din, while staking out some independence, are a phenomenon of the first half of the twentieth century. Thereafter, the decline of provincial Jewry rendered such proposals obsolete. In terms of the wider historiographical concerns of this book, reflecting on migration and religious authority in a transnational framework, this chapter cast light on these issues from a local perspective, seeking to disrupt the predominance of external assessment of the power struggles in Britain's religious Jewish communities. Indeed, I would argue that absolute population numbers are not, and should not be, the determinant in arguments for or against independent *batei din* and other community institutions. Instead, we may think of the mental maps of local populations that push, on the one hand, for independent decision-making or, on the other hand, for increased centralisation of authority. In his sphere of influence, Salis Daiches, I would contend, argued for more independent rabbinical leadership because it gave impetus to a thriving local religious life, not only because it was necessary for controlling conflicts between large numbers of immigrants and a small resident Jewish community or because it would simply have strengthened his hand in dealing with local power games.

The brief population swell in the 'provinces' generated much activity, and the discussion about regional authority structures affords a glimpse into the thriving microcosm of religious Jewry in the United Kingdom from the perspective of its religious leadership. This world is now largely gone and accessible only via historical research and memory. Daiches's work in Scotland, and particularly in Edinburgh, however, left a lasting mark on the Jewish community. Mention Daiches's name in Edinburgh and many associated with the present-day Jewish congregations will have something to share, a memory of Salis Daiches, or his two sons – Lionel, a prominent advocate, and David, the literary critic – or his son-in-law David Daiches Raphael, who married his daughter Sylvia, or his granddaughter Jenni, the writer and academic who lives in Edinburgh. At the University of Edinburgh, David Daiches is remembered as the initiator and founder of IASH, the Institute for Advanced Studies in the Humanities which, since 1969, has provided scholars with space to think and write in a supportive community of intellectual exchange.[79] The wider Edinburgh and Scottish communities are likely to reference the generation of Salis Daiches's children and grandchildren more readily than the rabbi but, nonetheless, the name Daiches elicits a response. Indeed, the final chapter of this book will reach into the present and explore traces of Jewish life and the work of the Daiches family in Edinburgh's urban geography of the present.

CHAPTER 4

Traces and Spaces: Jews and/in the City of Edinburgh

For six years I walked past the Daiches's family home in 6 Millerfield Place every working day, often twice, taking my children to and from their nursery at the end of the same street. Turning into the quiet cul-de-sac, my daughters would run ahead, jumping into puddles and delighting at the resulting splashes of water, or they would balance on the low walls which no longer sport the historic iron railings. We had to stop at a small elevation in front of number 16 so that one or both girls could recite the nursery rhyme 'I'm the king of the castle' at the top of their voices. I imagine the rabbi's children enjoying themselves similarly though perhaps not within earshot of their parents. Today, one side of the street is still largely residential, families occupying a whole house or sharing a front door leading to separate flats. The other side of the street of terraced houses was, until 2016, part of the Royal Hospital for Sick Children, the Sick Kids, as it is affectionately known, and the last in the row, backing on to the yard of Sciennes Primary School, was a nursery primarily for NHS staff. Millerfield Place, which is located on the Southside of the city just across the Meadows which separate the city centre from the southern residential areas of Edinburgh, was (and remains) a thoroughly genteel street occupied by generously proportioned houses with back gardens – in contrast to the tenements in the next street over, which have back greens, shared between all flats and designated solely for the drying of laundry.

When the Daiches family moved to 6 Millerfield Place in 1920,[1] the Meadows were still used as grazing land for cattle belonging to the city's many dairies. Indeed, until the early eighteenth century, the Meadows were a loch, providing drinking water for the city and for the adjoining breweries, while the streets beyond were known as Kamchatka, considered as remote as this far-eastern Russian province. On the surface, Edinburgh's cityscape has remained relatively unchanged across the centuries. War did not bring destruction to the city and town planners, while moving individual streets, did not reroute the main arteries serving the city. Thus, to the visitor, Edinburgh easily creates the impression of timelessness and a certain degree of majesty. On closer inspection, however, residents find that a lot has changed, particularly within the last century, as neighbourhoods transformed through changes to the local population, as renovations revealed (and concealed) historical detail, as shops opened and closed and as the soundscape altered through changes to the mode of transport, the business conducted and the vernacular of the residents. Local history initiatives, such as the Edinburgh Southside Heritage Group, collect stories from living memory and this Group has made these available online and through a small museum display in a community hall.[2] Thus, residents and visitors are invited to explore the various ways in which their neighbourhood may be 'storied' or narrated. Memoirs recalling early twentieth-century life, in particular, sit alongside tourist guides to Edinburgh, each pressing a different agenda onto their readers. And coffee-table publications refract the contemporary city through many layers. Walking tours offered by various groups reflect yet other ways of accessing the city: literary pub crawls combine the consumption of drink in the watering holes of famous Edinburgh writers with the recitation of poetry; ghost tours promise thrilling walkabouts on graveyards in the footsteps of the famous pair of graverobbers and murderers, Burke and Hare, who, in the early nineteenth century, supplied fresh corpses from the city's cemeteries to professors at the medical school for teaching and research purposes. These are joined by historical and architectural tours and tours catering for other, more specialised, interests. In 2017, Edinburgh's offering of walking tours was joined by a Jewish history tour: *Jewish Edinburgh on Foot*, taking place five times during that year's summer months, and now available as a self-guided tour on an app.[3]

This chapter explores 'Jewish Edinburgh' as a physical and mental space associated with the city. The chapter connects historical and memorial discourses by tracing the evidence of Jewish life in the city and in the memories of its residents. Here, the discussion turns to the present time and seeks to detect, discover and mark traces of Jewish life in the physical environment of the city of Edinburgh and in the imaginings of the city by its Jewish (and non-Jewish) residents. Thereby, traces of early twentieth-century spatial, communal and demographic movements can be uncovered and illustrated. Another aspect of this chapter is the imaginary space occupied by 'Jewish Edinburgh' in memories (and memoirs) of the city. The chapter is framed by an intersection of a number of different narratives that ground the analysis of 'Jewish spaces' in the Scottish capital. Firstly, the analysis draws heavily on David Daiches's memoir of his childhood in early twentieth-century Edinburgh. *Two Worlds: An Edinburgh Jewish Childhood*, first published 1956, is a landmark in the memory of the Jewish community in Edinburgh. Intimately connected to both the author's and his father's connection to the city, *Two Worlds*, in a sense, puts the Jewish community of Edinburgh on the map of the British and international Jewish imagination.[4] David Daiches weaves a portrait of his father central to his childhood recollections so that Salis Daiches's life and work emerge vividly from his son's memoir. While David Daiches's childhood is the ostensible reason for writing *Two Worlds*, he quickly becomes aware of the book's status in the city's sociocultural history.[5] The son's fame as one of the twentieth century's most important literary critics and public intellectual voices in the United Kingdom, and specifically in Scotland, attracts readers from outwith the Jewish community.[6] For the Jewish community, that David Daiches is a son of the Edinburgh community coupled with the fame of his father Salis – still the most significant Edinburgh and perhaps the most significant Scottish rabbi since the community's founding in the early nineteenth century – account for *Two Worlds*' prominent status, as does the fact that there is no comparable account of Edinburgh's Jewish landscape and experience from this period. Secondly, the route charted by the walking tour, *Jewish Edinburgh on Foot*, follows the movement of the Jewish population from the city centre to the Southside and traces demographic, economic and religious patterns of development across two centuries. An analysis of the 'Jewish spaces' identified, visited, inhabited, remembered and (re-)narrated in *Two Worlds* and *Jewish Edinburgh on Foot* offers a prism of various perspectives on the Scottish capital. In this chapter, the book's and the tour's themes, movements, locations and languages, and related narratives, are explored in their relationship to memory, community and audience. Pierre Nora's concept of *les lieux de mémoire* is used as a reference point in relation to texts, landscape and people, refracted and critiqued through Julia Creet's astute and illuminating argument that 'migration has an effect on how and what we remember and that displacement intensifies our investments in memory, illuminating the *topos* of memory itself. Memory is always migrating, generating its own topological demands.'[7]

Thus, rather than assuming that place is static, I argue, with Creet, that migration and the memory of migration affect how place is invested with meaning in any given social context. Indeed, for minorities, and particularly those with migration histories, the narratives of memory attaching to place shift and meander. We can extend this observation with Doreen Massey's suggestion in *For Space*: 'If space is rather a simultaneity of stories-so-far, then places are collections of those stories, articulations within the wider power-geometries of space.'[8] Narratives of place are therefore infinitely malleable given their retelling through different constellations of people, time and space.

In relation to the city, these ways of creating places are captured well by Roland Barthes who suggests that

> The city is a discourse and this discourse is truly a language: the city speaks to its inhabitants, we speak our city, the city where we are, simply by living in it, by wandering through it, by looking at it.[9]

This oft-quoted statement can be understood as a guiding maxim that is variously refracted in the explorations that follow. The theoretical underpinnings of the following explorations of Edinburgh's 'Jewish spaces' are formed by Henri Lefebvre's ground-breaking study of the social practices which produce our understanding of space,[10] Barthes's work on the city

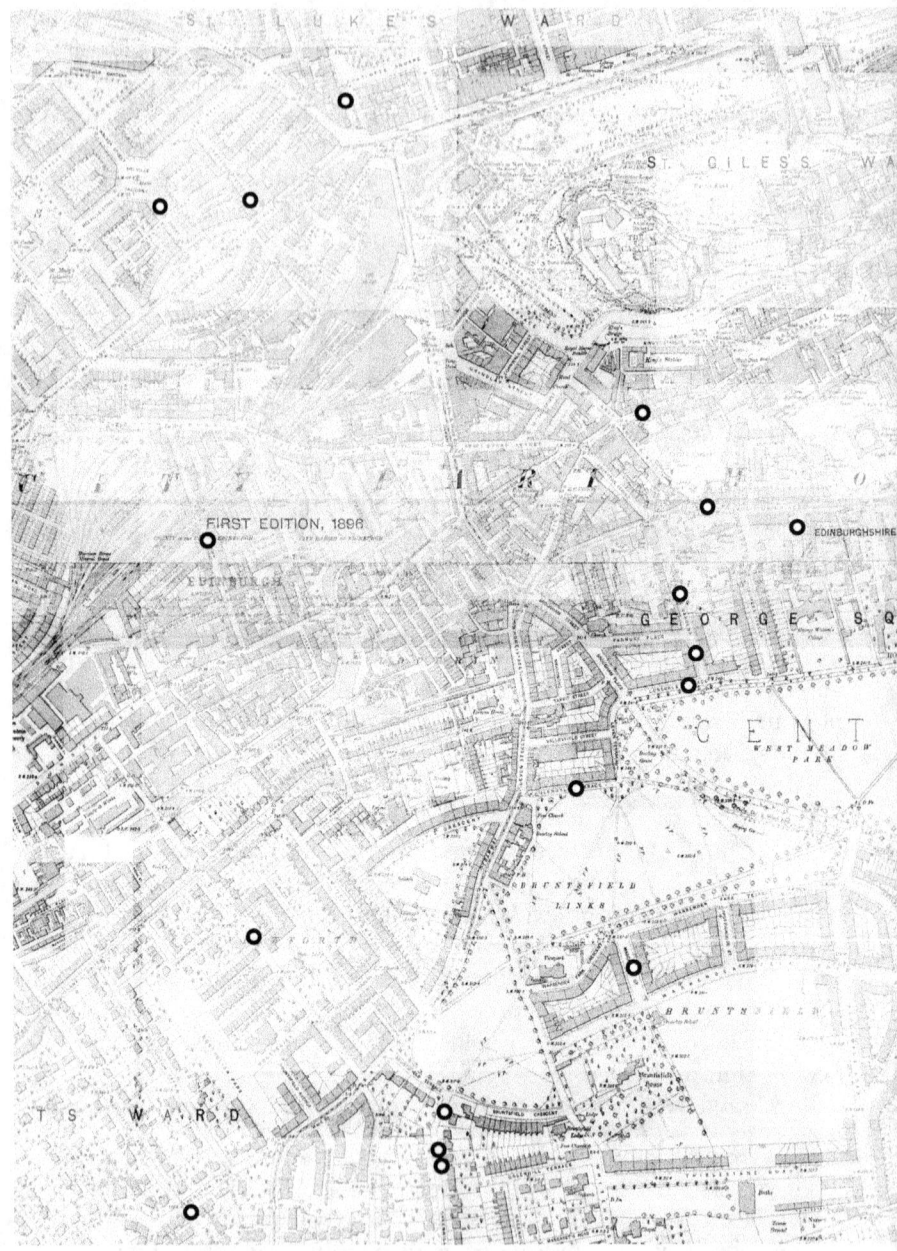

Figure 4.1 This map, designed by Piotr Leśniak, is based on the 1893 Ordnance Survey of Edinburgh. The map's artwork preserves a trace of the approach taken for the map's original purpose, the 2013 exhibition *Edinburgh Jews*. The shaded areas, achieved by layering maps, point to the parts of the city with a higher Jewish population: the darker the shade, the greater the number of Jewish residents. The map also shows the distribution of Jewish businesses derived from the 1911 Post

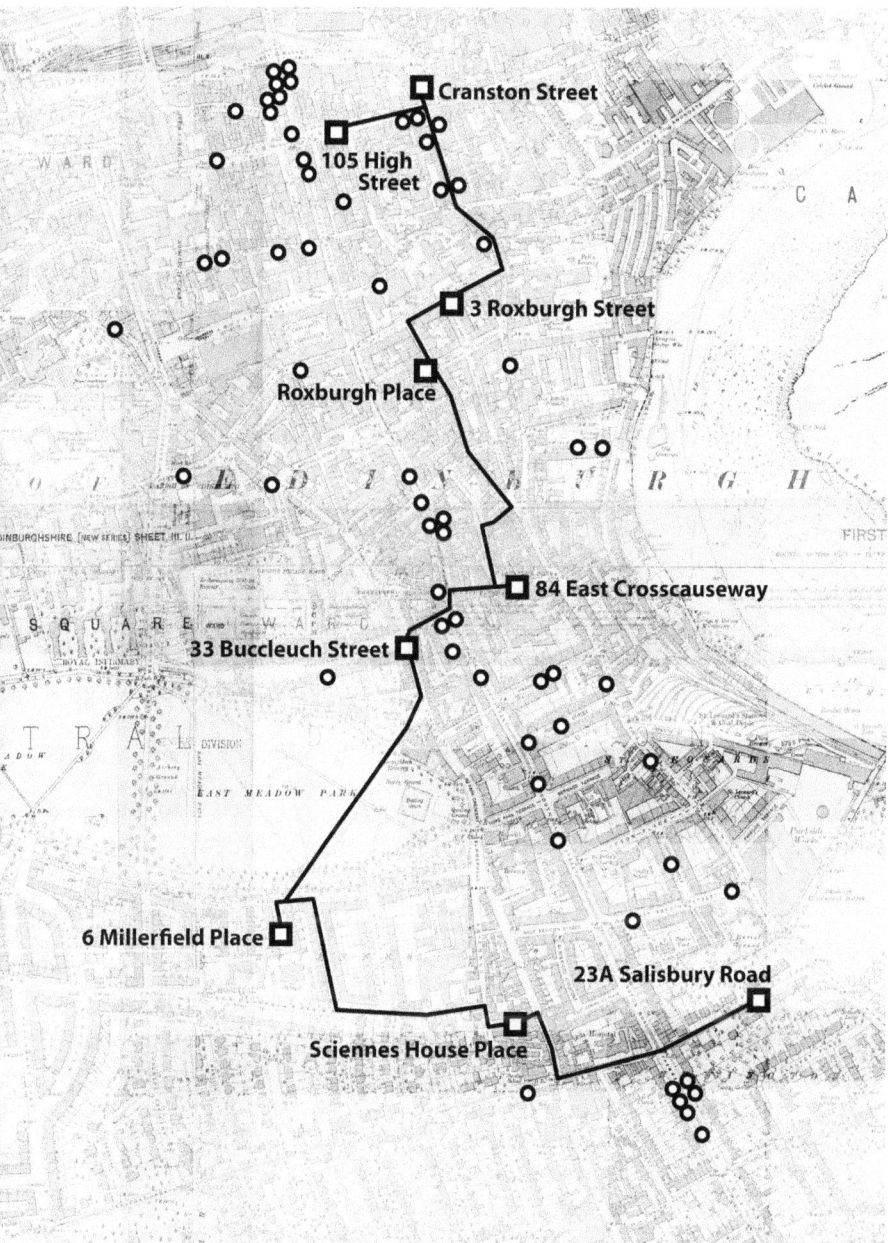

Office Directory. Business addresses were often identical to the residential address of the proprietor, as many lived 'above the shop', and so the map here offers an additional insight into the distribution of Jewish residents. More information can be found here: <https://jewishstudies.div.ed.ac.uk/mapping-jews-in-edinburgh/> (last accessed 25 October 2018). Lastly, the map also outlines the route of the walking tour *Jewish Edinburgh on Foot* developed in 2017.

and Nora's conceptualisations of place; Lefebvre's, Barthes's and Nora's work is further developed through Creet's approach to the experience of migration.

The map (Figure 4.1) shows settlement patterns of Jewish immigrants as they arrived in the city and as they formed communities and moved across the city. It also shows the route taken by the walking tour *Jewish Edinburgh on Foot*, and thus helps to anchor reflections on the contemporary self-perception of Jews in Edinburgh.[11] Indeed, Doreen Massey argues that we invent places by investing them with stories that define and name locations as markers of social relations. By their very nature, social relations are subject to constant change, necessitating continually renewing or reinventing place narratives.[12]

Tracing Jewish Edinburgh with *Two Worlds* involves delving into aspects of urban geography and communal memory comparable to those traced in Tony Kushner's accounts of Southampton and Nils Roemer's study of Worms.[13] Southampton's Jewish history is as 'provincial' as Edinburgh's and, in this respect, Kushner's work has a direct connection to the kind of investigation I am conducting in this chapter. Worms is a city rich with Jewish references and has a resonance far beyond the local, thus making it a Jewish place – geographical, physical, material, literary, and memorial – of inter- or transnational significance, connecting people in various corners of the world. In that respect, Worms may be compared with Edinburgh's secular and Scottish significance as a centre of the Enlightenment and with the place of Edinburgh and Scotland in the history and memory of the migrations that created a Scottish diaspora across the world. Roemer's investigation showcases what is also operative in Southampton, Edinburgh and any number of Jewish congregations whose descendants are now found in all corners of the globe. Those who remember Worms and relate to its intellectual, material and ritual history are connected through their narratives of the city and continue thus to evolve the meaning of landmarks visible in the geographical place of Worms.[14] Similarly, *Jewish Edinburgh on Foot* offers a small case study of the evolving meaning of Edinburgh's Jewish places, spaces and narratives across the globe. Time and again, the walking tours will bring together former and contemporary Jewish residents who share their own memories of Jewish life in the city; they are joined by others who connect to the wider Scottish Jewish community in all corners of the world, bound together by shared habits, traditions, cultural references and memories.

This chapter interprets *Two Worlds* as a *lieu de mémoire*, primarily for Edinburgh's Jewish community but also for others who associate the Daiches family, and specifically David Daiches, with Scotland and Scottish intellectual traditions. I explore the way in which the urban geography of Edinburgh emerges from the book as a landscape rich with Jewish memories, and the city becomes a locus of relationships between immigrant Jewish and resident non-Jewish Scottish communities. By joining up the sights, sounds and smells of early twentieth-century Edinburgh, David Daiches not only recalls his own memories of the city as experienced by a young Jewish boy but he also creates a textual memorial to his father and to the Jewish community of this city. *Two Worlds'* evocation of a vanishing world in which Jew and gentile lived together, albeit in parallel worlds, with crossing points from one to the other and largely devoid of animosity, is also an abiding reference point for positive Jewish/non-Jewish relations and thus very useful for Jewish and non-Jewish residents in narrating a positive Scottish national identity.[15] Furthermore, the chapter places *Two Worlds* in creative tension with the narrative traced across the city by *Jewish Edinburgh on Foot*, a story that traverses the city and may, in time, become another *lieu de mémoire* for residents and visitors. In many ways complementary, the walking tour nevertheless offers possibilities for a less nostalgic and more gritty engagement with the Jewish history of the city. In one further respect, too, the use David Daiches's book is put to, and the various ways in which it might be interrogated, find a helpful counterpoint in the walking tour which allows participants and narrators to invoke social spaces *in situ*, referring backwards and forwards in history, and making connections with other, parallel and interwoven historical concerns.

Two Worlds and Jewish Edinburgh on Foot as *lieux de mémoire*

In the terms of Pierre Nora's work on place and memory, *Two Worlds* can be understood as a *lieu de mémoire*, a 'site of memory, because there are no longer *milieux de mémoire*, real environments of memory,'[16] on account of the dwindling size of the Jewish community in Edinburgh whose links with the late nineteenth- and early twentieth-century waves of immigration are rapidly dissolving. A *lieu de mémoire* is a place that functions as a place holder for memories that can no longer be accessed directly through a lived reality. As a textual *lieu de mémoire*, *Two Worlds* occupies a unique position in the historical landscape of the city owing to the identity of its author.

By contrast, *Jewish Edinburgh on Foot* was researched, written and delivered by comparatively recent immigrants to the city. All four authors are members of Edinburgh's religious Jewish communities and all are active participants in the Edinburgh Jewish Literary Society, the oldest of its kind in Britain and the only one still operating.[17] Only one of the four authors is also a Scot by birth. Similarly, membership of the Lit., as the society is affectionately known, is still composed largely of recent migrants to the Scottish capital, most of whom hail from Britain's south or the wider anglophone and Jewish world. That the desire and commitment to connect to the fast-disappearing traces of early twentieth-century Jewish history in Edinburgh stem from a group whose members are not descended from the migrants who populated the Southside of the city during the time of mass migration and until the middle of the twentieth century gives pause for reflection. As in many Jewish communities in Britain, those rescuing, collecting, archiving and curating local Jewish history are often not 'indigenous' members of the local Jewish community.[18] Three of the authors of *Jewish Edinburgh on Foot* spent the majority of their working lives in the city; all four are academics; and three retired within the last decade. Many landmarks of Jewish life in Edinburgh vanished within the active memory of the tours' authors, and these and other places containing more recent resonances are now being inscribed with additional Jewish references to a century or more earlier. Thus, while the walking tour is a vehicle for historical discovery and for making history present in the texture of the city, the intersection between historical research, personal memory and recovery of place is what makes the guided tours actual 'memory events' that can be understood, with the help of Nora, Lefebvre and Creet, as a different kind of *lieu de mémoire*. And yet, their communal and communicative function as a *lieu de mémoire* is limited for at least two reasons: firstly, actual guided tours took place on only five instances during the summer of 2017, after which they became self-guided tours via the *Curious Edinburgh* app. Secondly, the ability to connect personal memory with specific places and relate the memories to historical data are contained within the present generation of residents connected to the Jewish community who can remember at least as far back as the 1950s. In short, the passing of the last eyewitnesses to the Jewish life of the community, descended from the late nineteenth-century wave of migration, is in sight. Their descendants largely no longer live in Edinburgh, or even in Scotland, being scattered across the globe, forming yet another Scottish diaspora; the largest community of Scottish Jews outwith Scotland today is found in the State of Israel. Hence, for *Jewish Edinburgh on Foot* to become a *lieu de mémoire*, that can be activated by residents, newcomers and tourists across a number of generations, the narratives connected with it need to solidify such that they can be inscribed into the evolving Jewish landscape of the city. And for such narratives to have resonance in the wider Scottish and Jewish historical consciousness, they need to speak to the current memory discourses of Scotland and of the Scottish and Scottish-Jewish diaspora.

The need for 'solidity' or the ability physically to reference aspects of historical memory narratives, so that they become part of a public discourse of the city, is as much an opportunity as it presents a danger. As soon as history is inscribed and acquires a certain shape as a public historical reference point, the plasticity and elasticity of historical interpretation is limited. And public history has the uncanny habit of rendering the meaning of history more static than the historical evidence warrants. All historical data can be narrated in multiple ways; what the historian finds and what she or he misses and what is lost, what he or she chooses to emphasise and what to leave out, to whom she/he tells the story and why and when, all influence the structure, content and meaning of the data. In short, context matters in finding, presenting and receiving historical information. Public history is never far from political opportunity.[19] The stories that communities, cities, regions and nations tell about themselves are subject to many imaginings and purposes and, as such, are never value free. And thus, public history is more likely than not to obscure complexity in favour of simplicity, to obliterate ambiguity in order to render a narrative not only accessible but also open for various identifications audiences may make. Thus, local historical complexities are subordinated to wider public and political agendas so that local stories acquire wider relevance.[20]

Treating *Two Worlds* and *Jewish Edinburgh on Foot* as complementary perspectives on the Jewish historical and remembrance cityscape of Edinburgh, then, is an attempt to bring into the present aspects of the questions guiding the research presented in the previous three chapters. Salis Daiches's memory is a touchstone for narratives about Edinburgh's Jewish history and the rabbi is just moving out of the reach of communicative memory.[21] His legacy in the form of the contemporary Orthodox Jewish community, focused on the synagogue in Salisbury Road, is a tangible marker of Daiches's achievements and of his ideology. Thriving 'provincial' centres of Jewish life have declined since the middle of the twentieth century. The relationship between the Chief Rabbi and the 'provinces' is closer as congregations face an uncertain future and, as it is difficult to recruit rabbis to serve in 'remote' communities, the authority of the Chief Rabbi is not only accepted but actively promoted. Chapter 4 closes the explorations of immigration, ideology and religious leadership opened in Chapter 1 by seeking to locate traces of the early twentieth-century struggles in the city's twenty-first-century landscape, now filled with Jewish memories and different forms of contemporary Jewish life.

In *David Daiches: A Celebration of his Life and Work*, Caroline McCracken-Flesher finds traces of Robert Louis Stevenson's portraits of Edinburgh in Daiches's memoir. McCracken-Flesher opens up a discussion of the perception and function of the city in literature, addressing aspects of a *lieu de mémoire*. Stevenson, she contends, 'may have given Daiches his Edinburgh voice', that is, David Daiches gained the strategy to reflect Edinburgh as the city of his father Salis's life and work from Robert Louis Stevenson: Daiches mirrored Stevenson's technique of offering various perceptions of the city so that he was able to show 'the multiple perspectives allowed by his [D. Daiches] literary, his religious and his topographical locations'.[22] Rather than remaining distanced from his new environment as an incomer – he was born in 1912 in Sunderland – and as a son of an immigrant to the United Kingdom, David Daiches uses his own 'otherness' to explore the diversity inherent in Edinburgh itself. In this he is akin to Stevenson who was wrestling new interpretations from the city whose meaning had previously been determined by his ancestors. Here 'two worlds' becomes Daiches's interpretive device to situate himself in his new environment and to forge his own relationship with Edinburgh and wider Scotland, independent of, and yet related to his father and to Scottish literature, thought, geography and culture. Edinburgh thus becomes David Daiches's own city, so much so that his long-term friend and colleague Michael Lister comments:

> But for me, the spirit of Daiches is very much alive, particularly in his numerous writings about this city. And here on the Southside, so rich in its association with his family, as Yeats once wrote about Swift and Dublin, I feel that, here in Edinburgh David Daiches is 'always just around the next corner'.[23]

In order that David Daiches may be anticipated 'around the next corner', his significance to the city has to be established in each generation. The reader needs to be motivated to pick up his memoir. Whether he is perceived to be prominent as a member of the Jewish community or as a leading light in the city's intellectual landscape, David Daiches needs to be situated or located again, and again and again. But, even without the seminal text in one's hand, David Daiches is invoked within the Jewish community where his memoir remains a reference point. And his daughter's presence in the city as a resident writer keeps the Daiches family connection alive beyond the confines of text and memory as does the Daiches archive in the NLS which is a reservoir for further investigation into Salis Daiches's life and work and his significance to the history of the Scottish capital. While these may be Jewish and literary *lieux de mémoire*, however, as well as those of historians of Edinburgh, they are not tangible or even accessible outwith specific interest groups. Even the guided tours of *Jewish Edinburgh on Foot* in the summer of 2017 attracted primarily those who had a prior connection to the Jewish community of Edinburgh, of Scotland or of their own home towns but did not (yet) pick up passing tourists. Be that as it may, the Jewish walkabout of the following paragraphs offers the opportunity to connect this monograph's research with concrete spaces and places in the Scottish capital.

Movements, locations, language(s)

Two Worlds, as a *lieu de mémoire* for Edinburgh's Jewish community, offers a perspective on the city and the Jewish community in early twentieth-century Edinburgh and anchors the memories of David Daiches with Scottish local and national narratives. As a city, Edinburgh is rendered as a place rich with relationships between the various Jewish groups and between Jews and non-Jews as David's life intersects with the wider social circles of his classmates at George Watson's College and the University of Edinburgh. Edinburgh as a place becomes tangible in the narrative which, in itself, becomes a memorial to his father, the Jewish community and the city.

Similarly, *Jewish Edinburgh on Foot* creates a trail that, in total, can be understood as a *lieu de mémoire* by tracing places of significance to Jewish history in Edinburgh and by attaching narratives to these places. Indeed, against Nora, the entire route of the walk can be understood as one *lieu de mémoire* carving out a Jewish perspective on the city. Rather than assume that the topography of the city anchors our historical narrative, the tour produces both history and memory for its authors and participants through its tracing of historical events and data which had never before entered the public realm. If we were to represent the trail of the walk on a map and allowed participants, authors and the historical actors referred to in the tour to populate that map with their perception of places of significance, readers of the map would be able to configure their understanding of the city from these multiple perspectives.[24] The trail woven by *Jewish Edinburgh on Foot* is driven by a multiplicity of factors, ranging from archaeological surveys, analysis of census data, historical photographs, building plans, maps, archival records, memoirs and memories offered through oral history interviews. During the summer of 2017, the walking-tour narrative was rendered as flamboyant and discursive as those delivering it were able and willing to make it, and thus it is pliable to suit the different temperaments of the four authors cum tour guides. The narrative offered during these walking tours was at once more malleable and less integrated than that of *Two Worlds* and other, more standardised, tours. Configured as an app. which walkers can use to guide them to the locations and to read the vignette for each stop, the tour loses the immediacy of the oral narrative but gains the opportunity for more varied inscriptions of meaning by vastly different audiences.

Three distinct aspects shared by *Two Worlds* and *Jewish Edinburgh on Foot* will be explored as ways to characterise 'Jewish spaces and places' in Edinburgh: movements, locations and languages. All three are tied together by reflections on Jewishness and its interaction with various other possible modes of being and interpretations of 'Jewishness' itself.

Movements

'Yon's the rabby'; 'the walking rabbi was an Edinburgh institution. Everybody knew who he was. Strangers would tip their hats to him. Policemen saluted him' writes David Daiches in 'Promised Lands: A Portrait of My Father' published in 1997 as a supplement to *Two Worlds*.[25] Rabbi Dr Salis Daiches is a prominent figure already in *Two Worlds*, shaping large parts of the narrative of his son David's memoir. In many ways, this memoir, published just a decade after Salis Daiches's death in May 1945 and by an arguably young author not yet of an age to be writing memoirs, is also a way of coming to terms with his relationship to his father. David repeats and expands his reflections in the twilight of his own life when he had returned to live in the city of his childhood. Hence, not only David's own life but particularly that of his father and the community he led occupy centre stage of the two parts now constituting *Two Worlds*.

The movements of David Daiches's own family across the city reflect the move into the suburbs for many in the community: the family lived for the first few weeks as guests of a congregant in Lonsdale Terrace on the north side of the Meadows and then on their southern edge in 6 Millerfield Place while worshipping mainly at Graham Street Synagogue at the Meadows' northern boundary. The opening of the Synagogue in Salisbury Road in 1932 is accompanied by a move further south to a house on Crawfurd Road. Thus, from the beginning, the rabbi's family lived close to the community on the one hand. On the other hand, from the very beginning, the Daiches family was already one step removed and higher up the social ladder, first in gentrified Marchmont, rather than just outwith the old city, and then in Crawfurd Road which is firmly in the 'suburbs'. The rabbi thus represented the aspirations of the community. Edinburgh is a city of short distances; the heart of the city can be circumnavigated on foot in less than one hour. Until Daiches moved deep into the Southside – to Crawfurd Road – he was never more than 15 minutes away from the area of settlement of recent immigrants around North and South Bridge and the northern part of Newington. Graham Street Synagogue, home to the anglicised part of the community, was less than 15 minutes on foot from the immigrants' *shul* in Park Place. Salisbury Road Synagogue was a further 10 to 15 minutes walk to the south. This represented already a significant 'move to the suburbs', and was intended to reflect the understanding that the Jewish community had 'arrived' and was now established in an area no longer dominated by recent immigrants.

Walking is the primary activity of *Jewish Edinburgh on Foot*, leading participants from the Royal Mile in the centre of town to the synagogue of the Edinburgh Hebrew Congregation in the south of Newington. And, in terms of the tour's narrative, movement is a key structuring factor, charting the movement of Jewish immigrants across the city from the late eighteenth century onwards. The tour does not move chronologically – it starts in the middle of the nineteenth century, moves back to the eighteenth century and then jumps forward into the early twentieth century, only to move back to 1817/1820 twice over before ending simultaneously in 1932 when the synagogue in Salisbury Road was built, and, in the present, as this is where the Edinburgh Hebrew Congregation still worships and where the Lit. holds most of its events. Hence, the tour asks a certain degree of chronological agility on the part of its participants alongside a willingness to roam across a range of themes, including migration, health, religion, culture, and occupation and trade.

Movement across the city for a number of purposes is a significant trait in *Two Worlds*: 'We walked, skipped and ran unnoticed distances.'[26] Walking, running, traversing parts of the city on foot are recounted frequently in *Two Worlds*. Waverley Station marks the arrival point for the Daiches family in February 1919: Rabbi Dr Salis Daiches, his wife Flora and their three children Lionel, David, Sylvia, aged nine, seven and six. And Waverley is the location for many departures from, and returns to, the city by Salis as well as David. Since his migration from Russia via Germany, Salis Daiches's life was punctuated by frequent travels across the United Kingdom to lecture and consult. *Two Worlds*, however, mentions only two significant long-distance journeys since Salis's arrival in the United Kingdom: first we have the journey from his father's house in Leeds to Edinburgh, a largely fictional rendition as Salis was moving from Sunderland to Edinburgh having already served in British congregations for a decade and a half. In the book, this (imagined) journey is a narrative device establishing the contrast between Eastern European Orthodoxy transplanted to the United Kingdom and the new synthesis between modern Orthodoxy and enlightened secular culture in Edinburgh. The second journey is Salis's travel to Palestine in 1925 to the opening of the Hebrew University in Jerusalem, testifying to the rabbi's Zionism while also marking his commitment to his own life in the diaspora.[27] These two trips to and away from the city thus serve as markers for ideological journeys, covering physical miles but also signifying changing intellectual ground. Leeds, functioning here as the United Kingdom's version of 'old world' Orthodoxy, and Jerusalem, projected as the centre of the Jewish national future, serve as contrasts to what Rabbi Daiches envisaged as Edinburgh's enlightened Orthodox life. As we noted in the previous chapter, the rabbi's intellectual vision was not reflected strongly by his community. Salis Daiches, however, appeared to have the ability to relate just as well to the *Yiddish*-speaking inhabitants of the Southside as he did to the president of the Edinburgh Hebrew Congregation and other anglicised families, perhaps not embracing the former but definitely tolerating their Old-World ways as a necessary stepping stone into his vision of a confident Jewish future in Scotland.

And yet, Edinburgh's locations are not without a sense of tension, at least for Salis's son David: 'Normally I had no difficulty at all in living in two worlds at once; both seemed to be satisfactorily related to the physical environment of Edinburgh.'[28] *Two Worlds* charts movement within and between worlds, not necessarily their overlap, even though Daiches maintains that 'the two worlds, in my childhood, were not really separate'.[29] Home and the city, Jewish Orthodoxy and the non-Jewish environment, form a strong dialectical theme in the text.

> In the long summer evenings, when the sabbath seemed to be stretching on for ever, we would go for sedate walks through the more genteel streets to the south, carrying a sort of invisible wall with us as we moved through a working and playing world. It never occurred to me to resent this restriction on my freedom to feel ill-used because I could not join the wild street play of the children who were often my casual playmates on other days of the week. But I preferred to avoid passing them, and to walk in the quieter ways where they were not likely to be.[30]

While home and city, Jewishness and secularity intersect, they simultaneously remain separate, though each reflecting the other. This mutual reflection of each world in the other is also underscored by the choice of vocabulary: *sabbath* from the city's perspective, while at home and in the community *shabbos* is the familiar term, feast or fast vs *yom tov*, and so on. In terms of Jewish life, the city is portrayed as an unchanging, open backdrop for the family's religious pursuits at home and in the Jewish community which have an impact on David's life when he needs to miss school or cannot attend events because of religious observance.

Jewish Edinburgh on Foot subtly reflects the general movement of Jewish immigrants into Scottish life while throughout also preserving a sense of Jewish separation from any Scottish mainstream. Indeed, what makes the walking tour work is a new way of accessing the city from a distinct and separate perspective. The perceived distinctive Jewishness functions as an attraction that offers a new view on a well-known city, or, as in the case of long-term Jewish residents of Edinburgh, the tour validates, refreshes and adds to their understanding of the Jewish spaces of the city. For tourists, the walking tour offers a perspective complementary to those of other sightseeing opportunities in Edinburgh and further afield in relation to Jewish-themed walking tours of London's East End or New York's Lower East Side. Indeed, the *Yiddish*-speaking immigrants attracted more attention from participants in the 2017 walking tours than the anglicised Jewish 'establishment'. The following portrait of Edinburgh's Jews, recollected from his childhood by Lionel Daiches, elder son of Salis Daiches, is evoked at 33 Buccleuch Street, the seventh stop of the tour deep in the Southside:

> They were devout observers and regular supporters of the synagogue; they worshipped at the Graham Street Synagogue and the Central Synagogue in Richmond Street. They bore themselves with dignity and were respected by their neighbours. Most of them were foreign born immigrants from Lithuania and other parts of the Russian empire; they arrived in Edinburgh and starting with little or nothing succeeded in establishing a modestly successful living, educated their children and managed to integrate themselves in the life of the general community. A few became rich. But not very many.
>
> They lived mostly in the South Side of Edinburgh in the area around about Nicolson Street, Summerhall Square and Hope Park Terrace. Quite a number of families lived in Buccleuch Street and some of the most active among them, related to each other, lived in number 33, a tenement which was affectionately referred to by its residents as *Drei und Dreissig*. Few realised at the time that the Scots-Yiddish speaking parents in *Drei und Dreissig* would produce doctors, scientists and men of learning whose names have now become famous in the English-speaking world.[31]

The iconic references to Jewish immigrant cultures in other places, notably New York City, but also London's East End, are thus tagged in the walking tour as a familiar trope.

While chosen 'Scottishness' was writ large across Salis Daiches's self-understanding,[32] David is more cautious in straightforwardly claiming this inheritance: 'In my secret heart I wanted to wear a kilt, but I knew that I had no hereditary right to one [...]'.[33] Indeed, differences in appearance made David uncomfortable: 'walking through a group of boisterously playing classmates when I was dressed up in my festival clothes I found uncomfortable'.[34] He thus recalls his discomfort when walking home from Graham Street Synagogue which was in close proximity to the then location of George Watson's College. Thus separated from his classmates, David also diagnoses a separation between himself as the rabbi's son and other Jewish children in the community which set him apart from easy companionship: 'I felt at least as strong a barrier dividing me from the Jewish boys of Edinburgh as from my Christian schoolfellows and playmates.'[35] David Daiches may have traversed the same city and engaged with the same culture as his Jewish and non-Jewish peers but the web of connections and meanings he derived from these co-ordinates of his life placed him in parallel, though not mutually exclusive, worlds: 'the city had no barriers against me; the sights and sounds and smells of Edinburgh crowded in upon my senses day after day and year after year'.[36] Not only with regard to David Daiches's relationship with his family and his peers is movement between locations and ideas significant, travel also becomes a metaphor for the transformations necessitated by daily life in two worlds.

Indeed, travel metaphors abound. Thus, Daiches describes his father's migration, from the Lithuanian part of Russia to Germany and further on via England to the Scottish capital, as a journey from the confinements of exile to the freedoms of home:

[...] he was aware of the long journey he had made. He saw himself as a small boy in Vilna, where he had been born almost thirty-nine years before, [...] Studying Talmud with his father from the age of five [...] then a schoolboy across the border [...] at the Königsberg *Gymnasium* in East Prussia, then as a young man studying rabbinics at the Hildesheimer rabbinical seminar in Berlin and simultaneously studying philosophy at the university – what a complex cultural journey he had made [...] Hume was the bridge. It was Hume who brought him [...] to relinquish his Polish–Lithuanian–German background to become a British citizen [...] that marked his final break with the Yiddish speaking *golus* and a re-birth into a promising world of cultural pluralism with which his Jewish traditions could be comfortably domiciled.[37]

While Salis Daiches travelled, adapted and changed to forge a synthesis between the two worlds – the Jewish and the secular – and modelled his life to reflect the happy coincidence of his Jewish with his secular pursuits, the same was not possible for his son. In David's life, the secular world occupied a contrasting point to that of his home life and ultimately proved to be determining for his professional and personal life; indeed, as a student, the relationship between the two worlds of his life became more strained, such that he perceived them divided by an 'abyss'.[38] Salis's life marked the journey from the world of Jewish Orthodoxy into the secular world, uniting the two by giving Orthodoxy precedence in forging the foundations of the secular life of the mind.[39] David's intellectual foundations were shaped by his secular education which he could not synthesise with Orthodox principles. In the son's life Ortho*doxy* gave way to ortho*praxy*, and secular principles paved the way for an almost complete transitioning into the secular part of the two worlds of his childhood.[40] Salis Daiches lived in two worlds which he sought to synthesise. David Daiches found he needed to choose one world without synthesising it with the other; of the two worlds of his childhood he left one behind though it continued to resonate. Salis Daiches was part of the last generation for whom both worlds were equally accessible, particularly as he appears to have migrated to follow opportunity after opportunity rather than fleeing economic hardship or persecution. By contrast, his father remained intellectually in the 'Old World' while physically residing in Leeds, having left his native land later in his life and perhaps in flight. For his son David, the Old World is not accessible any more and thus cannot be successfully synthesised into the new. The social and intellectual environments outside his home demand a different sort of engagement. Just as his father Salis's Orthodox religious passion embraced and integrated the study of philosophy, David's passion for the study of literature embraces and integrates his Jewish life and learning; for father and son the dominant cultural environment of their youth forms the basis for the cultural choices in their adult life.[41] As such, David Daiches's journey appeals to many descendants of first-generation immigrants and may thus be attractive as an eloquent blueprint, a transferable *lieu de mémoire*, for reflecting on their own lives. These journeys and movements are enabled by specific locations.

Locations

Three types of places triangulate the lives of father and son in the city:

1. home (Lonsdale Terrace, Millerfield Place, Crawfurd Road).
2. places of work: the synagogue(s) (Graham Street/Park Place, Salisbury Road)/school (George Watson's College) and the University of Edinburgh.
3. other places: holidays (the Fife coast, mostly Crail, and the Highlands).

Home and synagogue mark the Jewish aspects of Daiches's Edinburgh geography, alongside the locations of Jewish settlements in the city centre and on Edinburgh's Southside, and the trains which took travelling salesmen to various Scottish towns and villages. School and university mark out the secular locations in the city, as do the holiday destinations in Fife.

These worlds are connected by walking, taxis and trains, various idioms and cognitive dissonances. By their very nature, these places are all locations of Jewish/non-Jewish interaction, and David Daiches offers a narrative that connects them all without any apparent conflict but also without significant overlap. There is a 'Jewish city' within the city, distinguished by the ease with which the Jewish inhabitants can cross back and forth between the different spheres of their lives lived in one or the other. Daiches's grandfather had already enjoyed regular *sabbath* afternoon walks with a Catholic priest in Russia,[42] his father Salis enjoyed the professional contact with Edinburgh University's professor of Hebrew, and local Christian ministers, and shared conversations with Church of Scotland clergy on holidays in Fife.[43] While there is a sense of disconnect in these encounters, David Daiches's writing is permeated by the aims of the ethnographer, to record, to show and to preserve but to withhold any value judgement. He observes and explores but, to a certain degree, stays aloof, allowing himself both the immersion in his childhood experiences and his adult detached but emotionally close spectatorship, thereby opening up his narrative for others to connect their own experiences.

Jewish Edinburgh on Foot plots its storyline along a series of stops at once relevant to Jewish history and congenial to assembling a group. Thus, the tour moves from gravesides to residences, shops, and places of worship, education and leisure, rendering local history through anecdotes and memories. While the narrative of *Two Worlds* is framed as a memoir, the walking tour is at once a community event, a tourist attraction, a history lesson and a research project, framed by pragmatic decisions about where to walk, at what pace and the likely attention spans of participants. Stopping on the High Street/Royal Mile is a challenging opener owing to the amount of traffic, both pedestrian and motorised. Calton Hill, the first Jewish burial ground, acquired as a private mausoleum by Heyman Lion in 1795, is accessible to the walkers only by imagination, as the tour pauses on Cranston Street just off the Royal Mile and opposite the observatory that sits on top of the burial chamber. The following locations on the Southside are quieter streets whose layout has changed since the early twentieth century, such that tour participants may stand in the correct geolocations but experience vastly different architecture. This is particularly true when observing the place of the first synagogue in a tenement house in Richmond Place which cannot be accurately located even on historical maps. The tour, which proceeds in linear fashion but not chronologically, then hits easier territory as it is possible to visit the actual locations of the last Jewish bakery and butcher's shop in Newington district which closed in 2005 and 1986 respectively.[44] Three of the tour's authors have their own memories of picking up *challah* every week at Kleinberg's and eating salt-beef sandwiches for lunch at Lurie's which was conveniently located adjacent to university buildings on Buccleuch Street (and which is now a coffee shop). 33 Buccleuch Street, opposite Lurie's, requires more imagination as the historical facade has been replaced with a modern one. From there on, the locations are simpler to find and their history can be mapped more easily on to the experience of the contemporary tourist/walker.

Jewish Edinburgh on Foot and David Daiches's tracing of life in the city can alert the reader also to absences and silences, particularly when reflecting on locations. Edinburgh's public Jewish memory is decidedly male and not matched by an exploration of locations significant for Jewish women in the city. While *Two Worlds* is dedicated to his mother, Flora Daiches née Levin from Liverpool, women do not occupy centre stage; they stay at home. Yet 'home' does not then become a location in which Daiches actively situates his mother. She is often absent through illness, manages and serves the household, and thus is seen to set the rhythm but perhaps not the content of his life even though she undoubtedly has shaped significant aspects of her children's lives, not least their musical education. And yet, in contrast to David's father, the rabbi, his mother occupies hardly any space in the memoir. Women, it seems, either remain invisible and unseen enablers, or serve as markers of transition and separation.[45] The latter category is most prominently represented by David Daiches's wife, Isobel, who was not born Jewish and therefore marks the definite transition of David out of his father's house into the secular world. Isobel's conversion to Judaism while in the United States and the subsequent reconciliation with his father constitute another boundary crossing, this time hovering uneasily between two worlds.[46] In short, in *Two Worlds*, women signify important points in David's life but they only implicitly shape its trajectory. At least in the memoir of his childhood, Salis Daiches, the rabbi and public figurehead of Scottish Jewry, is seen to exert the stronger influence on his son. This may, of course, also have something to do with the memoir's function of coming to terms with his father's death while his mother lived to see her children's careers develop and families thrive. What Scotland's capital city looked like for women in the early twentieth century remains unexplored in most historical engagements with Jewish Edinburgh. David Daiches's Edinburgh Jewish places, in public as well as in private, appear dominated by men.[47] By the same token, at least in its first rendition, *Jewish Edinburgh on Foot* has the lives of men leading the narrative, having no stop which focuses on a woman. Again, women remain in the background and are explicitly cast in supporting roles such as companions and helpers or interlocutors.[48]

Men are also David Daiches's main interlocutors when he explores the significance of language in *Two Worlds*. His passion for language developed early, growing up in a multilingual environment, and he carefully listens to immigrants and residents alike to understand their characters and their lives. By contrast, as we shall see, *Jewish Edinburgh on Foot* focuses on today's *Yiddish* scene of the city while referencing public spaces dominated by male *Yiddish* speakers.

Language(s)

David Daiches reflects, unsurprisingly for someone in love with the richness of the English language and a competent speaker of a few more, a lot on the linguistic distinctions and fusions between Jewish and Scottish Edinburgh. He recalls

> the traditional chanting of Hebrew prayers brings back the Meadows and Lauriston Place and the Vennel and the old synagogue in Graham Street [. . .] with its mixed congregation of Yiddish-speaking immigrants and native-born Edinburgh Jews with their strong Edinburgh accents even in the singing of Hebrew hymns.[49]

Here we encounter the diversity of the Jewish population of Edinburgh in the early twentieth century. Daiches the ethnographer offers an anecdote-rich insight into the lives of the '*trebblers*', the travelling salesmen who populated one dedicated train carriage from Waverley to Dundee on Monday and back again on Friday in time for the *sabbath*. The blending of *Yiddish* with the local Scots dialect formed an idiom unique to this generation of immigrants and died with them, largely without having been recorded. Daiches dedicates an entire chapter of his memoir to these first-generation immigrant salesmen, one of the few surviving descriptions of these men and their language.[50] Writing in the mid-1950s, Daiches suggests that '1912–1940 was the period of its [Scots–Yiddish] flourishing [. . .] and while there is an occasional old man in Edinburgh who speaks it today, one has to seek it out in order to find it, and in another decade it will be gone forever.'[51]

The *trebblers* are a significant link in the history of Edinburgh Jews. Their vernacular, *Yiddish*, was not superseded by English but adapted to include enough (Scots) English to make a living by peddling goods in the Highlands. While others began to speak English to conduct their business, but continued to speak *mameloshn* at home, their children's command of *Yiddish* declined with their proficiency in English. There were no Jewish mainstream schools in Scotland until Calderwood Lodge Primary School opened long after World War II. Hence, all Jewish children attended mainstream schools and were educated solely in English, with Hebrew and religious education taking place at synagogues and other community institutions. As we have seen, Salis Daiches organised Hebrew and religion classes in Sciennes Primary School but there was no opportunity for children to be formally educated in *Yiddish*. Within one generation, *Yiddish* almost vanished from the everyday lives of Scottish Jews.

Like many immigrants, Salis Daiches's mother tongue was *Yiddish*. Already in his youth, however, this was soon superseded by Hebrew as 'the language of Jewish culture'[52] and followed by German as the language of secular scholarship and culture. By his mid-twenties English had become his dominant vernacular. In contrast to other migrants, in Salis's life *Yiddish* was quickly devalued and then largely abandoned in his quest for a synthesis of Jewish orthodoxy with secular culture although he continued to use it in conversation and preaching when necessary. This synthesis rested on moving out of the 'ghetto' – intimately associated with *Yiddish* as a Jewish vernacular and lingua franca – and which he associated with backwardness and the sufferings of the *golus*, of Exile. Salis Daiches sought to leave the 'ghetto' and its baggage behind with his move to the West. In Edinburgh, however, as much as in his previous appointments in Hull and Sunderland, his background in Lithuanian *Yiddish* culture served him well in his endeavour to unite a community split between recent immigrants and Scottish-born Jews. In *Two Worlds*, David Daiches is empathetic towards his father's ideology as much as he is towards the *trebblers* on the trains to the Highlands, fully conscious that both worlds will soon be irretrievably lost. Ultimately, his father's journey from Russia to Scotland was also a linguistic journey which discarded *Yiddish*, preserved Hebrew and added German and English as languages of modern secular cultures. Salis Daiches was able to hold these languages and their corresponding cultures together in a synthesis founded on traditional Jewish values and bridged by the intellectual adventure of the Enlightenment. As David Daiches demonstrates throughout his memoir, this kind of synthesising was no longer possible for the following generations.

Today, *Yiddish* is alive in the city of Edinburgh. Jews and non-Jews populate a community-run *Yiddish* class. Klezmer music is at home in Scotland, with a number of highly regarded musicians associated with Edinburgh. The current desire to (re-)connect with the *Yiddish* language and aspects of *Yiddish*-speaking culture in music, theatre, literature and poetry in Edinburgh mirrors the revival of *Yiddish* and associated cultural production across the Western world and in Central and Eastern Europe. It is stretching Nora's concept beyond what he might be willing to recognise but I would argue that this revival of language and culture and the new cultural productions borne of this are *lieux de mémoire*. These places of memory, in the landscape and on paper, in the minds and on the stage, transmit historical practices into the present and inscribe them with new meanings for those who engage with them. Around such practices new communities arise which connect the *Yiddish*-speaking Jewish history and culture brought to Scotland by migrants with the current immigrant and Scottish-born inhabitants of Edinburgh, thus transforming both. Indeed, rather than pointing to Edinburgh as another 'virtually Jewish' space,[53] we may observe the continued reinscription and changing meanings of Jewishness in the urban landscape of the Scottish capital by its Jewish and non-Jewish inhabitants and visitors.

Conclusion

Millerfield Place remains a quiet suburban street. The Daiches family home is still occupied by a family; and the sound of children playing continues to reverberate on the street and echo up from the Meadows. With the move of the Sick Kids to the large hospital complex of the Royal Infirmary on the southern edge of the city, Millerfield Place, once again, will become a solely residential street. Gone, however, is the Jewish community which once populated this area. The Sciennes district of Edinburgh is located between Marchmont, until the 1950s heavily populated by Jews, and the Grange, an area many Jews aspired to live in but few could afford to. Today, most who are associated with either or both of the Jewish religious congregations of the city live further afield and are spread out across and beyond the city. Nonetheless, it is the Southside, with its districts of Newington, Marchmont, Sciennes, and the Grange, which remain, in local memory, associated with Jewish life.

The sequel to *Two Worlds, Was: A Pastime from Times Past* (first published in 1975), has David Daiches embrace the multiple strands of his heritage exclaiming:

> I claim you, I adopt you all equally as ancestors, Scot and Lot, Celt and Semite, mystic, wonderful. I came to pass, here I am, *hineni*. From a multiple past I came to pass, creating a new past as I pass.[54]

This fusion of 'othernesses', of distinctive heritages which are difficult to hold in balance, I would argue opens Daiches's memoir *Two Worlds* to others who migrated to the city and experience Edinburgh refracted through multiple cultures. The expression of dissonance and its welding into new meanings for immigrant cultures in the city may account for the significance attaching to *Two Worlds*; this is what makes it into a *lieu de mémoire*. Precisely because the Edinburgh of *Two Worlds* is no more, it is possible to use this text to inscribe the narratives of other immigrants and newcomers to the city in the topography of the memoir. For the Jewish community, however, *Two Worlds* also expresses a sense of mourning and loss, a city no longer holding together the old with the new, no longer being a place in which Scottish and Jewish cultures fuse into a new Scottish–Jewish idiom.[55] Perhaps the street on the eastern edge of Edinburgh named after Salis Daiches, 'Daiches Braes', is a fitting memorial to this vanished world in which the newcomer is ultimately fused with the city such that his divergent, separate but connected, history is no longer apparent to the contemporary resident.

Those who engage in memory work which addresses both the Jewish community and the wider public, ironically, are not the descendants of the early twentieth-century immigrants. Rather, they are more recent Jewish migrants from other parts of the United Kingdom, Europe and the Americas who settled in Edinburgh for personal and professional reasons. Thus, the small group who authored the walking tour *Jewish Edinburgh on Foot* is composed of retired academics in the social sciences and myself. Similarly, the move to commemorate Rudolph Bing, refugee from Nazi Germany and founder of the International Festival, is carried forward by a very recent arrival in the city.[56] All are active in the Edinburgh Jewish Literary Society, which is seen by many associated with the religious communities or far from religious engagement, as a 'neutral' Jewish meeting ground. Curiously, this meeting ground and arising activities are largely not led by those born as Scottish (or even Edinburgh) Jews but by much more recent Jewish immigrants to the city. This raises questions about the location of memory, about the possibility of (re-)creating a *milieu de mémoire* but also about identifying *lieux de mémoire*. Such questions concern the addressees of these initiatives to remember and inscribe a Jewish narrative into the cityscape and the representativeness of the narratives offered. Indeed, it could be argued that these initiatives are, on the one hand, inscribing memories while, on the other hand, they are constructing specific historical narratives identified by academics and shaped by their disciplinary backgrounds. As such, the contexts in which such narratives are created shape their audiences as much as the discourses to which they are addressed have an impact on the stories told. Thus, the public sphere, governed by the need to show the public impact of research, and the agendas of local communities, heritage groups and touristic enterprises not only inform but also produce aspects of *Jewish Edinburgh on Foot*.

Such questions point to the wider themes underlying this monograph which position a small 'provincial' Jewish community within the currents of migration history and transnational narratives. The contribution of these chapters to the historiography of an Edinburgh and Scottish religious and ethnic minority, to British Jewish history and historiography, and to works on migration and transnationalism is focused in the considerations about to whom this history is told, for what purpose and by whom. I shall attempt to draw out the broader implications of the issues explored in this monograph in the Epilogue.

Epilogue

Founded in 2015, the Edinburgh Jewish Dialogue is a cross-community organisation that seeks to discern and enable future Jewish religious and cultural life in the city. Edinburgh Jewish Dialogue, on the one hand, was born out of the realisation that the membership of the Edinburgh Hebrew Congregation is aging rapidly without being replenished with younger members and, as a result, the community is growing smaller and smaller, such that the upkeep of the synagogue building and the employment of staff are threatened. On the other hand, the Dialogue's founders observed that Sukkat Shalom – Edinburgh Liberal Jewish Congregation – is growing but finds itself in no position to purchase its own building or employ full-time local staff. In addition, about 50 per cent of the Jews resident in Edinburgh and the surrounding region are not affiliated with a synagogue community. Edinburgh Jewish Dialogue wishes to embrace all those self-identifying as Jewish so that they may contribute to the future of Jewish life in the city. The momentum propelling the activities of the Dialogue demonstrates that there is a groundswell of enthusiasm for this project which is now being taken forward as a Scottish version of JW3 London Jewish Cultural Centre. While the fragmented nature of the Jewish communities and residents of Edinburgh today is not directly comparable to the conflicts plaguing the community in the early twentieth century, there are some instructive parallels that my research is able to draw out. Migration plays a huge part in the developments then and now. In the late nineteenth and the early twentieth centuries Jews moved to Scotland mainly from Russia. Today we see their descendants, that is, Scottish Jews, move away from Scotland and Jews from across the world, not least from Israel, move to Scotland. The impact this has on the communities can be best understood within a transnational framework. Salis Daiches was engaged to come to Edinburgh to unite the communities and to present Jewish religion and culture to the non-Jewish public. Edinburgh Jewish Dialogue, founded from within the communities, is engaged in a similar exercise: seeking shared ground between different Jewish religious and non-religious orientations and expectations and presenting Jews and Judaism in a confident, outward-facing way as a positive factor in a multicultural Scotland. Judaism, in the terms of the Dialogue, not only can, but should, claim a prominent public space in the city.

The Epilogue seeks to draw the book's themes together and reflect on opportunities for future research. This book took the cue from Rabbi Dr Salis Daiches who dedicated his life to small Jewish communities in Britain.

His commitment to an authentic religious Jewish life made him care about the structures which support it. For him *halakhic* work was a source and foundation of religious life, not a constraint. *Halakhah*, for Daiches, is an authority that enables and clarifies and that has the potential for unifying a religious community. Indeed, a united community in itself, as we have noted in this book, is a source of authority and a strength that support and enable the life of its members. To reach these insights, it was necessary to pursue a transnational analysis of the surviving records of Daiches's life and work. The analysis has, I hope, demonstrated that these and similar documents are worth our scholarly attention because they allow us to evaluate the religious life of Jewish leaders and their communities from the inside, enabling us to view these men from a perspective that does not limit the interpretation of religious politics to a function of formal clashes over hard power interests. Rather, placing the rabbis and their work in the context of a transnational inquiry in local settings shows the possibility of recreating patterns of authority and of authority structures which were anchored in the biographies of these men.

Chapter 1 demonstrated that the educational, cultural and experiential background of immigrant and resident Jewish religious functionaries strongly influenced their views of what constituted a religious (*halakhic*) authority and, hence, how communities should be organised. The analysis expanded the current range of interpretations of the 'clash' between resident and migrant Jews in early twentieth-century Britain by focusing on the biography of an individual rabbi and interpreting his life journey in a transnational framework. The transnational framework established the cultural and religious contexts the rabbi was exposed to and in which he was educated. As a result, it was possible to locate specific, divergent approaches to community organisation, religious leadership and *halakhic* authority between immigrants themselves and between immigrant and resident Jews. Having done so for this one example, we propose that further research on Salis Daiches's contemporaries is warranted. The transnational approach piloted here suggests that a broader investigation of migrant rabbis active in Orthodox Jewish communities in early twentieth-century Britain would yield a more complex picture of the mental maps of immigrants that contributed to the heated discussions on religious leadership at the time. Such an approach would also allow for a more nuanced understanding of the impact of migration on Jewish communities in Britain than the currently dominant paradigm of a 'culture clash' allows, including a more detailed assessment of the relationships between immigrant and resident Jews. This, in turn, could give rise to a revision of our understanding of acculturation and assimilation in the first half of the twentieth century, and a better grasp of various models of 'anglicisation'.[1]

Chapter 2 focused on the Conferences of Anglo-Jewish Ministers and the discussions about the reorganisation of British Jewish 'provincial' communities. The analysis showed how the leadership, authority and educational background acquired in the formative years of a rabbi's or minister's education influenced the discussions on the devolution of rabbinic authority in early twentieth-century Britain. Attacks on the institution of the Chief Rabbi, his authority, and the centralisation of power in the hands of one rabbi and his Beth Din were related to the realities facing Jewish communities across the country. A focus here was the differences in educational background of immigrant rabbis and resident ministers in which the *halakhic* competence of the former met with a lack of *halakhic* education of the latter, a situation that gave rise to conflicts over knowledge and authority. By paying greater attention to the nuances of the debate, the interventions of the Chief Rabbi, and the religious and cultural assumptions brought to the discussion, this chapter was able to offer a more nuanced interpretation of the insider perception of the conflicts erupting in Britain's Orthodox communities. The findings of Chapter 2 suggest that a further expansion of the transnational approach and more detailed attention to specific locations across the United Kingdom would be profitable and contribute to a revision of the reigning historiographical models that quickly gloss over cultural clashes and conflicts and see them as expressions on the path of 'anglicisation'.

Chapter 3, then, narrowed the focus of analysis further by homing in on the situation between the World Wars in the Scottish capital city of Edinburgh. The investigation of the local, again through a transnational lens, allowed detailed attention to perspectives from within the Jewish community, on issues such as leadership, religious guidance and representation of issues relevant to the Jewish community in relation to the outside world. Insider perspectives at the time offer a view into a microcosm of Jewish identifications and self-expressions which have, to date, not been investigated in detail. The analysis of Salis Daiches's work in Edinburgh shows that such explorations need to be extended to his contemporaries in Glasgow and in other locations across Britain, continuing the work begun by Bill Williams for Manchester and myself for Edinburgh. Rather than a simple clash between anglicised residents and an undifferentiated mass of Eastern European immigrants, we see that, at the local level, the educational and cultural backgrounds of leaders mattered and that the communities were split along a number of different lines of religious observance and ideology. Thus we find Scottish, Lithuanian, Russian, Polish, traditional Orthodox, modern Orthodox, and Hasidic forms of observance matched with care about, or indifference to, specific religious ideologies. Who trusted whom in relation to standards of religious observance is a complex matter only partly unravelled to date. Again, the transnational framework pursued in Chapter 3 chimes with the research of Adam Mendelsohn and David Feldman in seeking to interrogate models of interpreting the consequences of the great migration of Jews into Britain.

Finally, Chapter 4 sought to locate the historical discussion of the previous chapters in the urban landscape of present-day Edinburgh and in the memories of Edinburgh's Jewish communities today. The analysis of David Daiches's *Two Worlds* and *Jewish Edinburgh on Foot* as complementary *lieux de mémoire* fits into the transnational framework of the book by exploring the memory work by those resident Jews (and non-Jews) who are themselves immigrants to the Scottish capital. Local memorial discourses thus join the increased interest in British Jewish heritage evident since the 1980s, thus closing the discussion in this book by a reflection on 'Jewish spaces' in the city. What is recalled, narrated and made visible in the city depends on a number of variables which have as much to do with contemporary interests as with the availability of historical data. Thus, the final chapter also reflects on the practice of historiography and its implications for local communities.

At the conclusion of this monograph we may be able to appreciate the exploration of Salis Daiches's biography in the preceding chapters as an example of a strategy of enquiry which would benefit from further work. Research on religious leaders in smaller communities across the anglophone world at the turn of the twentieth century and, more specifically, within the United Kingdom would allow a more nuanced understanding of the expectations, structures and lines of authority among immigrant and resident communities. Such research would contribute to a more detailed interpretation of the religious transformation of British Jewry in the first half of the twentieth century and shed new light on the relationship between the Chief Rabbi and the London Beth Din and on the leadership of smaller Orthodox communities across the British Isles. I contend that there are issues to explore with regard to multifaceted religious ideologies, leadership styles and understandings of religious authority which have, as yet, not been investigated in depth. As noted in the Introduction, we are now fortunate to have a number of excellent, in-depth studies of the Chief Rabbis from the Adlers through to Jonathan Sacks, studies that focus on their education, training, ideology, leadership and politics. What we lack are corresponding studies of community rabbis and ministers who were tasked with leading their congregations and balancing a relationship with the central and supreme *halakhic* authority in the Empire, the Chief Rabbi.

More generally, we may wish to think about the move from an immigrant to a settled community as an example of a complex web of cultures in transition, a transition which continues throughout the life of the community but which peaks at the time the first generation of immigrants hands over the reins of the community to the next generation.[2] Anne-Marie Fortier, in an article about the relationship between a place and its memories, suggests that

> generations, in immigration discourses, are the living embodiment of continuity and change, mediating memories of the past with present living conditions, bringing the past into the present and charged with the responsibility of keeping some form of ethnic identity alive in the

future. Called upon as bearers of an 'original' identity and culture, and an 'adopted' one, they embody both continuity and change, 'identity-as-conjuncture' and 'identity-as-essence' that decant into each other and combine in the formation of a distinct émigré identity.[3]

Such movements of continuity and change have been highlighted and examined in the chapters of this monograph, and particularly Chapter 4 is witness to the possibility of a continually self-renewing sense of continuity with the past while also keeping a firm eye on the promise of a Jewish future in the Scottish capital. Rather than assuming a 'distinct émigré identity', however, this monograph shows that generational transitions give rise to new forms of Jewish identification and religiosity and that, when we are able to witness some of the movements of transitions through the historical records, we are able better to understand the traces of Jewish life we find in the present.

Glossary

Terms listed are italicised in the main text.

Alrightnik: Jewish immigrant who had done well economically and mediated between their fellow and much poorer immigrants and the British Jews who had acculturated one or more generations previously. The *alrightniks* somewhat challenge the idea of an outright clash between immigrant and resident Jews.

Ashkenazi (adj.) (noun: **Ashkenazim**): Jews originating in northern Europe, *Ashkenaz* is the *Yiddish* name for Germany.

Austrittsgemeinde. See also **Einheitsgemeinde**: Secessionist Orthodox community which separated from the *Einheitsgemeinde*. Secession took place following the passing in 1876 of a law in Prussia which allowed individuals to retain their Jewish status on relinquishing membership of the official, state-sanctioned, Jewish community, the *Einheitsgemeinde*. Well-known *Austrittsgemeinden* were located in Frankfurt and Berlin.

Av beth din: Literally, the 'father' of the court, that is, the chair or leader of the *beth din*.

Bar mitzvah: Ceremony celebrating the religious maturity of a Jewish boy at the age of thirteen. The boy demonstrates his competence in and his ability to take responsibility for, his religious observance by leading part of a service and by reading from the *Torah*.

Bat mitzvah: Ceremony introduced in the late twentieth century to celebrate the religious majority of Jewish girls at the age of twelve or thirteen. Non-Orthodox communities often hold identical ceremonies for both genders while Orthodox ceremonies largely omit the observances connected with public acts of worship, such as reading from the *Torah*.

Beth din (pl. **batei din**): Jewish religious courts which deal, among other things, with issues affecting Jewish status, determining whether a person is Jewish, issuing marriage licences and divorce documents, and conducting conversions to Judaism.

Chalitzah: Ceremony liberating a childless widow and her brother-in-law from the obligation to marry each other.

Challah: White, sweet bread, baked for *shabbat* and festivals.

Cheder: Religion school for children of nursery and primary school age.

Chief Rabbi: Head of the Jewish community; often an appointment made by the state or municipality. In Britain, the Chief Rabbi is not appointed by the state but from within the Orthodox community by a complex election process. He serves as the community's most senior rabbi and as head of the London Beth Din.

Dayan (pl. **dayanim**): Religious judge, always a rabbi, who serves on a *beth din*.

Derasha: Sermon interpreting a *Torah* passage.

Einheitsgemeinde. See also **Austrittsgemeinde**: State-sanctioned Jewish community, in particular in Germany, which catered for congregations of various religious outlooks and practices within one organisational structure.

Get: Religious divorce document issued by the husband to his wife in the presence of a *beth din*.

Giyur (Hebrew): Conversion to Judaism.

Golus (Yiddish; Hebrew: **galut**): Exile; also used to describe life in the diaspora, that is, Jewish life outwith the land of Israel while remaining centred on the land of Israel.

Gymnasium: Grammar school in Germany.

Halakhah: Jewish religious law.

Haredi: Literally 'trembling'; refers to Jewish groups that distinguish themselves from mainstream Orthodoxy through beliefs and practices that encourage or favour firm social boundaries against secular and non-Jewish society. These developments originate in the large-scale social and political changes Jews experienced in eighteenth-century central Europe. From the outside, *haredi* Jews can be most easily identified through the dress style of men: black suits and hats, white shirts, often sporting full beards and sidelocks.

Hazan (pl. **hazzanim**): Cantor.

High Holidays: The festivals of Rosh Hashanah (Jewish New Year) and Yom Kippur (Day of Atonement), celebrated in the autumn.

Kashrut: Jewish dietary laws.

Kehillah: Jewish community of a city or town.

Kosher (adj.): Permitted food prepared according to the laws of *kashrut*.

Litvak: A Jew from Lithuania.

Mameloshn: Mother tongue; alternative term for *Yiddish*.

Minhag (pl. **minhagim**): Religious customs which have acquired the force of law such as, for example, the covering of one's head for prayer.

Minyan: In Orthodox Jewish practice a quorum of ten Jewish men required for public prayer and the recitation of certain parts of the service.

Pale of Settlement: Area of Tsarist Russia where Jews were permitted to live.

Parashah (pl. **parashot**): Passage of the *Torah*, the Pentateuch. The complete Pentateuch is read in Orthodox synagogues on an annual cycle. For this purpose the biblical books are divided into *parashot* which are assigned to the weeks of the Jewish year.

Rabbi: Literally, teacher. In Orthodox Judaism someone who has been trained in *Talmud* and law codes, and is qualified to make *halakhic* decisions, that is, someone who has been given *semicha*, rabbinical ordination.

Since the nineteenth century, in Western Europe, a rabbi was also tasked with pastoral work, and the German title *Rabbiner* could also be tied to the functions of community leadership rather than solely identify someone ordained as a rabbi.

Rabbonim (pl.): Rabbis trained in Eastern Europe. Can be used pejoratively.

Rav: A well-respected *rabbi* who is able to act as a unifying authority across congregational boundaries.

Responsa: Rabbinic genre of writing in which a question is answered by extensive *halakhic* discussion. Many rabbis collect and publish their *responsa*.

Sabbath: See *shabbat*.

Semicha: Rabbinical ordination. See also *yoreh, yoreh, yadin, yadin*.

Shabbat (Hebrew; Yiddish: **Shabbos**): Seventh day of the week dedicated to rest. *Shabbat* begins at sunset on Friday and ends at sunset on Saturday.

Shechita: The butchering of *kosher* animals according to Jewish law by a qualified butcher, a *shochet*.

Shochet (pl. **shochetim**): *Kosher* butcher.

Shtetl: Small towns in Eastern Europe, and the Pale of Settlement, with a large Jewish population.

Shtille chuppe: Marriages conducted without a registrar acting as the representative of civil law.

Shul: Synagogue.
  Englisher shul: Synagogue frequented by acculturated Jews.
  Griner shul: Synagogue frequented by recent immigrants.
  Russisher shul: Synagogue frequented by recent immigrants from Russia.

Sukkah: (Temporary) structure erected for the celebration of the festival of *sukkot*, recalling the biblical narrative of the dwelling of the Jewish people in the desert following their liberation from Egyptian slavery. Many synagogues will have a part of the building which can be used as a *sukkah* by opening the roof.

Sukkot: Festival remembering the story of the dwelling of the Jewish people in the desert following the Exodus from Egypt.

Tallit: Prayer shawl. Garment worn, in Orthodox Judaism, by Jewish men during the morning service and during services at which the Torah is read.

Talmud: The most significant text of rabbinic learning and instruction.

Talmud torah: Religious learning for its own sake.

Tevilah: Immersion in a ritual bath (*mikveh*). This is a requirement for an Orthodox conversion. In Orthodox practice Jewish women immerse in a *mikveh* at the conclusion of the menstrual cycle, and Jewish men may choose to immerse before festivals.

Torah: The Pentateuch. By extension the entirety of Jewish law, *halakhah*. *Torah Judaism* refers to particular forms of Orthodox Judaism.

Torah im derekh erets: Literally, '*Torah* in the ways of the land', meaning the observance of Torah while engaging positively, if pragmatically, with the economic, social and intellectual traditions of the host society. The modern use of the term originates with Samson Raphael Hirsch.

Torah min hashamayim: Literally, '*Torah* from heaven', pointing to an Orthodox understanding of the divine origin of the text of the *Torah*. In some interpretations this may mean the precise letter-by-letter revelation of the Pentateuch in its current form.

Torah u'maddah: A combination of traditional religious with secular learning which had grown in German-speaking lands since the middle of the nineteenth century. Rabbis Esriel Hildesheimer and David Zvi Hoffmann were key advocates of this joining of Jewish and secular learning.

Wissenschaft des Judentums: The scientific, that is, historical–critical, study of Jewish texts and Jewish history arising in the nineteenth century.

Yeshivah (pl. **yeshivot**): Religious Jewish high school for boys.

Yiddish: The mothertongue (*mameloshn*) of *Ashkenazi* Jews. A Jewish lingua franca of northern Europe which arose from medieval German and includes Hebrew and Slavic vocabulary.

Yom tov (Hebrew; Yiddish: **yontef**): Festival day, such as Jewish New Year, the Day of Atonement, *Sukkot* etc.

Yoreh yoreh, yadin yadin: Literally, 'can he teach? He can teach; can he judge? He can judge'. Formula recited at the ordination (*semicha*) of Orthodox rabbis, designating two different levels of *halakhic* competence.

References and Notes

Notes to Preface and Acknowledgements

1. See, for example, Brinkman 2008, Green 2008, Kobrin 2008 and Feldman 2018.
2. Definitions of terminology italicised in the main text can be found in the Glossary.
3. Please note that Vilna, rather than Vilnius, is used throughout, thereby clearly indicating the name of the city in contemporary Russian, German and English usage.
4. For an explanation of the terminology chosen in this book and alternative ways of referring to Jews in Britain, please see the Introduction.
5. Endelman 2002:12. The designation of 'provinces' for Jewish communities outwith the greater London area, and thereby outwith the London-based United Synagogue, is explored in the Introduction.
6. See also Dee 2017, particularly Chapter 4.
7. It is also worth mentioning that specific varieties of Jewish religious practice have flourished in Britain since the late nineteenth century, not least *haredi* communities in London, Gateshead and Manchester.
8. The maps forming the basis of Figure 4.1 in Chapter 4 are reproduced with the permission of the National Library of Scotland. The maps were part of the 1893 Ordnance Survey of Edinburgh and can be accessed at <https://maps.nls.uk/geo/explore/side-by-side/#zoom=18&lat=55.9429&lon=-3.1850&layers=73&right=BingHyb> (last accessed 25 October 2018).

Notes to Introduction

1. Other than the moves required in pursuit of his education, from Vilna to Königsberg and on to Berlin and Leipzig, I have not been able to trace whether he had travelled across the European continent or even further afield before migrating to Britain.
2. For an exploration of this terminology please see below.
3. Mendelsohn/Kahn 2014:2.
4. Panayi 2010:2f.
5. Kushner 2006; 2012:6.
6. Brinkmann 2012; Kushner 2012; Mendelsohn/Kahn 2014.
7. See, for example, Mendelsohn/Kahn 2014; Mendelsohn 2017.
8. See, for example, Endelman 2002, 2010; Gilfillan 2019.
9. For a helpful working typology of the spectrum of Jewish ideological orientations at the time see Elton 2009:40ff.
10. Alderman 1990, 1993; Freud-Kandel 2006; Persoff 2008, 2013; Elton 2009.

11. The most prolific author on Scottish Jewish history is Kenneth Collins, a retired physician, and a cofounder of the SJAC Centre. More academically oriented works of note include Nathan Abrams's study of small communities, *Caledonian Jews* (2009), Billy Kenefick's comparative work between Jewish and Irish immigrant groups, and a handful of PhD theses by Paul Vincent, Ben Braber, Linda Fleming, and Mark Gilfillan which, with the exception of Braber and Gilfillan, remain unpublished.
12. Like the British Jews who founded the Jewish Historical Society of England in 1893, Jews in the Americas and Jews in South Africa and Australia founded historical societies whose journals and pamphlets narrate local Jewish history and offer an opportunity for lay and professional historians to connect with community heritage and history.
13. See Parry-Jones/Abrams 2018 whose special *Jews in the Celtic Lands* has its origins in a 2011 conference entitled 'Jews on the Celtic Fringe'; Collins/Newman/Wasserstein (eds) 2018 which presents the fruits of a two-year genealogical and demographic project funded by the International Institute for Jewish Genealogy celebrating *Two-hundred Years of Scottish Jewry*; and the special issue of *Shofar* (2019, 37:3) entitled *Narrative Spaces at the Margins of British-Jewish Culture(s)*, edited by Phil Alexander, Hannah Holtschneider and Mia Spiro.
14. See, for example, the bibliography on the theme of 'religion' compiled by the Southern Jewish Historical Society which is regularly updated: available at <https://www.jewishsouth.org/category/themes-and-subjects/religious-life> (last accessed 2 February 2018).
15. Indeed, studies on Scottish migration predominantly do not engage with Jews. For example, the following books and anthologies do not refer to Jews: Brock 1999; McCarthy 2006 and (ed.) 2007; Campbell et al. 2011; McCarthy/MacKenzie (eds) 2016.
16. See, for example, Newman 1981; Green 1983; Cantor Berrol 1994; Lichtenstein/Sinclair 1999; Diner 2000; Bial 2002; Mendelsohn 2009.
17. The chapters were originally published in 2010 in a special issue of the journal *Jewish Culture and History*.
18. Mendelsohn 2014, 2015, 2017; Brinkmann 2012; Schloer 2014, 2016.
19. See Abrams 2018; Parry-Jones, 2018; Hansen 2018; see also *Shofar* (2019, 37:3); and Collins/Newman/Wasserstein (eds) 2018.
20. Cesarani 1990a:2.
21. Ibid. 3. For a more recent overview see Kershen 2000, and Kushner/Ewence 2010.
22. Endelman 2010:30f.
23. Ibid. 33.
24. Ibid. 31f.
25. See also Kenefick 2007 and 2013 on comparative work on Jewish and Irish immigrants to Scotland.
26. Though Gartner and Endelman dedicate significant sections of their monographs to the clashes between immigrant religiosity and the sensibilities of the established British Jewish community.
27. Alderman 1990, 1993, 1998, 2008; Freud-Kandel 2006; Persoff 2008; Elton 2009.
28. Endelman 2010:36.

29. Cesarani 1992:30. The Jewish Historical Society of England was founded in 1893 in an effort to showcase Jewish history and culture not primarily to Jews but to British mainstream society, demonstrating Jewish patriotism to Britain (Cesarani 1992:32).
30. Kushner 1992b:13f. See also Kushner 1992a.
31. For an overview of the contemporary landscape of Jewish archives in Britain, see Robson 2010.
32. Endelman 2010:39. See also Kushner 2009.
33. Green 2008:287.
34. Ibid. 288.
35. Green 2008; Mendelsohn 2014 and 2017.
36. Feldman 2017.
37. Frankel 1992:31.
38. Feldman 2017:135.
39. Williams 1990.
40. Feldman 2017:136.
41. An alternative and complementary framework would be the examination of the thought of religious leaders and reflecting this back into the social and religious politics of the day. This approach is evident in the work of Ben Elton and Miri Freud-Kandel as well as Jeffrey Gurock and Adam Ferziger, to name but a few examples.
42. Reasons for this paucity of sources can be gleaned from a 1992 article by Tony Kushner, 'A History of Jewish Archives in the United Kingdom' (1992a), which outlines the practices and politics of collecting Jewish historical material in the United Kingdom. While, for much of the time, there was a focus on medieval Jewish history in Britain, the sources collected for the history from 1880 onwards are scarce and many have been lost when communities closed and buildings were reused. In addition, a substantial number of documents remain in private hands.
43. This book was found in May 2016 in the synagogue of the Edinburgh Hebrew Congregation in Salisbury Road and has now joined the Daiches family papers in the NLS.
44. This conclusion is likely because the first letter in the 1925-1932 correspondence book is addressed in gratitude to the person who suggested this method of filing correspondence to the rabbi. When the book was filled, it seems Salis Daiches simply did not keep up this filing system.
45. There are no rich personal sources which would allow us to delve deeper into the reasons for the immigration of the Daiches family to the United Kingdom (and the United States) and the journey made. David Daiches offers a stereotypical reason for his grandfather Israel Hayyim Daiches's move to Leeds: the 'call' from Beth Hamedrash Hagadol synagogue came at an opportune moment when the family was concerned that their son, who had died as an infant and that death being unrecorded, would be called up to serve in the Russian Army. Emigration was the alternative to penalties (Daiches 1997:166). There is no way to verify this account or to contradict it but we note that it is part of the standard repertoire of migrant narratives (see Cesarani 1996). There is, to my knowledge, no surviving private correspondence from Israel Hayyim Daiches and his sons in the lead-up to their immigration to the United Kingdom. Similarly, local records, which speak of their personal lives and reflect on their time in

Leeds, Hull, Sunderland, and then Edinburgh, largely do not appear to have survived whereas community records have.
46. NLS Acc.12278 Inventory.
47. Aspects of titles, addresses and areas of competence of religious functionaries will be discussed further in Chapters 1 to 3. See Chapter 1 for a more detailed discussion of the differences between rabbi and minister in British Jewish Orthodoxy.
48. For an overview of the collection of documents pertaining to provincial Jewish communities see Williams 1975.
49. Another recent article which reflects on a set of correspondence between a Scottish community and the Chief Rabbi's office is detailed in Abrams 2018.
50. Collins 1990; Abrams 2009. See also the critical history of the *Jewish Chronicle* (Cesarani 1994).
51. A few copies of the *Jewish Times*, published in *Yiddish* around the turn of the twentieth century, survive in the SJAC. The *Jewish Times* was followed by the *Glasgow Jewish Evening Times* and the *Glasgow Jewish Weekly Times*, published from 1914. At that time, Zevi Golombok also launched the *Yiddish* monthly *Die Yiddishe Shtimme* which survived until the mid-1920s.
52. The SJAC and the Mitchell Library in Glasgow each holds a complete set of the *Jewish Echo*.
53. The *Edinburgh Star* is available as a complete set in the SJAC.
54. For a fuller discussion see Chapter 1.
55. Daiches 1928:xii.
56. This is another project altogether, most likely there is a viable PhD project in a reconstruction and evaluation of Salis Daiches' sermons which are now all lodged with the NLS Acc.12278.
57. *The Scotsman* 3 May 1945:4.
58. For example, Rabbi Shmuel Isaac Hillman who was co-opted as *dayan* on the London Beth Din in 1912 (but was only able to take up this position in 1914) had held the de facto position of 'Chief Rabbi of Glasgow' since his appointment brought him to Glasgow from Russia in 1908. Hillman had been appointed by the Glasgow Jewish Communal Council (founded 1907 following the break-up of the United Synagogue of Glasgow [1898–1906]) to serve the migrants settled in the Gorbals, an inner-city neighbourhood predominantly populated by Jews. Hillman's appointment was ratified by the anglicised Garnethill Synagogue and thus his tenure inaugurated a period of relative calm in the struggles of leadership in the Glasgow Jewish community. Hillman was succeeded by Rabbi Jacob Lurie though his status did not command the same citywide authority as that of his predecessor. Rabbi Atlas at the Great Synagogue in the Gorbals was another significant personality in the city who engaged in discussion about a Scottish Beth Din. For detailed discussion see Chapter 3.
59. Sperber (2012) points rightly to the German origins of the British Chief Rabbinate as created by Nathan Adler. Cohen (1967), however, balances this view somewhat because, in Britain, the Chief Rabbinate was not used directly as an instrument of state control. For alternative models of rabbinic leadership and authority see Gurock 1983, Liebman 1965 and Ferziger 2005.
60. See also Abrams 2018.
61. See also McBride 2013:121f.

62. Kushner 2009:258.
63. Ibid. 264 (emphasis original).

Notes to Chapter 1

1. Cf. Alderman 1990.
2. Mendelsohn 2014:143f.
3. Ibid. 146.
4. Shapiro 2000:76. See also Elton 2009:54 ff.
5. Below, we shall explore a number of positions on the study of secular subjects and on the academic study of Jewish texts and history.
6. Elton 2009:57. By contrast Samson Raphael Hirsch understood *Wissenschaft des Judentums* as 'a purely academic pursuit with no purpose in strengthening Judaism or increasing Jewish commitment' (Ibid. 54).
7. The section 'Placing philosophy in relation to modern Orthodox Jewish thought' will explore Orthodox approaches to *Wissenschaft des Judentums*. See also Yedidyah 2011.
8. Elton 2009:59. It is also worth noting that in the early twentieth century the lines between what is today considered Orthodox and Conservative Jewish ideology and practice were considerably more blurred than they are today. What made the difference for individual rabbis hinged on who ordained them rather than where they had studied. Hence, Chief Rabbi Hertz's training at JTS, the seminary associated with Conservative Judaism since the tenure of Solomon Schechter, was not an impediment to his employment by Orthodox congregations (Ibid. 211): before Schechter's leadership JTS was a 'traditionalist centre of the scientific branch of the acknowledgement school'). Similarly, Salis Daiches's lenient attitude to some *halakhic* issues – such as flicking an electric light switch on *shabbat* – was less contentious than it would be today.
9. For an overview of the growth of rabbinical organisation and resulting authority structures in North America see Gurock 1983 and, more generally, Schwarzfuchs 1993 and Liebman 1965, as well as Jacobson 2016.
10. While Daiches illustrates the Scottish context well, research on other local contexts would enable a fuller picture of the Orthodox Jewish landscape of early twentieth-century Britain. Indeed, similar investigations into the biographies of Hildesheimer graduates are lacunae in current scholarship.
11. The biographical work in this chapter is the prerequisite for my examination of the relationship between Daiches and the two Chief Rabbis in Chapter 2.
12. See Freud-Kandel 2006; Elton 2009; Persoff 2013.
13. The United Synagogue, in its extension across Britain as the United Hebrew Congregations, may have intended to unify the disparate congregations. Locally, however, it was more often than not perceived as centralising, that is as imposing its aims and ambitions on congregations, rather than offering an opportunity for joint or united policymaking.
14. See Gartner ³2001; Alderman 2008; Endelman 2002 and 2011.
15. There are studies of individual rabbis who made the transition to North America: see, for example Goldberg 1989. For the following see also Feldman 2017 for a proposed change in the approach to immigration history.
16. Freud-Kandel 2006; Elton 2009; Persoff 2013.
17. Feldman 2017:143f. in his examination of London's East End, highlights the

co-operation between immigrant synagogues and the established British Jewish leadership, and points to various lines of conflict across immigrant and resident leaders. Thus, he implicitly suggests that further, more detailed attention of the religious divisions and co-operations with the Jewish community in the early twentieth century is warranted.

18. See also Williams 1990:31f.
19. Wertheimer 1987:155.
20. Ibid. 98.
21. Ibid. 99.
22. In 1905 Salis Daiches was ordained as a rabbi by Rabbi Solomon Cohen, then Chief Rabbi of Vilna; three further ordinations followed, from Rabbi Ezekiel Lipshitz, Chief Rabbi of Kalish, his father Rabbi Israel Hayyim Daiches (*Jewish World* 14 August 1908:18). In 1912 Daiches also received rabbinical ordination from the Hildesheimer Seminary (Eliav et al. [eds] 2008: 97). Why Daiches decided to seek this ordination in 1912 when he was already established in the United Kingdom is unclear.
23. See Wilke 2003, 2013 for a discussion of the historical development of the modern rabbinate. For the present purpose, it is helpful define as rabbis those religious officials who were ordained either by a seminary, such as the Hildesheimer, or by traditional *yeshivot* or by individual rabbis who recognised their learning and whose ordination (*semicha*) included the traditional formula of *yoreh, yoreh, yadin, yadin* which acknowledges the candidate's proficiency in Jewish law and authorises him to make *halakhic* judgements. As will be explored in the section 'Education and ideology', the United Synagogue preferred the majority of its religious officials educated in Britain not to progress to rabbinical ordination, instead conferring the title of 'minister', and reserving both the title and authority of rabbi for the Chief Rabbi and the *dayanim* of the London Beth Din.
24. Already in 1904, Moses Gaster wrote to congratulate Daiches on his 'Candidatur' (which most likely is his taking a position in Hull) with the following endorsement: 'Leute Ihrer Bildung und von Ihrer academischen Schulung sind nicht zu haeufig in England anzutreffen und gewiss nicht unter Candidaten fuer die Stellung eines "Minister"; umso groesser muss die Befriedigung sein, dass endlich auch eine andere Schule anfaengt hier Fuss zu fassen. Ich bin fest überzeugt dass, so sehr man Ihnen zu diesem Erfolg Glueck wuenschen darf, die Gemeinde, welche Sie anstellt, sich auch dazu gratulieren muss' (NLS Acc. 12278/1).
25. For correspondence see LMA Acc. 2805/04/02/44, letters from 1914/15. Hillman was installed at the London Beth Din and took up office as *dayan* only in 1914, even though he had been appointed in 1912 (see Elton 2009:213, 233).
26. Elton 2009:140, 213ff.
27. This rivalry may best be thought of as a reflection of the different 'characters' of the cities which had come about as a result of their different historical fortunes. In the early twentieth century, Glasgow was the fourth largest city in Europe and thrived on its industrial and technical productivity and inventiveness. By contrast, at that time, Edinburgh's reputation largely rested on the Scottish Enlightenment of a century previously and its echoes in literature and heritage. For an overview see, for example, Crawford 2013.
28. See Chapter 3 for a detailed exploration of the relationship between Hertz and Daiches.

29. NLS Acc.12278/27.
30. Daiches 1903.
31. For example, Israel Hayyim Daiches initiated the conference of immigrant rabbis which took place in 1910 in Leeds, where proceedings were carried out predominantly in *Yiddish* (Gartner ³2001:217f, 243f; see also Chapter 2), and carried on scholarly publishing activity in Hebrew aimed at the same socioreligious context. The latter activity was economically unsuccessful as none of the journals he founded survived more than a few editions (Gartner ³2001:247f.). David Daiches's recollections of his grandfather's house are of stepping into the cultural world of Eastern Europe, and he records his father's discomfort with exposing his children to the culture still inhabited by their grandparents (Daiches 1997:90ff.).
32. Murray Freedman quotes Rabbi Y. Shemaria about Israel Hayyim Daiches's outlook as follows: 'Yet Rabbi Daiches, although very much a traditional Eastern European Rav, held "views concerning the importance and value of secular education which would not find support amongst some like minded rabbinical leaders today"' (Freedman 2004:22).
33. Wertheimer 1987:98ff., 155; Wilke 2013:97f., 102ff.
34. See Chapter 4 for a reflection on the success of this synthesis from the perspective of the following generation.
35. Wertheimer 1987:98f.
36. Ibid. 155.
37. Ibid.
38. Ibid. 156. See also Brinkman 2008.
39. Wilke 2013:86ff.
40. Levin in Wertheimer 1987:155.
41. See list of graduates in Eliav/Hildesheimer et al. (eds) 2008:49–271.
42. Ellenson 1990:159.
43. In contrast to Germany and other places in Continental Europe, Jewish communities in Britain were, and are, entirely self-funding. Hence the salary of the minister was (and is) largely determined by the finances of the congregation and often amounted only to that of lower-class professionals (Newman 1976:87f.).
44. Ellenson 1990:159; 182 note 13; Wilke 2013:102. And Daiches's own certificate of ordination from the Hildesheimer Seminary (NLS Acc. 12278/26).
45. Eliav et al. (eds) 2008.
46. Ellenson 1990:159.
47. See Daiches 1997:162.
48. Letter from A. Philips to S. Daiches 21 October 2018 (NLS Acc. 12278/1).
49. Chapter 3 will establish the local context(s) of Salis Daiches's work and evaluate how his background and abilities had an impact on his work in Edinburgh.
50. Elton 2009:84ff.
51. Ibid. 166, 180ff.
52. Ibid. 190.
53. Baumel 2013:21.
54. Ben Elton suggests that Hertz 'wanted his ministers to looks more traditional and rabbinic' (email to author 5 May 2016), hence placing an emphasis on their beards and even encouraging (or rather seeking to mandate) them to wear beards (Elton 2009:210). Daiches, however, along with many others, appears to have ignored this.

55. As we shall explore in more detail in Chapter 3, they exchanged regular correspondence on *halakhic* concerns regarding marriages and conversions. Hertz also invited Daiches to contribute to his Torah commentary; and Daiches asked Hertz's career advice when contemplating 'calls' from South African congregations. Yet, Daiches's vocal contributions to the Conference of Anglo-Jewish Ministers/Preachers, and his tendency to act decisively in local cases concerning Jewish status, sometimes strained the relationship with the Chief Rabbi. Similarly, Daiches's contribution to Hertz's Torah commentary on Leviticus was not included in the eventual publication of the commentary, and the correspondence around this subject is a little intemperate (see Meirovich 1998:29ff.).
56. Webber 1955:14.
57. Though, as we shall see in Chapter 2, Samuel Daiches's work in Sunderland and his participation in the conferences of Jewish ministers during Hermann Adler's tenure as Chief Rabbi suggest that, like his brother Salis, he was highly critical and very vocal on the topic of the centralisation of *halakhic* authority in London.
58. Alderman 1998:92ff.
59. Endelman 2002:115. Though, as discussed below, without succeeding in bringing all Ashkenazi congregations under its umbrella.
60. Ibid. 115f.
61. Goulston 1968:73ff.
62. Endelman 2002:119.
63. Alderman 1998:93; Newman 1976:87; Goulston 1968:63.
64. Cesarani 1998.
65. We shall observe in Chapters 3 and 4 how this message resonated with their congregants.
66. Daiches 1997:9.
67. These epithets, undeniable invocations of the tensions between the *shuls*, were both likely to have been used in the pejorative sense by the opposing congregations.
68. See also Saperstein 2008:32f.
69. Ibid. 2f. Prior to these developments, sermons were rarely delivered and concentrated on a close reading of the week's *parashah*.
70. Even a cursory glance at the *JC* from 1905 to 1945 and local, secular, papers in Hull, and Sunderland, as well as *The Scotsman* and Glasgow's *Jewish Echo* reveal that Daiches spoke in various Jewish clubs and organisations on topics of the day: Zionism, Jewish education, spirituality, modernity, the war, to name but a few. The papers also contain summaries of his talks, and sometimes also of his sermons.
71. Daiches 1997:98.
72. Professor Macdonald Webster was exasperated by Daiches's frequent press contributions and complained that, 'more and more it is being said that no one in Scotland today can say "Jew," but Rabbi Daiches must needs rush into print' (Levison 1989:149).
73. Gilfillan 2019:142ff.
74. Daiches 1997:34, 102, 168, 175.
75. Elton 2009:205.
76. Mendelsohn 2017:146. Mendelsohn also demonstrates that Jewish communi-

ties throughout the Anglophone world emulated the practices of missionary societies regarding education and social welfare in an effort to combat missions, a move which resulted in the large-scale modernisation of Jewish communities (Ibid. 147ff.).

77. *The Scotsman* 3 May 1945:4.
78. A large collection of manuscripts of Salis Daiches, including many sermons, is now in the NLS. These were found in a wooden box in the Edinburgh Hebrew Congregation during research for the present book. Accessing these for research purposes requires extensive preservation work at the same time and thus I have not been able to include these texts in the research for this book. These handwritten sermons and essays await a capable researcher seeking a viable PhD or post-doctoral project (NLS Acc. 12278).
79. See Chapters 3 and 4 for reflections on how Salis Daiches's approach resonated with his Edinburgh congregation. David Daiches remembers that his father's demeanour would change when interacting with *Yiddish*-speaking immigrants, emulating the sing-song of talmudic discussion and seamlessly adapting his habitus to the expectations of his interlocutor (1997:182). The *JC* listed the topics of sermons, and Daiches appears to have sent in his topics on almost a weekly basis. The themes he preached on ranged from the topics found in the week's *parashah* or the festival to immediate concerns of the community, such as mixed marriages and the duties of children towards their parents and vice versa.
80. There may be further examples of speeches in the recently found, and as yet unresearched, manuscripts of Salis Daiches in the NLS.
81. Daiches 1928:11.
82. Hermann Cohen (1842–1918) is most closely associated with the neo-Kantian philosophical movement of the late nineteenth century which, no doubt, also influenced Salis Daiches. Cohen reworked his interpretation of Judaism through his reading of Kant. This work was published posthumously in 1919 as *Religion of Reason out of the Sources of Judaism*. The resulting ethical foundation of Judaism dispenses with some of the distinctive ethnic and practical elements that Daiches would have considered essential.
83. David Daiches suggests that Kant and Hume were the two secular philosophers most relevant to his father's synthesis (Daiches 1997:89f., 168).
84. Daiches 1928:55.
85. Ibid. 61.
86. Ibid. 56.
87. Ibid. 57.
88. Yedidya 2011:74; see also Solomon 2012, particularly 204f. when discussing David Zvi Hoffmann's (1843–1921) approach to the biblical text. Hoffmann had been one of Daiches's teachers at the Hildesheimer Seminary.
89. In 1943/44 Salis Daiches authored a series of articles on the themes of faith, conduct, person, home, prayers, festivals, law, religion and Zionism for *B'Derekh*, a periodical issued by the Joint Emergency Committee for Jewish Religious Education in Great Britain (NLS Acc. 12278/16).
90. Anecdotally, in my own observations during conversations, *Two Worlds* is often (falsely) remembered to have been entitled 'Between Two Worlds', indicating a separation stronger than then boundaries perceived by Salis and remembered by David Daiches.

Notes to Chapter 2

1. *Proceedings of the Conference of Anglo-Jewish Ministers* held at Jews' College, London, 26–8 December 1909:14, LMA Acc.2805/01/03/02/01.
2. Elton points to Hermann Adler's recognition that *rabbis*, and hence authority figures among recent immigrants, were needed to facilitate the acculturation of the new arrivals (Elton 2009:131).
3. Ibid. 133ff., 200, 216.
4. Freud-Kandel 2006:88.
5. Braber 2007:146ff.
6. Cf. also Feldman 2017:135; and for Scotland in particular see Evans, 2018.
7. Endelman 2002:127.
8. Alderman 2008:93.
9. Ibid. 97.
10. Williams 1990:31.
11. Gartner ³2001:246.
12. Endelman 2002:127, 145, 176ff.; Newman 1986:223ff.; Taylor 2014:52, 61, 83ff.
13. Endelman 2002:178.
14. Finestein 1999:242.
15. Newman 1986:223ff.
16. The Adlers officiated as Chief Rabbis from 1844 to 1911: Nathan Adler 1844–90; Hermann Adler 1891–1911. See also Black 1988:26ff.
17. See, for example, the struggle of the London Beth Din with Machzike Hadath which concluded only in 1905 with Machzike Hadath accepting the jurisdiction of the Chief Rabbi (Gartner ³2001:207ff.).
18. Freud-Kandel 2006:18ff.
19. For example, Elton 2009:114ff.; Persoff 2013:106ff.
20. See also Dee 2017:149ff.
21. Cf. Goulston 1968, and Sharot 1973, as well as Freud-Kandel 2006 and Elton 2009.
22. Freud-Kandel 2006:9ff.; Goulston 1968:62.
23. Thus, congregations as far afield as South Africa and Australia had to negotiate practices and *halakhic* decisions via the London Beth Din.
24. Englander 1988:249ff.; Freud-Kandel 2006:37f.; Goulston 1968:64.
25. Freud-Kandel 2006:11ff.; Sharot 1973:171f.; Goulston 1968:62.
26. Sharot 1973:168ff.
27. Freud-Kandel 2006:14f. Elton suggests, however, that the Chief Rabbi differentiated between rabbis working within the United Synagogue and those in other congregations in Britain and the Empire. While he refused the former the title of rabbi, at least in his English correspondence, he addressed the latter by their full title in Hebrew and in English (Elton 2009:140f.). Elton's observation is certainly borne out in the case of Salis Daiches.
28. Goulston 1968:73ff.
29. See Gurock 1983 and Liebman 1965 as well as Ferziger 2005 and 2015.
30. Goulston 1968:63ff. For a detailed exploration of the status and education of Jewish religious functionaries in Britain since the middle of the nineteenth century see Goulston 1968 and Sharot 1973.
31. Adler was very aware of the need to 'bridge the gap' between immigrant and

resident Jews and, in his final letter, called for his successor to be someone who would 'appeal to both "East and West"' (Goulston 1968:70).

32. For a detailed account of the election process and background negotiations see Freud-Kandel 2006:42–51: 'A Chief Rabbi for East and West'. See also Persoff 2013:90ff., in particular; and Sharot 1973:172ff. Regarding the hegemony of the establishment see also Cesarani 1990b.
33. Elton 2009:164ff.
34. Freud-Kandel 2006:63.
35. Elton 2009:200f.
36. Ibid. 202.
37. Freud-Kandel 2006:42f.
38. Elton 2009:213.
39. Ibid. 213.
40. Freud-Kandel 2006:79ff. Derek Taylor illustrates the dispute between Robert Waley Cohen, President of the United Synagogue, and Hertz on the issue of strict religious practice as favoured by the Chief Rabbi in characteristic anecdote-rich form (Taylor 2007:353ff.).
41. See Persoff 2013:70 for a brief description of the proposals and their opposition in the British Jewish establishment, personified in *dayanim* Hyamson and Feldman. Persoff considers these issues in relation to the election of Joseph Hertz as Chief Rabbi and discusses various motions to influence the selection process originating with the Conference and the vocal opposition to Hertz's candidature from within the Conference.
42. Freud-Kandel 2006:43.
43. The atmosphere had already been brewing since the death of Nathan Adler (Goulston 1968:65). And so, high expectations of congregants combined with a lack of educational opportunities and a poor salary gave rise to discontent and rebellion (Goulston 1968:67ff. and 78f.).
44. Daiches 1997:29. While the approach was shared by father and son, Israel Hayyim did not go as far as permitting the active use of electricity on *shabbat*.
45. About which I have not been able to find any further information.
46. Gartner ^{3}2001:217f.
47. Elton 2009:141.
48. Ibid.
49. Ibid.
50. Ibid.
51. Ibid. 142.
52. Ibid. 140ff.
53. Ibid. 133ff.
54. Ibid. 111f.
55. Alderman 2008:97f.; Goulston 1968:71ff.
56. Daiches 1907:4.
57. Ibid. 5.
58. Ibid. 7.
59. See his passionate intervention in the *JC* in relation to the second Conference of Anglo-Jewish Ministers, *JC* 23 June 1911.
60. *JC* 28 February 1913:14.
61. *Proceedings of the Conference of Anglo-Jewish Ministers* held at Jews' College, London, 26–28 December 1909:2ff. (LMA Acc. 2805/4/01/4/03).

62. The need to recognise at least the concerns of ministers in the 'provinces' was also understood by the leadership of the United Synagogue although concrete steps to such recognition were not agreed upon (Finestein 1999:239).
63. *Proceeedings of the Conference of Anglo-Jewish Ministers* held at Jews' College, London, 26–28 December 1909:52–9 (LMA Acc.2805/01/03/02/01).
64. Ibid. 56 (LMA Acc. 2805/01/03/02/01).
65. *Proceeedings of the Second Conference of Anglo-Jewish Ministers* held at Portman Rooms, Baker Street, London, 12–14 June 1911:67–72 (LMA Acc. 2805/01/03/02/02).
66. Rabbi Jacob Rabinowitz, an immigrant from Lithuania, had taken, in 1899, a leadership position at the Edinburgh New Hebrew Congregation, a splinter group from the Edinburgh Hebrew Congregation. He remained in office until 1917 when he moved to London to serve in Dalston in the Montague Road Beth Hamedrash which was part of the Federation of Synagogues. We shall meet the Edinburgh New Hebrew Congregation again in Chapter 3 when we consider the fragmentation of congregations in Edinburgh and Salis Daiches's work from 1919. Here, it is sufficient to note that Rabinowitz was on the traditionalist end of the Orthodox spectrum and deeply opposed to the leadership of the Chief Rabbi, a position evidenced also by his later employment in the Federation.
67. *Report of the District Organisation of Provincial Congregations Sub-Committee* 1911:3 (LMA Acc. 2805/01/03/01/01).
68. Ibid. The subcommittee's recommendations were approved by the Conference's Standing Committee and presented the 1911 Conference for adoption.
69. Ibid. 3f.
70. Goulston 1968:71ff.
71. *JC* 12 January 1912:25f.
72. Minutebook of the Standing Committee, 20 March 1912 (LMA Acc. 2805/01/01/01/01:108ff.).
73. *JC* 31 December 1909:38 and *JC* 16 June 1911:24ff. See also Goulston 1968:72f.
74. See also the opinion piece on Samuel Daiches' involvement in the 1911 conference published in the *JC*: *JC* 23 June 1911:8f.
75. And yet, the Federation, Reform, Liberal and other alternatives were able to co-opt wealthy members of the British Jewish elite.
76. See Goulston 1968:71.
77. Organising Committee Minute Book, LMA Acc.2805/01/03/01/01:152.
78. This falls outwith our period of consideration: both Daiches and Hertz had died before the 1949 conference.
79. See also Finestein 1999:239f.
80. See Hertz's notes for his speech at the beginning of the 1914 Conference (HLS MS175/50/08:2ff.).

Notes to Chapter 3

1. Gilfillan 2019:15ff.
2. Letter of appeal detailing the situation of the Edinburgh Hebrew Congregation to the readership of the *JC* for contributions to the building fund for a new synagogue in Edinburgh (*JC* 13 June 1930:27).
3. Collins 1987:41.

4. Gilfillan 2019:66.
5. *JC* 9 July 1892:16.
6. Gilfillan 2019:83ff.
7. *JC* 14 July 2011:22.
8. Gilfillan 2019:37f.
9. MOEHC 1921–31.
10. Gilfillan 2019:69. Abel Phillips's collection of the annual reports of the Edinburgh Hebrew Congregation from 1911 onwards details the often precarious financial position of the synagogue community (Record Book of the EHC).
11. Gilfillan 2019:110ff.
12. MOEHC 29 September 1918 and 8 December 1918. The two congregations had been seeking a leader independently of each other and both had sought out Daiches (Gilfillan 2019:128).
13. Daiches–Hertz, 10 December 1918 (LMA Acc. 2805/04/02/121).
14. Levy 1956:137.
15. Even a cursory glance at the *JC* from 1905 to 1945 reveals a steady stream of contributions by Salis Daiches and entries about his activities at least on a monthly basis.
16. Daiches was 'called' by the Edinburgh Hebrew Congregation because he was an ordained rabbi (MOEHC 8 December 1918).
17. The *JC* and the *Jewish World* published a long biographical piece announcing Daiches's appointment to Sunderland, praising his intellectual pedigree and standing in the Jewish community to underline the appropriateness of Salis succeeding his brother Samuel in Sunderland (*JC* 14 August 1908:6; *Jewish World* 14 August 1908:18). Similarly, Daiches's departure from Sunderland to Edinburgh received a long entry in the *JC* highlighting the successes of his ten-year service to Sunderland's Jews (*JC* 7 February 1919:21).
18. Daiches 1997:102. Indeed, even when Chief Rabbi Hertz visited in 1928, Daiches asked him to present a *derashah* in *Yiddish* on *shabbat* afternoon at the synagogue in Graham Street (NLS Acc. 12278, Salis Daiches's Correspondence Book 281, letter to Hertz dated 10 February 1928).
19. See the frequent entries about Daiches's appearances at local occasions, and reports on his talks and sermons in Jewish and non-Jewish communities as reported in *The Scotsman*, Glasgow's weekly the *Jewish Echo*, and the *JC*.
20. See Salis Daiches's regular contributions and the frequent entries about his activities in the *JC*, the *Jewish Echo*, *The Scotsman* and the *Glasgow Herald*.
21. Salis Daiches reported on the activities of this Movement in the *Bulletin of the Society of Christians and Jews* in December 1942, shortly after the founding of the national society (NLS Acc. 12278/28).
22. *JC* 17 February 1933:8.
23. Letter from Goodman to Hertz 18 January 1933, LMA Acc. 2805/04/02/112.
24. Daiches/Cameron 1939.
25. For a detailed account of Daiches's engagement with the Christian missions to the Jews see Gilfillan 2019:135ff.
26. See, for example, his use of the secular press: *The Scotsman* 19 November 1920:9. Indeed, it appears that Daiches's work in Edinburgh contributed to a national campaign against missions by B'nai B'rith in 1929 (*JC* 1 March 1929:5).
27. The letter of appeal for contributions to the building fund of a synagogue in Edinburgh made a case for the need for an adequate building to represent

Judaism by referring to 'the beauty and impressiveness of the many Christian Churches and houses of worship of all denominations which render the capital of Scotland so attractive to other religious bodies' (*JC* 13 June 1930:27).

28. Daiches interpreted the United Kingdom as a quasi-secular state, notwithstanding the status of the Church of England as the established Church with the monarch simultaneously serving as head of state and as head of the Church.
29. Gilfillan 2019:132, 144; *Jewish Echo* 28 February 1936:10 for report on Daiches's intervention regarding the marriage laws; the legal situation changed only in 1939, however [Gilfillan 2019:142]); *JC* 25 January 1929:28; *JC* 15 February 1929:18.
30. For coverage of the case at the time see *JC*, particularly 7 November 1924. See also the account given in Gilfillan 2019:132ff.
31. *JC* 14 January 1922:16.
32. For an overview of the debates surrounding *shechita* in early twentieth-century Britain, see Alderman 1993.
33. For an account of *shechita* conflicts and resolutions in Glasgow, see Vincent 1966:54ff.
34. For the following, see Gilfillan 2019:132ff. There were no Jewish day schools in Scotland until well after World War II. Calderwood Lodge Primary School was founded in 1962 and remains the only Jewish school in Scotland.
35. Gilfillan 2019:131f.
36. The minutes of MOEHC 21 October 1923, record a reprimand to religious officials who were lax in their attendance of weekday services so that a *minyan* could not always be guaranteed. Even after the new synagogue had been opened, Daiches felt compelled to send a letter to his congregants urging their commitment to attend a *minyan* on weekdays (MOEHC 26 January 1933).
37. MOEHC 1921–31; 1931–6.
38. For a similar conclusion see Gilfillan 2019:156f. For an exploration of the social changes in British Jewry from the interwar years until after World War II, see Cesarani 1998.
39. Cesarani 1998.
40. Hertz to Daiches 11 December 1918 (LMA Acc. 2805/04/02/121).
41. For the following see Braber 2007:146ff. For a summary overview of Jewish religious life in Glasgow in the period under consideration see Collins (ed.) 1987:26–30.
42. The United Synagogue of Glasgow was disbanded in 1906 because of internal conflicts (see Collins 1990:83ff. for an account of the United Synagogue of Glasgow; see also Braber 2007:147).
43. Collins 1990:198.
44. Vincent 1966:54.
45. Collins 1990:169f.
46. This is where we hit a paucity of sources. For our time period, I have been unable to locate any correspondence by Glaswegian rabbis other than I. K. Cosgrove. Perhaps none has survived; or it has not yet been found because it remains in private custody.
47. See, for example, the mention of Daiches's correspondence in the Minutebooks of Garnethill Synagogue (SJAC MOGHC 1912–23 and 1925–9).
48. For example, Rabbi Atlas published a series of four articles on 'Problems of Judaism' in 1935 (*Jewish Echo* 8 February 1935:5; 22 February 1935:4; 8 March

1935:14; 5 April 1935:13). And the *Echo* frequently carried reports of sermons and other addresses delivered by Glasgow's rabbis and ministers.

49. Aside from the series of three articles on the reorganisation of Scottish Jewry in 1928 (29 June 1928:2; 6 July 1928:2; 13 July 1928:2) Daiches himself did not contribute much to the *Jewish Echo*. He did put in Rosh Hashanah message(s) and congratulated on the anniversary of the publication but, otherwise, he is mostly mentioned as someone who makes a lot of speeches and participates in events.
50. See Braber 2007:146ff.
51. Collins 2016:74ff.
52. There are various proposals but, it seems, no solution was reached during the war years. R. Lurie comes out as favoured by Hertz, that is, trusted by him to oversee *shechita* and *giyur* (for correspondence between Glasgow and the Chief Rabbi see LMA Acc. 2805/04/02/44 letters from 1914 onwards; see also Braber 2007:15; Collins 1990:198f.; Collins 2016:74).
53. In 1929 the Glasgow Beth Din was constituted by Rabbis Lurie, Balkin and Atlas with Revd E. P. Phillips as secretary (*Glasgow Jewish Yearbook* 1937–8:47; 1938–9:47).
54. For an account of various *shechita* disputes in early twentieth-century Glasgow, see Collins 1990:245ff., 212; Vincent 1966:54ff. Vincent suggests that the single unifying factor in the *shechita* disputes was the passage of the Slaughter of Animals Act for Scotland of 1929.
55. *Jewish Echo* 19 June 1928:2, 1 July 1928:2, 13 July 1828:2.
56. See the responses by Rabbis Lurie, Atlas and Balkin in the *Jewish Echo* 17 July 1928:3 (Lurie), 3 August 1928:4 (Atlas), 10 August 1928:4 (Balkin).
57. *Jewish Echo* 3 August 1928:4.
58. *Jewish Echo* 3 August 1928:4. Ideologically, Rabbi Atlas and Rabbi Daiches did not see eye to eye. Atlas declared that the 'endeavour to prove that the precepts of our Torah and the customs of Israel are in full agreement with the lay customs of the world and the conclusions of science, I experience a rent in my soul [...]'. Daiches, as we have seen, aimed to show that nothing in science could challenge the authority of Torah, even though the ways of the world need some correction through the divinely ordained morality and ethics of Torah. For Atlas's attitude towards Jewish engagements with secular society see Vincent 1965:52f.
59. *Jewish Echo* 28 February 1936:4.
60. See, for example, the correspondence relating to regularising the Jewish status of a boy of an intermarried couple who was being cared for by his Jewish relatives in Sunderland. The boy's Jewish father had been killed in action and Daiches called an ad hoc *beth din* to effect the boy's acceptance into the Jewish faith: letters between Daiches and Hertz 11 and 18 June 1917, LMA Acc. 2085/04/02/121. Daiches justifies his course of action by saying that 'As we have no permanent בית דן [*beth din*] here' – a reminder of his continuing quest for devolution of *halakhic* responsibility – he needed to form a quorum 'for the occasion'. The Chief Rabbi replied that 'in the circumstances', he is 'willing to comply with your request' of admitting the boy but the disapproval of going it alone is obvious. See also, the letter from the secretary of the Chief Rabbi to Daiches, dated 5 May 1925, in which he is 'particularly annoyed that the reception of the bridegroom into Judaism was made without reference to the Beth

Din here [in London] and without their previous knowledge and consent'. The letter closes by asking Daiches to constitute an ad hoc local *beth din* which is now authorised to 'confirm the reception of the bridegroom into Judaism' and to include *tevilah* (LMA Acc. 2805/04/02/40).
61. Cape Town offered £900 a year and Pretoria £1,200 (LMA Acc. 2805/04/02/04 correspondence from July 1919 and July/August 1920).
62. Daiches to Hertz 31 July 1919, LMA Acc. 2805/04/02/041.
63. The annual salary of £350, which Daiches had negotiated when he was appointed, was a sum that would have assured a decent living standard for the Daiches family and which was fully in line with the earnings of other Jewish religious functionaries. Yet, it is also understandable that the tight financial circumstances of the Edinburgh Hebrew Congregation, particularly during the economic difficulties of the 1920s, made a salary increase challenging (MOHEC 29 October 1922 report a deficit in the budget and an inability to raise Daiches's salary; indeed, the Council of the community asked Daiches to consider a reduction of his salary to help the community). The EHC's decision to purchase a new plot and build a synagogue from scratch added to the strain on the community's finances. From Daiches's perspective, however, already in 1919, he would most likely have compared himself to Garnethill's minister in terms of local significance. Phillips, lacking rabbinical ordination, at that time received almost twice as much a year. Similarly, Edinburgh's Christian clergy, particularly those appointed to prominent parishes, could command more than twice the salary Daiches received. He thus may quite rightly have felt that his salary was not matching the respect his position commanded (email from S. J. Brown 17 June 2016). He accepted the terms and salary, however, and decided to stay rather than seek more lucrative employment elsewhere. His decision made, despite the community's dire financial situation, from 1922, and possibly in response to the repeated call Daiches had received from the Cape Town congregation, Daiches drew a salary of £624 a year from the Edinburgh Hebrew Congregation (MOEHC, 24 December 1922). No further increases to this salary are reported; indeed, in 1925, a letter informed the rabbi that his salary was to be regarded as permanent (letter from Abel Philips [honorary secretary of the congregation] on behalf of the Edinburgh Hebrew Congregation 25 December 1925, NLS Acc. 12278/2).
64. Hertz to Phillips 12 September 1919, LMA Acc. 2805/04/02/041.
65. Daiches to Hertz 3 December 1919, LMA Acc. 2805/04/02/041.
66. Letter dated 27 July 1922, LMA Acc. 2805/4/02/11.
67. LMA Acc. 2805/04/02/040.
68. Hertz to Daiches 24 March 1927, HLS MS175/50/9. The years before World War I had seen a quarter of Jewish marriages in Scotland take place outwith the authority structures of British Orthodoxy and, while such a trend was not observable in the interwar years, the London Beth Din was, understandably, a little concerned: 'Between 1880 and 1901 (with some gaps in the records), 419 Authorization Forms were located for Jewish Marriages in Scotland but, in the corresponding periods, 558 Scottish Statutory Marriage records were extracted claiming to be the product of a Jewish marriage ceremony, [*sic*] It follows that 139, or 1 in 4 Scottish Jewish religious marriages were conducted without prior authorization (causing no small disquiet in the Chief Rabbi's Office)!' (Lamdan 2015).

69. HLS MS189/AJ383/17.
70. For example, Daiches to Hertz letter exchange May 1925, LMA Acc. 2805/04/02/040, and letter exchange Daichesto Hertz July 1931, LMA Acc. 2805/04/02/112.
71. Daiches to Hertz 5 February 1920, LMA Acc. 2805/04/02/041.
72. Hertz to Daiches 22 February 1920, LMA Acc. 2805/04/02/041. Hertz, however, does not engage with Daiches's suggestions on this topic.
73. The Jacobs Affair 1961–64 under Chief Rabbi Israel Brodie.
74. Daiches 1997:146ff.
75. Ibid.
76. See the frequent contributions by and about Cosgrove's work in the *Jewish Echo*.
77. See also Cesarani 1998.
78. Website of the Manchester Beth Din: available at <http://mbd.org.uk/site/page/family-division> (last accessed 12 February 2018).
79. Available at http://www.iash.ed.ac.uk/history-institute> (last accessed 16 October 2017) although the website does not acknowledge David Daiches's founding contribution.

Notes to Chapter 4

1. Apparently, the same address housed another writer–resident in the previous century, the Scottish children's writer Robert M. Ballantyne (1825–94).
2. Available at <https://sites.google.com/site/southsideheritagegroup/> (last accessed 18 September 2017).
3. Available via the *Curious Edinburgh* app for both iOS and Android, at <https://jewishstudies.div.ed.ac.uk/edinburgh-jewish-walks/> (last accessed 13 February 2018).
4. Even though an early review found it difficult to think of 'Jew' and 'Scot' belonging together in the same phrase (Bellow 1956:19: 'in spite of Mr. Daiches's matter-of-fact tone the idea of a Scottish Jew is a little startling').
5. Daiches 1997:3.
6. As far as I am aware, *Two Worlds* and other writings by David Daiches, which address Jewish themes, have not received any scholarly discussion.
7. Creet in Creet/Kritzmann 2011:10.
8. Massey 2005:130.
9. Barthes 1986:92.
10. Lefebvre 1991.
11. See also Rebecca Solnit's maps of various American cities, making visible the different ways the city is inhabited and storied: for example, in Solnit 2010.
12. Massey 1995:188:

    The invention of tradition is here about the invention of the coherence of a place, about defining and naming it as a 'place' at all. It is for this reason that it may be useful to think of places not as areas on maps but as constantly shifting articulations of social relations through time; and to think of particular attempts to characterise them as attempts to define, and claim coherence and a particular meaning for, specific envelopes of space–time.

13. Kushner 2009; Roemer 2010.

14. Roemer 2010:6.
15. See the recent publications in association with the SJAC, such as Collins/Kaplan/Kliner 2013 and Collins 2016, which celebrate the idea of integration and the virtual absence of antisemitism in Scotland such that conflicting or more complex experiences of Jewish migration to Scotland and relating Jewishness to Scottish belonging and identification are obscured or silenced.
16. Nora 1989:7.
17. When its original remit of educating recent immigrants about British culture became obsolete, the Lit. changed its constitution to refocus on things Jewish so that today's annual programme includes talks of Jewish religious, cultural and historical interest (https://ejls.org/ [accessed 19 October 2017]).
18. See Williams on Manchester (Williams 1985) but also Cesarani and Kushner about collecting Jewish heritage (Cesarani [ed.] 1990; Kushner [ed.] 1992). Scotland may perhaps constitute something of an exception as the SJAC was initiated and continues to be led by Scottish Jews.
19. See, for example, Pearce 2014 and the insightful discussion about 'Holocaust consciousness' in contemporary Britain.
20. There are also contexts, however, in which we find examples of a division of perspective which is part of the story being told: Yael Zerubavel's work on Israeli national memory, as narrated at sites relevant for a national story, demonstrates how groups draw on different political accounts precisely as part of the contest over what the nation is (Zerubavel 1995).
21. Assmann 1988.
22. McCracken-Flesher 2008:88.
23. Lister in Baker/Lister 2008:8.
24. Such representational technique draws on the work of Rebecca Solnit (see, for example, Solnit 2010).
25. Daiches 1997:205.
26. Ibid. 7.
27. Ibid. 178ff.
28. Ibid. 11; see also 64.
29. Ibid. 9.
30. Ibid. 12.
31. Lionel Daiches 1989, *Edinburgh Star* 3:22f.
32. Daiches 1997:83.
33. Ibid. 14.
34. Ibid. 13.
35. Ibid. 16.
36. Ibid.
37. Ibid. 162.
38. Ibid. 150.
39. Ibid. 34.
40. Ibid. 34, 149ff.
41. David Daiches's many publications on the literary landscapes of the British Isles, on Scotland and Edinburgh and the nation's and city's literary connections, do not once reference Jewish themes or Jewish writers. This is in addition to showing a male bias which eclipses the literary production of women – including Jewish women – from the canon referenced. See, for example, Daiches 1980, 1981 and 1986; and Daiches/Flower ²1981.

42. Daiches 1997:92.
43. Ibid. 80f.
44. *Kosher* baking continues in Edinburgh, however, first through a local German bakery in Bruntsfield and, from 2017, through an Israeli bakery located in Haymarket. Having shut shop in the Southside in the east of the city, bakeries in the west of Edinburgh have taken on providing for the community.
45. Though David Daiches does acknowledge the personal sacrifices his mother made when marrying his father, namely a complete resignation from any career of her own, talented musician that she was. He also notes his father's traditional expectations of marriage which did not allow for a spouse with her own career and ambitions: Daiches 1997:58f.
46. Ibid. 150ff.
47. Though the *Edinburgh Star* regularly publishes recollections of congregants and many of these are penned by women. Similarly, the frequent obituaries in the magazine are an opportunity to recall the lives of women.
48. Ironically, three of the tour's authors are professional women with careers independent of those of their spouses.
49. Daiches 1997:17.
50. Ibid. 121ff. See also Denton 1991:33 where he remembers his father's train journey as just such a salesman to Fife.
51. Daiches 1997:123.
52. Ibid. 88.
53. Gruber 2002; see also Kushner 2009:264.
54. Daiches ²1990:223. In the third part of his autobiographical texts, *A Third World*, David Daiches traces his strong emotional attachment to Scotland, to his childhood but claims it as part of his heritage through the acquisition of an intellectual legacy of Scottish history and literature realised in his life's work (Daiches 1971:50f.).
55. Edinburgh's Jewish residents, however, are planning a Jewish cultural centre in which Jews and non-Jews can come together to experience and participate in Jewish religious and cultural events, and host events of other groups in the city: *JC* 24 November 2017, available at <https://www.thejc.com/news/uk-news/edinburgh-council-chiefs-back-6m-jewish-culture-centre-1.448957> (last accessed 13 February 2018).
56. Available at <https://www.scojec.org/noticeboard/files/17_bicentenary.pdf> (last accessed 7 November 2017).

Notes to Epilogue

1. See also Feldman 2017.
2. Ibid.
3. Fortier 1999:55.

Bibliography

Archives and primary sources

Edinburgh Hebrew Congregation:
  Minute Books, MOEHC
  Abel Phillips's record book: Record Book of the EHC
Hartley Library Southampton: HLS
London Metropolitan Archives: Records of the Anglo-Jewish Community, LMA Acc. 2805 (Office of the Chief Rabbi)
National Library of Scotland: Daiches Family Papers, NLS Acc. 12278
Scottish Jewish Archives Centre: SJAC
Minute Books of the Garnethill Hebrew Congregation (MOGHC)

Edinburgh Star, community magazine 1989–
Glasgow Herald
Glasgow Jewish Year Book
Jewish Chronicle
Jewish Echo
Jewish World
The Scotsman

Daiches, David 1997, *Two Worlds: An Edinburgh Jewish Childhood*, Canongate Classics 7, Edinburgh.
Daiches, David ²1990, *Was: A Pastime from Times Past*, Richard Drew Publishing, Glasgow.
Daiches, David 1971, *A Third World*, Sussex University Press, Brighton.
Daiches, Sally 1903, *Über das Verhältnis der Geschichtsschreibung D. Humes zu seiner praktischen Philosophie*, Alexander Edelmann, Leipzig.
Daiches, Samuel 1907, 'Judaism in England: Congregation and Minister', Sermon delivered on Sabbath, the 2nd of Adar, 5667 (15 February 1907) at the Sunderland Synagogue, offprint, n.p.
Denton, Howard and Wilson, Jim C. 1991, *The Happy Land*, Ramsey Head Press, Edinburgh.

Secondary literature

Abrams, Nathan 2009, *Caledonian Jews: A Study of Seven Small Communities in Scotland*, McFarland, Jefferson, NC.

Abrams, Nathan 2018, 'English Centre vs. Celtic Periphery: The Chief Rabbi, *Shechita* and Dundee, 1883', *Jewish Culture and History* 19:2 (Jews in the Celtic Lands), pp. 154–68.

Alderman, Geoffrey 1990, 'The British Chief Rabbinate: A Most Peculiar Practice', *European Judaism* 23:2, pp. 45–58.

Alderman, Geoffrey 1993, 'Power, Authority and Status in British Jewry: The Chief Rabbinate and *Shechita*', in *Outsiders & Outcasts: Essays in Honour of William J. Fishman*, (eds) Alderman, Geoffrey and Holmes, Colin, Duckworth, London, pp. 12–31.

Alderman, Geoffrey 1998, *Modern British Jewry*, Oxford University Press, Oxford.

Alderman, Geoffrey 2008, *Controversy and Crisis: Studies in the History of the Jews in Modern Britain*, Jews and Jewish Life, Academic Studies Press, Boston, MA.

Alexander, Phil, Holtschneider, Hannah and Spiro, Mia (eds) 2019, *Narrative Spaces at the Margins of British-Jewish Culture(s)*, Shofar 37:3.

Altman, Alexander 1974, 'The German Rabbi: 1910–1939', *Leo Baeck Yearbook* 19:1, pp. 31–49.

Assmann, Jan 1988, 'Kollektives Gedächtnis und kulturelle Identität', in *Kultur und Gedächtnis*, (eds) Assmann, Jan and Hölscher, Tonio, Suhrkamp, Frankfurt am Main, pp. 9–19.

Baker, William and Lister, Michael (eds) 2008, *David Daiches: A Celebration of his Life and Work*, Sussex Academic Press, Brighton.

Barthes, Roland 1986 (originally published in 1967), 'Semiology and the Urban', in *The City and the Sign: An Introduction to Urban Semiotics*, (eds) Gottdiener, Mark and Lagopoulos, Alexanders P., Columbia University Press, New York, pp. 87–98.

Baumel, Mosche 2013, *Orthodoxie und Wissenschaft: Der Weg von Rabbiner David Zwi Hoffmann*, Limmud – Beiträge zum Judentum 2, LIT Verlag, Münster.

Bellow, Saul 1956, 'Rabbi's Boy in Edinburgh', (review of *Two Worlds*) in *Saturday Review of Literature* 39 (24 March 1956), p. 19.

Bial, Raymond 2002, *Tenement: Immigrant Life on the Lower East Side*, Houghton Mifflin Company, New York.

Black, Eugene C. 1988, *The Social Politics of Anglo-Jewry 1880–1920*, Basil Blackwell, Oxford.

Braber, Ben 2007, *Jews in Glasgow 1879–1939: Immigration and Integration*, Vallentine Mitchell, London.

Brinkmann, Tobias 2008, 'From *Hinterberlin* to Berlin: Jewish migrants from Eastern Europe in Berlin before and after 1918', *Journal of Modern Jewish Studies* 7:3, pp. 339–55.

Brinkmann, Tobias 2012, *Migration und Transnationalität: Perspektiven deutsch-jüdischer Geschichte*, Schöningh, Paderborn.

Brock, Jeanette M. 1999, *The Mobile Scot: Emigration and Migration, 1861–1911*, John Donald, Edinburgh.

Campbell, Jodi A., Ewan, Elizabeth and Parker, Heather 2011, *The Shaping of Scottish Identities: Family, Nation, and the Worlds Beyond*, University of Guelph, Guelph, ON.

Cantor Berrol, Selma 1994, *East Side/East End: Eastern European Jews in London and New York, 1870–1920*, Modern Hebrew Classics, Praeger, Westport, CT.

Cesarani, David 1990a, 'Introduction', in *The Making of Modern Anglo-Jewry*, (ed.) David Cesarani, Jewish Society and Culture, Blackwell, Oxford, pp. 1–11.

Cesarani, David 1990b, 'The Transformation of Communal Authority in Anglo-Jewry, 1914–1940', in *The Making of Modern Anglo-Jewry*, (ed.) David Cesarani, Jewish Society and Culture, Blackwell, Oxford, pp. 115–40.

Cesarani, David (ed.) 1990, *The Making of Modern Anglo-Jewry*, Jewish Society and Culture, Blackwell, Oxford.

Cesarani, David 1992, 'Dual Heritage of Duel of Heritages? Englishness and Jewishness in the Heritage Industry', in *The Jewish Heritage in British History: Englishness and Jewishness*, (ed.) Kushner, Tony, Frank Cass, London, pp. 29–41.

Cesarani, David 1993, *The Jewish Chronicle and Anglo-Jewry 1841–1991*, Cambridge University Press, Cambridge.

Cesarani, David 1996, 'The Myth of Origins: ethnic memory and the experience of migration', in *Patterns of Migration, 1850–1914, Proceedings of the International Academic Conference of the Jewish Historical Society of England and the Institute of Jewish Studies*, UCL, London, pp. 247–54.

Cesarani, David 1998, 'A Funny Thing Happened on the Way to the Suburbs: Social Change in Anglo-Jewry Between the Wars, 1914–1945', *Jewish Culture and History* 1:1, pp. 5–26.

Cohen, Norman 1967, 'Non-Religious Factors in the Emergence of the Chief Rabbinate', *Transactions (Jewish Historical Society of England)* 21 (1962–67), pp. 304–13.

Collins, Kenneth, Kaplan, Harvey and Kliner, Stephen 2013, *Jewish Glasgow – An Illustrated History*, Scottish Jewish Archives Centre, Glasgow.

Collins, Kenneth (ed.) 1987, *Aspects of Scottish Jewry*, The Michael Press, Glasgow.

Collins, Kennth 1990, *Second City Jewry: The Jews of Glasgow in the Age of Expansion, 1790–1919*, Scottish Jewish Archives Centre, Glasgow.

Collins, Kennth 2016, *The Jewish Experience in Scotland: From Immigration to Integration*, Scottish Jewish Archives Centre, Glasgow.

Collins, Kenneth, Newman, Aubrey and Wasserstein, Bernard (eds) 2018, *Two Hundred Years of Scottish Jewry*, Scottish Jewish Archives Centre, Glasgow.

Crawford, Robert 2013, *On Glasgow and Edinburgh*, Harvard University Press, Cambridge, MA.

Creet, Julia and Kritzmann, Andreas (eds) 2011, *Memory and Migration:*

Multidisciplinary Approaches to Memory Studies, University of Toronto Press, Toronto.
Daiches, David and Flower, John ²1981, *Literary Landscapes of the British Isles: A Narrative Atlas*, Bell & Hyman Limited, London.
Daiches, David 1980, *Edinburgh*, Granada, London.
Daiches, David (ed.) 1981, *A Companion to Scottish Culture*, Edward Arnold, London.
Daiches, David 1986, *Edinburgh: A Travellers' Companion*, Constable, London.
Daiches, Salis and Cameron, Duncan 1939, *A Hebrew Grammar for Beginners*, Oliver & Boyd, Edinburgh.
Dee, David 2017, *The 'Estranged' Generation? Social and Generational Change in Interwar British Jewry*, Palgrave Macmillan, London.
Diner, Hasia R. 2000, *Lower East Side Memories: A Jewish Place in America*, Princeton University Press, Princeton, NJ.
Eliav, Mordechai, Hildesheimer, Esriel, Schütz, Chana, Simon, Hermann (eds) 2008, *Das Berliner Rabbinerseminar 1873–1938: Seine Gründungsgeschichte – seine Studenten*, Schriftenreihe des Centrum Judaicum 5, Henrich & Henrich, Berlin.
Ellenson, David 1990, *Rabbi Esriel Hildesheimer and the Creation of a Modern Jewish Orthodoxy*, Judaic Studies Series, The University of Alabama Press, Tuscaloosa, AL.
Elton, Benjamin J. 2004, 'Did the Chief Rabbinate Move to the Right? A Case Study: The Mixed-Choir Controversies, 1880–1986', *Jewish Historical Studies* 39, pp. 121–51.
Elton, Benjamin J. 2009, *Britain's Chief Rabbis and the Religious Character of Anglo-Jewry, 1880–1970*, Manchester University Press, Manchester.
Elton, Benjamin J. 2014, 'British Orthodox Jewry 1945–1990: Swing to the Right or Shift to the Centre?', *Journal of Modern Jewish Studies* 13:2, pp. 264–83.
Endelman, Todd M. 2002, *The Jews of Britain, 1656 to 2000*, University of California Press, Berkeley, CA.
Endelman, Todd M. 2010, 'Anglo-Jewish Historiography and the Jewish Historiographical Mainstream', *Jewish Culture and History* 12:1–2, pp. 28–40.
Endelman, Todd M. 2011, *Broadening Jewish History: Towards a Social History of Ordinary Jews*, Littman Library of Jewish Civilization, Oxford.
Englander, David 1988, 'Anglicized not Anglican: Jews and Judaism in Victorian Britain', in *Religion in Victorian Britain: I Traditions*, Manchester University Press, Manchester, pp. 235–73.
Evans, Nicholas J. 2018, 'A Staging Post to America – Jewish Migration via Scotland', in Collins, Kenneth, Newman, Aubrey, Wasserstein, Bernard (eds), *Two Hundred Years of Scottish Jewry*, Scottish Jewish Archives Centre, Glasgow, pp. 302–26.
Feldman, David 2017, 'Mr Lewinstein goes to Parliament: Rethinking the

History and Historiography of Jewish Immigration', *East European Jewish Affairs* 4:2, pp. 134–49.

Ferziger, Adam S. 2005, *Exclusion and Hierarchy: Orthodoxy, Nonobservance, and the Emergence of Modern Jewish Identity*, Jewish Culture and Contexts, University of Pennsylvania Press, Philadelphia, PA.

Ferziger, Adam S. 2015, *Beyond Sectarianism: The Realignment of American Orthodox Judaism*, Wayne State University Press, Detroit, MI.

Finestein, Israel 1999, *Anglo-Jewry in Changing Times: Studies in Diversity 1840–1914*, Parkes-Wiener Series in Jewish Studies, Vallentine Mitchell, London.

Fortier, Anne-Marie 1999, 'Re-Membering Places and the Performance of Belonging(s)', *Theory, Culture & Society* 16:2, pp. 41–64.

Frankel, Jonathan 1992, 'Assimilation and the Jews in Nineteenth-Century Europe: Towards a New Historiography', in *Assimilation and Community: The Jews in Nineteenth Century Europe*, (eds) Frankel, Jonathan and Zipperstein, Steven, Cambridge University Press, Cambridge, pp. 1–31.

Freedman, Murray 1995, *Leeds Jewry: A History of its Synagogues*, Murray Freedman, Leeds.

Freedman, Murray 2004, *25 Characters in Leeds Jewish History*, Murray Freedman, Leeds.

Freud-Kandel, Miri 2006, *Orthodox Judaism in Britain since 1913: An Ideology Forsaken*, Vallentine Mitchell, London.

Freud-Kandel, Miri, 2014, 'In Defence of Synthesis: A Response to Benjamin Elton', *Journal of Modern Jewish Studies* 13:2, pp. 284–91.

Gartner, Lloyd P. ³2001, *The Jewish Immigrant in England, 1870–1914*, Simon Publications, London.

Gilfillan, Mark D. 2019, *Jewish Edinburgh: A History, 1880–1950*, McFarland, Jefferson, NC.

Gilman, Sander L. 1999, 'Introduction: The Frontier as a Model for Jewish History', in *Jewries at the Frontier: Accommodation, Identity, Conflict*, (eds) Gilman, Sander L. and Shain, Milton, University of Illinois Press, Urbana, IL, pp. 1–25.

Gilman, Sander L. and Shain, Milton (eds) 1999, *Jewries at the Frontier: Accommodation, Identity, Conflict*, University of Illinois Press, Urbana, IL.

Goldberg, Hillel 1989, *Between Berlin and Slobodka: Jewish transition figures from Eastern Europe*, KTAV, Hoboken, NJ.

Goulston, Michael 1968, 'The Status of the Anglo-Jewish Rabbinate, 1840–1914', *Journal of Jewish Sociology* 10:1, pp. 55–82.

Green, Abigail 2008, 'Sir Moses Montefiore and the making of the Jewish International', *Journal of Modern Jewish Studies* 7:3, pp. 287–307.

Green, Joseph 1983, *A Social History of the Jewish East End in London, 1914–1939: A Study of Life, Labour, and Liturgy*, Edwin Mellen Press, Lewiston, NY.

Gruber, Ruth Ellen 2002, *Virtually Jewish: Reinventing Jewish Culture in Europe*, University of California Press, Berkeley, CA.

Gurock, Jeffrey S. 1983, 'Resisters and Accommodators: Varieties of Orthodox Rabbis in America, 1886–1983', *American Jewish Archives Journal* 35:2, pp. 100–87.

Homa, Bernard 1969, *Orthodoxy in Anglo-Jewry, 1880–1940*, The Jewish Historical Society of England, UCL, London.

Jacobson, Maxine 2016, *Modern Orthodoxy in American Judaism: The Era of Leo Jung*, Academic Studies Press, Brighton, MA.

Kadish, Sharman 2002, 'Constructing Identity: Anglo-Jewry and Synagogue Architecture', *Architectural History* 45, pp. 386–408.

Kadish, Sharman 2015, 'Jewish Heritage in Scotland', *Jewish Historical Studies* 47, pp. 179–216.

Kenefick, William 2007, 'Comparing the Jewish and Irish Communities in Twentieth Century Scotland', *Jewish Culture and History* 9:2–3, pp. 60–78.

Kenefick, William 2013, 'The Jews and Irish in Modern Scotland: Anti-Semitism, Sectarianism and Social Mobility', *Immigrants & Minorities: Historical Studies in Ethnicity, Migration and Diaspora* 31:2, pp. 189–213.

Kershen, Anne J. 2000, 'From Celebrationists to Confrontationists: Some Thoughts on British Jewish Historiography in the Twentieth Century', *Immigrants & Minorities: Historical Studies in Ethnicity, Migration and Diaspora* 19:2, pp. 91–106.

Kobrin, Rebecca 2008, '"When a Jew was a *Landsman*": Rethinking American Jewish regional identity in the age of mass migration', *Journal of Modern Jewish Studies* 7:3, pp. 357–76.

Kushner, Tony 1992a, 'A History of Jewish Archives in the United Kingdom', *Archives* 20:87, pp. 3–16.

Kushner, Tony 1992b, 'Heritage and Ethnicity: An Introduction', in *The Jewish Heritage in British History: Englishness and Jewishness*, (ed.) Tony Kushner, Frank Cass, London, pp. 1–28.

Kushner, Tony 2006, *Remembering Refugees: Then and Now*, Manchester University Press, Manchester.

Kushner, Tony 2009, *Anglo-Jewry since 1066: Place, Locality and Memory*, Manchester University Press, Manchester.

Kushner, Tony 2012, *The Battle of Britishness: Migrant Journeys, 1685 to the Present*, Manchester University Press, Manchester.

Kushner, Tony and Ewence, Hannah 2010, 'Whatever Happened to British Jewish Studies? In Search of Contexts', *Jewish Culture and History* 12:1–2, pp. 1–26.

Kushner, Tony and Ewence, Hannah (eds) 2012, *Whatever Happened to British-Jewish Studies?* Parkes-Wiener Series on Jewish Studies, Vallentine Mitchell, London.

Lamdan, Neville 2015, 'A Family Tree of Scottish Jewry: Records-Retrieval Stage Completed!', *Avotaynu Online: Jewish Genealogy & Family History* 29.4.2015, http://www.avotaynuonline.com/2015/04/a-family-tree-of-scottish-jewry-first-stage-complete/ (accessed 1 May 2015).

Lefebvre, Henri 1991, *The Production of Space*, translated by Donald Nicholson-Smith, Blackwell, Oxford.
Levison, Frederick 1989, *Christian and Jew: The life of Leon Levison, 1881–1936*, Pentland Press, Edinburgh.
Levy, A. 1959, *The Origins of Scottish Jewry*, n.p.
Levy, Arnold 1956, *History of the Sunderland Jewish Community*, MacDonald, London.
Liebman, Charles S. 1965, 'Orthodoxy in American Life', *The American Jewish Year Book* 66, pp. 21–97.
Lichtenstein, Rachel and Sinclair, Iain 1999, *Rodinsky's Room*, Granta Books, London.
McBride, Terence 2013, 'Introduction', *Immigrants & Minorities: Historical Studies in Ethnicity, Migration and Diaspora* 31:2, pp. 119–26.
McCarthy, Angela 2007, *Personal narratives of Irish and Scottish migration, 1921–65: 'for spirit and adventure'*, Manchester University Press, Manchester.
McCarthy, Angela (ed.) 2006, *A global clan Scottish migrant networks and identities since the eighteenth century*, Tauris Academic Studies, London.
McCarthy, Angela and MacKenzie, John M. (eds) 2016, *Global Migrations: The Scottish Diaspora since 1600: A Tribute to Professor Sir Tom Devine*, Edinburgh University Press, Edinburgh.
McCracken-Flesher, Caroline 2008, '"One City" of Fragments: Robert Louis Stevenson's Second (Person) City Through David Daiches' Personal Eye', in *David Daiches: A Celebration of his Life and Work*, (eds) William Baker and Michael Lister, Sussex Academic Press, Brighton, pp. 85–92.
Massey, Doreen 1995, 'Places and Their Pasts', *History Workshop Journal* 39, pp. 182–92.
Massey, Doreen 2005, *For Space*, Sage, London.
Meirovich, Harvey Warren 1998, *A Vindication of Judaism: The Polemics of the Hertz Pentateuch*, Jewish Theological Seminary of America, New York.
Mendelsohn, Adam 2014, 'The Sacrifices of the Isaacs: The Diffusion of New Models of Religious Leadership in the English-Speaking Jewish World', in *Transnational Traditions: New Perspectives on American Jewish History*, (eds) Adam Mendelsohn and Ava Kahn, Wayne State University Press, Detroit, MI pp. 11–37.
Mendelsohn, Adam 2015, *The Rag Race: How Jews Sewed their Way to Success in America and the British Empire*, New York University Press, New York.
Mendelsohn, Adam 2017, 'Great Britain, the Commonwealth, and Anglophone Jewry', in *The Cambridge History of Judaism volume 8*, Cambridge University Press, Cambridge, pp. 133–63.
Mendelsohn, Adam and Kahn, Ava (eds) 2014, *Transnational Traditions: New Perspectives on American Jewish History*, Wayne State University Press, Detroit, MI.
Mendelsohn, Joyce 2009, *The Lower East Side Remembered and Revisited:*

A History and Guide to a Legendary New York Neighborhood, Columbia University Press, New York.

Nadel-Klein, Jane 1991, 'Reweaving the Fringe: Localism, Tradition, and Representation in British Ethnography', *American Ethnologist* 18:3, pp. 500–17.

Newman, Aubrey (ed.) 1975, *Provincial Jewry in Victorian Britain*, Jewish Historical Society of England, London.

Newman, Aubrey 1976, *The United Synagogue 1870–1970*, Routledge & Kegan Paul, London.

Newman, Aubrey 1981, *The Jewish East End, 1840–1939*, Jewish Historical Society of England, London.

Newman, Aubrey 1986, 'The Chief Rabbinate and the Provinces, 1840–1914', in Sacks, Jonathan (ed.), *Tradition and Transition: Essays Presented to Chief Rabbi Sir Immanuel Jakobovits to celebrate twenty years in office*, Jews College Publications, London, pp. 217–25.

Nora, Pierre 1989, 'Between Memory and History: Les Lieux de Mémoire', *Representations* 26, Special Issue: Memory and Counter-Memory, pp. 7–27.

Opal, Elliot 2000, *The History of Hull's Orthodox Synagogues and the people connected with them*, Highgate Publications, Beverley.

Panayi, Panikos 2010, *An Immigration History of Britain: Multicultural Racism Since 1800*, Pearson Education Limited, Harlow.

Parry-Jones, Cai 2018, 'Jewish life in the British-Jewish periphery: an examination of North Wales Jewry', *Jewish Culture and History* 19:2 (Jews in the Celtic Lands), pp. 169–90.

Parry-Jones, Cai and Abrams, Nathan 2018, 'Introduction: Jews in the Celtic Lands', *Jewish Culture and History* 19:2 (Jews in the Celtic Lands), pp. 119–23.

Pearce, Andy 2014, *Holocaust Consciousness in Contemporary Britain*, Routledge Studies in Cultural History 27, Routledge, London.

Pelger, Gregor 2006, 'Konkurrent und Kompromiss: Das jüdisch-theologische Seminar im viktorianischen England', in *Kulturtransfer in der jüdischen Geschichte*, (eds) Wolfgang Schmale and Martina Steer, Campus Verlag, Frankfurt am Main, pp. 97–123.

Persoff, Meir 2008, *Faith Against Reason: Religious Reform and the British Chief Rabbinate, 1840–1990*, Vallentine Mitchell, London.

Persoff, Meir 2013, *Hats in the Ring: Choosing Britain's Chief Rabbis from Adler to Sacks*, Judaism and Jewish Life, Academic Studies Press, Boston, MA.

Phillips, Abel 1979, *A History of the Origins of the First Jewish Community in Scotland – Edinburgh 1816*, John Donald, Edinburgh.

Pollins, Harold 1987, *Hopeful Travellers: Jewish Migrants and Settlers in Nineteenth Century Britain*, Research Papers of the London Museum of Jewish Life 2, London Museum of Jewish Life, London.

Robson, Karen 2010, 'The Anglo-Jewish Community and its Archives', *Jewish Culture and History* 12:1–2, pp. 337–44.

Roemer, Nils H. 2010, *German City, Jewish memory: The Story of Worms*, Brandeis University Press, Waltham, MA.
Saperstein, Marc 2008, *Jewish Preaching in Times of War 1800–2001*, Littman Library of Jewish Civilization, Oxford.
Schloer, Joachim 2014, 'Means of transport and storage: suitcases and other containers for the memory of migration and displacement', *Jewish Culture and History* 15:1–2, pp. 76–92.
Schloer, Joachim 2016, 'Irgendwo auf der Welt: German-Jewish emigration as a transnational experience' in *Three-Way Street: Jews, Germans and the Transnational*, (eds) Geller, Jay Howard and Morris, Leslie, Social History, Popular Culture, and Politics in Germany, University of Michigan Press, Ann Arbor, MI, pp. 220–38.
Schwarzfuchs, Simon 1993, *A Concise History of the Rabbinate*, Jewish Society and Culture, Blackwell, Oxford.
Shapiro, Marc B. 2000, 'Rabbi Esriel Hildesheimer's Program of Torah u-Madda', *The Torah u-Madda Journal* 9, pp. 76–86.
Sharot, Stephen 1973, 'Religious Change in Native Orthodoxy in London, 1870–1914: Rabbinate and Clergy', *Journal of Jewish Sociology* 15:2, pp. 167–87.
Solnit, Rebecca 2010, *Infinite City: A San Francisco Atlas*, University of California Press, Berkeley, CA.
Solomon, Norman 2012, *Torah from Heaven: The Reconstruction of Faith*, Littman Library of Jewish Civilization, Oxford.
Sperber, Haim 2012, 'Rabbi Nathan Adler and the Formulation of the Chief Rabbinate in Britain, 1845–1890', *European Judaism* 45:2, pp. 8–20.
Stampfer, Saul 2012, *Lithuanian Yeshivas of the Nineteenth Century: Creating a Tradition of Learning*, Littman Library of Jewish Civilization, Oxford.
Taylor, Derek 2007, *British Chief Rabbis, 1664–2006*, Vallentine Mitchell, London.
Taylor, Derek 2014, *Chief Rabbi Hertz: The Wars of the Lord*, Vallentine Mitchell, London.
Vincent, Paul 1966, *A Social History of Glasgow Jewry, 1928–1963*, unpublished PhD thesis, Department of Sociology, University of Strathclyde, Glasgow.
Webber, George J. 1955, 'A Memoir' in *Essays and Addresses by Samuel Daiches*, (eds) Simon, Maurice and Levy, Isaac, The Samuel Daiches Memorial Volume Committee, pp. 9–29.
Wertheimer, Jack 1987, *Unwelcome Strangers: East European Jews in Imperial Germany*, Studies in Jewish History, Oxford University Press.
Wilke, Carsten 2003, *'Den Talmud und den Kant': Rabbinerausbildung an der Schwelle zur Moderne*, Netiva: Wege deutsch-jüdischer Geschichte und Kultur 4, Georg Olms Verlag, Hildesheim.
Wilke, Carsten 2013, 'Modern Rabbinical Training: Intercultural Invention and Political Reconfiguration', in *Rabbi – Pastor – Priest: Their Roles and*

Profiles Through the Ages, (eds) Homolka, Walter and Schöttler, Heinz-Günther, Studia Judaica 64, DeGruyter, Berlin, pp. 83–110.

Williams, Bill 1975, 'Provincial Anglo-Jewish History: A Note on Sources' in *Provincial Jewry in Victorian Britain*, (ed.) Newman, Aubrey, Jewish Historical Society of England, London, pp. 1–17.

Williams, Bill 1985, *The Making of Manchester Jewry, 1740–1875*, Manchester University Press, Manchester.

Williams, Bill 1990, '"East and West": Class and Community in Manchester Jewry, 1850–1914', in *The Making of Modern Anglo-Jewry*, (ed.) Cesarani, David, Jewish Society and Culture, Blackwell, Oxford, pp. 15–33.

Yedidya, Asaf 2011, 'Orthodox strategies in the research of the *Wissenschaft des Judentums*', *European Journal of Jewish Studies* 5:1, pp. 67–79.

Zerubavel, Yael 1995, *Recovered Roots: Collective Memory and the Making of Israeli National Tradition*, University of Chicago Press, Chicago, IL.

Index

Aberdeen, 73, 76
Abrams, Nathan, 7
acculturation, 5–6, 22, 26, 31–2, 35, 42, 64, 104
Adler, Hermann, 4, 22–3, 29, 31–2, 39, 42–51, 54, 56–8, 61, 63
Adler, Nathan, 4, 16–17, 20, 31–2
Alderman, Geoffrey, 8, 11, 44
Anglicisation, 2, 64, 104–5
Anglo-Jewry, Anglo-Jewish, 3, 6–9, 17, 32, 41, 43, 48, 76; see also British Jews
Anglophone world, 2, 4, 7–8, 12–13, 20, 22, 47
assimilation, 29, 104
Atlas, Benjamin Beinush, 71–3, 115n, 125n, 126n; see also Glasgow
authority, religious, 2–6, 8, 10, 12, 15–18, 20, 22–4, 31–2, 41–60, 65, 72–7, 79–80, 104–6

Balkin, Baruch, 71, 73, 126n; see also Glasgow
Barthes, Roland, 83, 86
Berlin, 15, 17–18, 20–3, 25–7, 95, 108
beth din/batei din, 16, 24, 41–3, 45, 49, 54, 57–9, 62, 75–6, 79–80, 108–9, 126n; see also Glasgow Beth Din; Leeds; London Beth Din; Manchester; Scottish Beth Din
Breslau Rabbinical Seminary see Rabbinical Seminary
Brinkmann, Tobias, 6
British Jews/Jewry, definitions, 3–4; see also Anglo-Jewry
Brodie, Israel, 8, 128n

Calder, Jenni, 12, 38
Calderwood Lodge Primary School see Glasgow
Caledonian Rubber Works see Edinburgh
Central Edinburgh Hebrew Congregation, Roxburgh Place see Edinburgh
Cape Town, 74–5
Cesarani, David, 6, 9–11, 69
Chevra Kadisha Synagogue see Glasgow
Chief Rabbi, 3–4, 8, 13, 15–17, 20, 22–6, 31–2, 41–60, 104–6, 108–9, 115n; see also Adler, Hermann; Adler, Nathan; Brodie, Israel; Hertz, Joseph; Jacobovits, Immanuel
Church of Scotland, 16, 65, 97
Collins, Kenneth, 112n
Conference of Anglo-Jewish Ministers/Preachers, 13, 41, 49, 51–8, 64, 77, 104–5
conference of immigrant rabbis, Leeds see Leeds
Conservative Judaism, 3, 28, 116n
conversion, convert, 24, 46, 72–3, 76, 98, 108–9, 126n
Cosgrove, I. K., 16, 79; see also Glasgow
Council of Christians and Jews (CCJ) see Jewish-Christian Fellowship Movement
Creet, Julia, 83, 86, 88

Daiches Raphael, David, 80
Daiches, David, 14, 17, 29, 32, 38, 80, 82–3, 86–7, 89–100, 106, 114n, 118n, 120n, 128–30n
Daiches, Israel Hayyim, 25, 50, 114, 117–18n, 122n
Daiches, Jenni; see Calder, Jenni
Daiches, Lionel, 38, 92, 94
Daiches, Samuel, 17, 25–6, 29, 31, 52–3, 56, 119n
Dalry synagogues see Edinburgh
Dundee, 73, 99

Edinburgh
 Caledonian Rubber Works, 63
 Jewish population of, 63, 69, 83–4, 99
 Meadows, the, 38, 68, 81, 92, 99, 101

Edinburgh (*cont.*)
  Newington, 92, 97, 101
  Sciennes, 62, 68, 101
  Sciennes Primary School, 66, 68, 81, 99
  Southside, 17, 68, 75, 78, 81–3, 87, 90, 92–4, 96–7, 101, 130n
  Waverley Station, 92, 99
Edinburgh Hebrew Congregation, 12, 19, 24–5, 33, 37, 63–4, 68–70, 74–6, 92–3, 103, 123n, 127n
  Graham Street Synagogue, 33, 63, 78, 92, 94–6, 99, 124n
  Salisbury Road Synagogue, 38, 61, 66, 68, 73, 89, 92, 96
Edinburgh Synagogues
  Central Edinburgh Hebrew Congregation, 63
  Dalry synagogues, 63
  Edinburgh New Hebrew Congregation, 123n; *see also* Rabinowitz, Rabbi Jacob
  Independent Edinburgh Hebrew Congregation, 67–8; *see also* Levison, Alexander
  see also Edinburgh Hebrew Congregation
education, religious, 21–9, 31–5, 41, 54–7, 65–6, 68, 70, 72, 99, 117n, 121n
Elton, Benjamin, 8, 21, 30, 44, 48, 51, 118n
Endelman, Todd, 7–8, 10–11, 31, 43

Feldman, David, 10, 105
Frankel, Zacharias, 21, 30
Freud-Kandel, Miri, 8, 44,

Garnethill Synagogue, 13, 16, 71–2, 77, 115n, 127; *see also* Glasgow
Gartner, Lloyd, 7–8
George Watson's College, 90, 95–6
Germany, German, 1, 3, 15, 19–20, 23, 26–30, 37, 92, 95, 99–100, 108–11, 118n
giyur see conversion
Glasgow, 8, 13, 62, 68–79, 105, 117n
  Calderwood Lodge Primary School, 99, 125n
  Glasgow Board of Shechita, 70, 72
  Glasgow Jewish Representative Council, 70
  Gorbals, 71–2, 115n
  Jewish population of, 15, 16, 24–5, 43
  United Synagogue of Glasgow, 70, 115n, 125n
Glasgow Beth Din, 42, 49, 126n
Glasgow Board of Shechita *see* Glasgow
Glasgow Jewish Representative Council *see* Glasgow
Glasgow ministers *see* Cosgrove, I. K.; Philips, Revd E. P.
Glasgow rabbis *see* Atlas, Benjamin Beinush; Balkin, Baruch; Hillman, Samuel/Shmuel; Lurie, Jacob David
Glasgow synagogues
  Chevra Kadisha Synagogue, 71
  New Central Synagogue, 71
  Queen's Park Synagogue, 65
  South Portland Street Synagogue, 71–2
  see also Garnethill Synagogue
Gorbals *see* Glasgow
Graham Street Synagogue *see* Edinburgh Hebrew Congregation
Greenberg, Leopold, 67
Gruber, Ruth Ellen, 18
Gurock, Jeffrey, 114–16n

Hebrew, 20, 26, 29, 30, 65, 66, 68, 99–100, 111, 118n
Hegel, Friedrich, 37
Hertz, Joseph, 16, 19, 22–3, 29–31, 34, 39, 42–4, 47–9, 52–3, 57–9, 62, 64–5, 67, 70, 72–7, 79, 116n, 118n, 119n, 122n
Hildesheimer, Esriel, 21, 27–8, 30, 48, 111
Hildesheimer Rabbinical Seminary, 4, 15, 20–5, 27–9, 37, 60, 95, 116n, 117n; *see also* Rabbinical Seminary
Hillman, Samuel/Shmuel, 24–5, 48, 51, 54, 72, 115n; *see also* Glasgow
Hirsch, Samson Raphael, 21, 28, 30, 48, 111, 116n
Hochschule für die Wissenschaft des Judentums see Rabbinical Seminary
Hoffmann, David Zvi, 29, 111
Hull, 12, 15, 25, 30, 35, 39–40, 42, 53, 61, 64, 100, 114n
Hume, David, 25, 19, 37, 95

ideology, Jewish, 20–5, 27, 29–30, 32–7, 116n

Index

immigration, 2, 4, 8–11, 15–18, 11–15, 29–33, 41–52, 54–60, 63–6, 68–9, 71–2, 76, 79–80, 86–7, 89, 92, 94, 98–107, 108, 110, 114n, 116n, 118n, 120n, 123n; *see also* migration
Independent Edinburgh Hebrew Congregation *see* Edinburgh; *see also* Levison, Alexander
Institute for Advanced Studies in the Humanities (IASH), 80
integration, 15, 27, 29, 31, 41–3, 51, 55, 66
Inverness, 73

Jacobovits, Immanuel, 23, 26
Jewish Chronicle, 14, 34, 40, 56, 58, 63–7, 70, 115n
Jewish Echo, 14, 25, 68, 70–3
Jewish status, 20, 24, 42, 45–6, 54–5, 70, 72, 75–6, 79–80, 108, 119n; *see also* Beth Din
Jewish Theological Seminary, New York (JTS) *see* Rabbinical Seminary
Jewish-Christian Fellowship Movement, 65–6
Jews' College, 31–2, 47, 53

Kant, Immanuel, 35–7, 120n
Kirk *see* Church of Scotland
Königsberg, 17–18, 25–7, 95
Kushner, Tony, 2, 6, 9–10, 17–18, 86

Leeds, 24–6, 29, 42–3, 63, 93, 96, 114n
  conference of immigrant rabbis, 50–1, 56, 118n
  Leeds Beth Din, 42, 49, 80
  see also Beth Din
Lefebvre, Henri, 83, 86, 88
Levison Case, 13, 67
Levison, Alexander, 67–8, 73; *see also* Independent Edinburgh Hebrew Congregation; Levison Case; Missions to the Jews
Liberal Judaism, 3, 19, 21, 103
lieu(x) de mémoire, 83, 86–90, 96, 100–2, 106
Lithuania, 1, 20, 25, 50, 63, 94–5, 100, 105, 109
Litvak, 25, 109
London Beth Din, 15–16, 20, 23–5, 31–2, 39, 41–2, 46–50, 52–60, 71–3, 76–7, 79–80, 105–6, 115n; *see also* Beth Din
Lurie, Jacob David, 71–3, 115n, 126n; *see also* Glasgow

Manchester, 10, 24, 43–4, 52, 63, 79–80, 105
Manchester Beth Din, 42, 49, 79–80
marriage, 24, 41–2, 45–6, 51, 55–6, 59, 65–6, 70, 72–3, 75–6; *see also shtille chuppe*
Massey, Doreen, 83, 86
Meadows, the *see* Edinburgh
memory, 2, 4, 6, 14, 17–18, 38, 66, 80, 82–3, 86–91, 97–8, 100–2, 106
Mendelsohn, Adam, 5–6, 10, 105
migration, 1–2, 4–6, 10–12, 15, 20, 22–3, 25–6, 38, 43, 45, 60, 62, 80, 83, 86–8, 95–6, 101–7, 113n; *see also* immigration
minister, 13, 16, 24, 28–32, 40–2, 44, 46–59, 64, 67, 70–2, 77, 104–6, 117n; *see also* rabbi
Missions to the Jews, 33–4, 65–7

New Central Synagogue *see* Glasgow
Newington *see* Edinburgh
Nora, Pierre, 83, 86–8, 90, 100

Orthodox Judaism, 1, 3–6, 15–17, 20–4, 28–31, 33–8, 41–4, 46–51, 59, 64–5, 69, 78, 89, 93, 96, 100, 104–6, 108–11, 116n, 123n

Panayi, Panikos, 2
Persoff, Meir, 8, 122n
Phillips, Revd E. P., 72, 127n; *see also* Glasgow
place, Jewish, 5–6, 10, 18, 83, 86–8, 90–1, 96–8, 100, 101, 106, 128n; *see also lieu(x) de mémoire*
Presbyterianism *see* Church of Scotland
Pretoria, 74, 127n
proselyte, 76; *see also giyur*
provincial Jews/Jewry, 3–5, 7–8, 17, 23–4, 31, 41–2, 45, 47–9, 52–9, 67, 70, 77, 79–80, 86, 89, 102; *see also* regional/national Jewish communities
Prussia, 17, 25–7, 95, 108

rabbi, 8, 13, 15–17, 20–8, 30–2, 41–5, 47–52, 54–60, 71–6, 104–6, 109–10; *see also* Chief Rabbi; minister
Rabbinical Seminary, 21–3
  Breslau, 21–2
  Hochschule für die Wissenschaft des Judentums (Liberal), 21–2
  New York (JTS), 21–2, 116n
  see also Hildesheimer Rabbinical Seminary (Orthodox)
Rabinowitz, Rabbi Jacob, 54, 123n; *see also* Edinburgh New Hebrew Congregation
Reform Judaism, 3, 28, 46
regional/national Jewish communities, 4–5, 7–11, 13, 15, 17, 39, 41–5, 49, 51–2, 54–60, 61, 67, 70, 79–80, 90, 103; *see also* provincial Jews/Jewry
Russia, 17, 20, 23, 25–7, 43, 62–3, 92, 94–5, 97, 100, 103, 105, 109–10, 114n, 115n

Salisbury Road Synagogue, 38, 61, 66, 68, 73, 89, 92, 96; *see also* Edinburgh; Edinburgh Hebrew Congregation
Schloer, Joachim, 6
Sciennes *see* Edinburgh
Sciennes Primary School *see* Edinburgh
Scottish Beth Din, 41–3, 54, 60, 62, 69–70, 72–3, 75–7, 79; *see also* Beth Din
shtille chuppe, 76, 110; *see also* marriage
South Africa, 1, 5, 48, 74, 113n
South Portland Street Synagogue *see* Glasgow
Southside *see* Edinburgh
space, Jewish, 5–6, 10, 17–18, 82–3, 86–7, 90–1, 94, 98, 100, 106; *see also* place, Jewish
status, Jewish, 20, 24, 41–2, 45, 54–5, 70, 72, 75–6, 79–80, 119n; *see also* beth din; *see also* giyur
Stevenson, Robert Louis, 89
Sunderland, 12, 15, 24–5, 30, 35, 39–40, 42, 52–3, 61, 64, 89, 93, 100

Torah im derekh erets, 30, 48, 110
Torah min hashamayim, 21, 111
Torah u'maddah, 20–1, 35, 37, 48, 111
traditional/authentic Judaism, 3, 20, 21–4, 26–37, 45, 48, 50, 65, 78, 100, 104–5, 116n
transnational, 2, 4–6, 11–12, 16–18, 22, 26, 47, 80, 86, 102–6
Two Worlds, 14, 17, 26, 32, 38, 82–3, 86–7, 89–93, 95–8, 100–1, 106, 120n, 128n

United Hebrew Congregations of the British Empire, 24, 46, 48, 53–4, 72
United Synagogue, 4, 15, 17, 20, 22–3, 39, 41–2, 44–8, 54, 56–7, 74, 121n
United Synagogue of Glasgow *see* Glasgow

Vilna/Vilnius, 17–18, 25–7, 40, 95, 112n

Waverley Station *see* Edinburgh
Wertheimer, Jack, 26–7, 29
Wilke, Carsten, 117n
Williams, Bill, 9–11, 44, 105
World War I, 15–16, 22–3, 27, 32, 42, 43, 50, 56–8, 62, 64, 69, 72, 79, 105
World War II, 2, 6, 15, 43, 61, 69, 77, 99, 105

Yiddish, 14, 24–6, 30, 33–5, 48, 50, 64–5, 69, 93–5, 98–100, 108–11

Zunz, Leopold, 21

EU representative:
Easy Access System Europe
Mustamäe tee 50, 10621 Tallinn, Estonia
Gpsr.requests@easproject.com

www.ingramcontent.com/pod-product-compliance
Lightning Source LLC
Chambersburg PA
CBHW070359240426
43671CB00013BA/2569